TRUMAN
AND THE
HIROSHIMA
CULT

TRUMAN
AND THE
HIROSHIMA
CULT

Robert P. Newman

Michigan State University Press

East Lansing

1995

All Michigan state University Press books are produced on paper which meets the requirements of American National Standard of Information Sciences—Permanence if paper for printed materials ANSI Z39.48-1984.

Michigan State University Press
East Lansing, Michigan 48823-5202

03 02 01 00 99 98 97 96 95 1 2 3 4 5 6 7 8 9

Library of Congress Cataloging-in-Publication Data

Newman, Robert P.
    Truman and the Hiroshima cult / Robert P. Newman.
        p.   cm. — (Rhetoric and public affairs series)
    Includes bibliographical references and index.
    ISBN 0-87013-403-5 (alk. paper)
    1. World War. 1939-1945—Japan—Hiroshima-shi. 2. Truman, Harry S., 1884-1972. 3. World War, 1935-1945—Japan—Nagasaki-shi. 4. Atomic bomb—United States—Moral and ethical aspects. 5. Hiroshima-shi (Japan)—History—Bombardment, 1945. 6. United States—Military policy—Moral and ethical aspects.. 7. United States—Foreign relations—Soviet Union. 8. Soviet Union—Foreign relations—United States. I. Title. II. Series.
    D767.25.N3N48 1995
    940.54'25—dc20   95-20263
                                                                              CIP

to

J. William Fulbright

who knew the difference between a just war

and an ignoble crusade

Even as the formal days of atonement in the Jewish and Christian calendar weaken, lose some of their traditional power, and attract fewer of the young to their rites, the age-old human impulse to critical self-scrutiny, with resulting acts of contrition to amend for past sins, takes on a new and more secularized form. The date is August 6. Its icon is a mushroom cloud. The sin to be expiated is America's. And the event is Hiroshima.

Andre Ryerson
"The Cult of Hiroshima"
in *Commentary*, October 1985

Contents

Preface

I take the meaning of "cult" from *Merriam-Webster's Ninth New Collegiate*: "a great devotion to a person, idea, or thing: esp: such a devotion regarded as literary or intellectual fad." The intellectual idea to which Hiroshima cultists are devoted is that since Japan was about to surrender when the bombs were dropped, the slaughter of innocents at Hiroshima and Nagasaki was not motivated by military reasons. It was instead motivated primarily by the desire to intimidate the Russians (so-called atomic diplomacy), by racism (we did not drop the bomb on Germany), by the desire of Robert Oppenheimer and company to experiment with a new toy, by the fear of Secretary of War Henry Stimson and others that Congress would investigate if their $2 billion dollar expenditure was found not useful, or by the sheer unthinking momentum of a bureaucratic juggernaut (Manhattan Project).

This cult has a shrine, a holy day, a distinctive rhetoric of victimization (it can also be called a Japanese-as-victim cult), various items of scripture (John Hersey's *Hiroshima*, The Franck Report, P.M.S. Blackett's 1949, *Fear, War, and the Bomb*), and, in Japan, support from a powerful constituency (Marxist). As with other cults, it is ahistorical. Its devotees elevate fugitive and unrepresentative events to cosmic status. And most of all, *they believe*.

The Hiroshima cult is the mirror image of the nuclear cult—those evangelists of the 1950s and 1960s who saw the energy of the atom as the means to make the desert bloom, to air condition whole cities for pennies (the electricity would be too cheap to meter), to power an airplane across the oceans on a thimbleful of fuel, and to do other wonderful things. Daniel Ford dealt with these matters in his 1982 book, *The Cult of the Atom*. *This* cult has demonstrated its bankruptcy.

But the Hiroshima cult is not bankrupt. It gained ascendancy in 1994 in the Smithsonian's Air and Space Museum, and its faithful still flock to the shrine in Japan. This book is about how things got that way, and it is judgmental. My focus, however, is not on the cultists as such; rather it is on the arguments they use to proselytize.

I first became interested in the Hiroshima event while working on a biography of Owen Lattimore. That irascible sinologue's heretical judgments were remarkably sound. He was almost alone in predicting in the early 1930s that Japan's invasion of China would founder. When the Pacific War broke out, his claim that this would mean the end of colonialism was also counter to the conventional wisdom. He made many other farsighted judgments.

In regard to the tricky problem of how to deal with the Japanese emperor, however, he thought attempting to shorten the war by allowing the emperor to remain in place was wrong; he thought the emperor was complicit in the war, and should be exiled. We now know that the Emperor was instrumental in ending the war, which without his startling intervention might have gone on much longer.

On the matter of the atomic bombs, Lattimore held two contradictory ideas. He agreed with Blackett's claim that the bombs were not necessary to secure Japan's surrender, but he denied there was any "Russian angle" in Truman's decision to use them.

I puzzled over these judgments, and sought to see the Pacific War in 1945 as Truman saw it from the White House. This led to reading newspaper accounts of the horrendous battle for Okinawa, and then to studying the conclusions of the United States Strategic Bombing Survey that inspired Blackett. I concluded that Blackett, and Lattimore, had been led down the garden path.

I also discovered some gaps in the discussions of Hiroshima that were puzzling. Nobody had ever studied the grounds on which the Bombing Survey issued its ukase that Japan would probably have surrendered by 1 November 1945 with no atom bomb, no Russian attack, and no invasion of the home islands; yet this conclusion was fundamental to most critiques of Truman's decision.

Few accounts of the end of the Pacific War disentangled the rhetoric of unconditional surrender from the reality that in the Potsdam Declaration, the United States had set out fairly explicit conditions while maintaining the tough slogan. The Japanese were aware that the Potsdam terms were reasonable conditions, certainly not destructive of the Japanese state; few writers on ending the Pacific War acknowledge this. Professional moralists who wrote about the bomb, especially Elizabeth Anscombe and Michael Walzer, were grossly ignorant of Pacific War history. Neither Hiroshima cultists nor professional moralists had even considered the possibility that Hiroshima and Nagasaki were legitimate retribution for the millions of deaths caused by Japan's fourteen-year rampage through China and the Pacific.

Also surprising was my inability to find an overall accounting of how many deaths could be attributed to the Greater East Asia Co-Prosperity Sphere (Japan's euphemism for its empire). There are many estimates of deaths caused by World War II in Europe, for deaths in Hitler's concentration camps, and deaths due to Stalin's crimes, but no similar figures on Japan. Also missing, until Ian Buruma's enlightening *The Wages of Guilt,* was any serious explanation of why Germany had publicly and adequately acknowledged its sins, while Japan never had. Likewise it was not clear how the Japanese-as-victims cult had taken hold not just in Japan, but in the United States.

Perhaps the most indefensible error of Hiroshima cultists is their linguistic legerdemain. "Japan was ready to surrender without the bomb," they tell us. Which Japan? Cultists talk as if the elites of the peace party *were* Japan. Of course those who favored peace wanted to end the war. *But they were not the effective government of Japan.* Minister of War Anami Korechika was *the* effective ruler as the Japanese government was then constituted. By resigning, Anami could bring down the government.

A second linguistic confusion common in cultist writing is one between "defeat" and "surrender." Saying that Japan was "defeated" by late 1944 means nothing if the effective government was determined not to surrender until it had crushed the first wave of an American invasion. In fact, Japan did not offer to "surrender"; the emperor spoke only of *shusen*—ending the war. A massive amount of bad argument is injected into the public arena by these linguistic confusions.

All these problems merit consideration.

I have approached them from the perspective of a student of policy argument, seeking to discover the pressure points of arguments for and against the bomb, evaluating the evidence on those points, and relating them to each other. I have also teased out the probable reasons for the prominence of the Hiroshima cult in the United States, an inquiry that leads to the postwar growth of the Atomic Energy Commission, the overkill of American and Soviet arsenals, and the rhetorical efficacy of the United States' ill-considered intervention in Vietnam.

As I was finishing this study, the bitter conflict over the end-of-the-war exhibit featuring the *Enola Gay* planned by the Smithsonian's National Air and Space Museum broke out. I was astounded to read that the text to accompany this exhibit originally included the statement "For most Americans, this . . . was a war of vengeance. For most Japanese, it was a war to defend their unique culture against Western imperialism." The second half of this statement is ludicrous. The Japanese, as much as the Germans, believed themselves to be a superior race, rightfully ruling Asia and the Pacific. En route to this objective, they saw nothing wrong with conscripting Korean and Chinese (and other) women as prostitutes for their army, herding Asian and Caucasian captives into lethal labor camps, or with slaughter and mayhem to the tune of many millions of victims. Since the Air and Space Museum controversy broke out, the Smithsonian has cancelled its exhibit, and the Japanese have gotten around to apologizing to the Korean and Chinese "comfort women." As they should.

My conclusions in this book have been improved, though not necessarily endorsed, by a number of remarkably conscientious prople who took time to critique the whole manuscript: John Butler, Alec E. Campbell, Terry Check, Hilary Conroy, Edward Drea, Marc Gallicchio, Cecilia Graves, Harold Hitchens, William Lanouette, Howard Martin, Rachel Mayer, Martin Medhurst, Morris Ogul, Beth Smarts, Roger Stemen, Mark Stoler, Jennifer Wood, Weiming Yao, and Edwin M. Yoder, Jr. Others rendered great service by commenting on specific chapters: Kurt Baier, Sir Michael Brock, Robert Butow, Sheldon Cohen, Bernard and Susan Duffy, George Feifer, James A. Field, Robert Frank, Waldo Heinrichs, William Hall, Sir Michael Howard, Dan Howe, Thomas Kane, David MacIsaac, Dale Newman, Don Oberdorfer, Raymond G. O'Connor, Ray Skates, Brian Loring Villa, and Geoffrey Warner. I only regret that correspondence with Barton Bernstein, far and away the most knowledgeable scholar in this field, came too late to be of maximum benefit. In those few areas where I differ with him, I do so with trepidation.

Stuart Creighton Miller and Don Goldstein furnished much stimulation and encouragement. Pat Colbert of Hillman Library was indispensable. Regina Renk put it all in a computer at the expense of many lost lunch hours. Paul and Elaine Tendler, Bruce and Wendy

Gronbeck, John Rowett, and Keith Sanders all helped a maverick 70th Calvary Reconnaissance Trooper recreate the closing months of World War II. And even though this book is not primarily an archive centered effort, the many helpful people at the Department of the Army Center of Military History, the George C. Marshall Research Foundation, the Modern Military History Branch of the National Archives, the U.S. Army Military History Institute, the Harry S. Truman Library, the Library of Congress Manuscript Division, and the Franklin D. Roosevelt Library provided vital documents.

Chapter two originally appeared in the May 1995 *Pacific Historical Review*, to which thanks are due for permission to reprint.

I am also indebted to the Modern History Faculty of Oxford University, the California Polytechnic State University, the University of Iowa, the University of Wisconsin—Stevens Point, and Northeast Missouri State University for furnishing critical audiences at early stages of my research.

This book follows the practice of most writers in giving Japanese family names first, with the exception of Japanese scholars resident abroad and publishing in English. My use of "casualties" includes dead, wounded, and missing in action; when I refer to deaths I do not say casualties.

1

Why Did Truman Drop the Bomb?

On 8 May 1945 German representatives ratified unconditional surrender of all their armies. There was much rejoicing in Washington and other Allied capitals, but it was muted by a daunting situation in the Pacific. Japan had to be brought to surrender; however, after V-E Day, every soldier in the army wanted to come home—immediately.

GIs who had escaped with their lives from North Africa, the Italian campaign, D-day, and the Battle of the Bulge dreaded the prospect of again risking everything to subdue Japan. Fifty years and several dozen crises have dulled American memories of the pressures to end the Pacific War in 1945. In addition to the soldiers and sailors, family, friends, and sweethearts were vocal about getting it over with.

The Ninety-fifth Infantry Division participated in the war against Germany for ten months, then was brought back to Camp Shelby, Mississippi, to train for the invasion of Japan. The division commander said, "there was a continuing and growing opposition to being ordered to the Pacific. A very disturbing situation arose approaching open sedition and mutiny."[1]

As early as 1943, after the exhausting battle against Gens. Rommel and von Arnim in Tunisia, rumors spread that the Americans who had participated in that campaign had "done their share" and would be sent home. Gen. Omar Bradley wrote, "When the men were told emphatically that this was not true, there was widespread rebellion. . . . many cases of self-maiming were reported."[2] As casualties began to mount in the Pacific, the morale of those being sent there, and of their families, suffered. The battle for Iwo Jima captured people's imaginations, largely because of the

1

stunning picture of the Stars and Stripes being raised on Mount Suribachi, but all was not upbeat. Geoffrey Perrett describes the trouble:

> . . . the cost of the war was beginning to wear on people's nerves. February [1945] brought a quarter of a million American casualties, including more than 50,000 dead. For the first time in its history the United States was in a war that would cost it more than 1,000,000 casualties. Letters and telegrams poured into government offices. One distraught woman wrote: "Please, for God's sake, stop sending our finest youth to be murdered in places like Iwo Jima. It is too much to stand, too much for mothers and homes to take. It is driving some mothers crazy. . . . It is most inhuman and awful—stop, stop."[3]

In the first part of August 1945, 115,000 troops passed through the Panama Canal en route to the Pacific.[4] Almost five million Americans were scheduled to make this trip.

They would not make it gladly. A committee of the Social Science Research Council, chaired by Frederick Osborn, made studies of the social psychology of American soldiers in World War II. Samuel A. Stouffer was the lead author of several of its reports, and among other predictions, Stouffer and his colleagues felt that morale was likely to drop precipitously after Hitler was defeated. This prediction was borne out: "In June 1945, just after VE Day, two thirds of the returnees in the United States and not eligible for discharge under the point system reported themselves as unwilling to go overseas again while another fifth asserted that they would be willing to go when needed."[5] But even the one-fifth "willing" to go had reservations; they did not actually believe they would be sent.

Secretary of War Henry Stimson was acutely sensitive about prospective casualties in the Pacific; he had conscripted the men whose lives were at stake. Gen. George Marshall was also worried about increasing casualties, and about the nation's will to fight; he told a biographer after the war that "A democracy cannot fight a Seven Years War."[6] Adm. Ernest King had even stronger doubts about American "stamina and commitment" for a long war. He told reporters in 1944 that "the American people will weary of it quickly, and that pressure at home will force a negotiated peace, before the Japs are really licked."[7]

The invasion of Iwo Jima was preceded by an immense air and sea bombardment; capture of this tiny island was to take three or four days. Instead, it lasted a month, from mid-February to mid-March 1945; there were 2,500 casualties the first day. Total casualties in taking these eight square miles were 6,821 marines killed and almost 20,000 wounded. This was the first battle in the Pacific in which the Japanese had inflicted more casualties than they had suffered, and this despite overwhelming American air and sea power.[8] The outcome sent a shudder through many a casualty-conscious army planner.

The *San Francisco Examiner*, among other papers, took a dim view of the cost of taking Iwo Jima. In an editorial on 27 February, the paper said American forces were paying too heavily for the island, and that they were "in danger of being worn out before they ever reach the really critical Japanese areas."[9] John Toland writes that after Iwo Jima:

> The War Department itself was searching for ways to reduce casualties on all fronts. The most controversial had already been suggested to Admiral Nimitz by General Marshall's office, which had previously had similar recommendations for the European Theater of Operations: the use of poison gas. There were large quantities on hand. Nimitz pondered its employment on Iwo Jima but concluded that "the United States should not be the first to violate the Geneva Convention."[10]

Also after Iwo Jima the U.S. Office of War Information warned that the public was uneasy about casualties in the Pacific War. Marshall took this to heart. In a speech to the Academy of Political Sciences in April, he warned that "we are approaching one of the most difficult periods of the war" when the "great impatience" of Americans to return to normalcy would interfere with maximum efforts against the Japanese.[11]

Marshall, and army planners generally, had no hope that navy blockades and air force bombardment would bring surrender before disillusionment set in. Germany had been bombed and blockaded and had held out to the bitter end, showing that despite claims of air strategy theorists, only the seizure of the enemy's territory forced capitulation.[12] And as the spring of 1945 developed, seizing Japanese territory became increasingly painful. There was trauma upon trauma. Iwo Jima was barely secure when American forces invaded Okinawa, and it became clear that Japanese forces were fighting more fiercely as the fighting got closer to the home islands.

Of the Okinawa battle, lasting from 1 April to 2 July, Hanson Baldwin's apocalyptic description is appropriate:

> In size, scope and ferocity it dwarfed the Battle of Britain. Never before had there been, probably never again will there be, such a vicious, sprawling struggle of planes against planes, of ships against planes. Never before, in so short a space, had the Navy lost so many ships; never before in land fighting had so much American blood been shed in so short a time in so small an area. . . . There have been larger land battles, more protracted air campaigns, but Okinawa was the largest combined operation, a "no-quarter" struggle fought on, under and over the sea and the land.[13]

American forces recorded 12,520 killed or missing, 36,631 wounded, and 93 missing in taking an area half the size of Rhode Island that the Japanese could not resupply or reinforce. The Japanese air force and navy were in tatters, but the Okinawa defenders had superbly dug-in defenses and hundreds of kamikaze volunteers; the latter sunk 36 American ships and damaged 368 more.[14]

Not just Okinawa, but all the battles of the Pacific War had shown the Japanese to be in the grips of a Masada complex. Like the Jewish Zealots defending that mountain fortress from Rome's tenth legion in A.D. 73, they would fight to the bitter end, and when fighting was no longer possible, they would kill themselves.[15] Only one organized Japanese unit surrendered during the entire Pacific War.[16]

On Okinawa, approximately 70,000 Japanese lost their lives, and 80,000 Okinawans, most of them civilians, many by a kind of "poor man's hara-kiri"—holding a grenade against their stomachs and blowing themselves to pieces. Only 7,000 surrendered to American forces when the battle was clearly over, and the Americans used some effective propaganda to get at least a few captives.[17] It was that bad, or worse, in every other battle. On Attu, of some 3,000 Japanese defenders, 29 surrendered; the rest were killed in battle or killed themselves. On Tarawa, of 5,000 Japanese defenders, only 150 were taken prisoner. On Saipan, of 30,000 Japanese soldiers, fewer than 1,000 allowed themselves to be captured; more than 1,000 civilian workers committed suicide. On Iwo Jima, of 23,000 men, only 216 surrendered.[18]

The Japanese code required victory or death. Ruth Benedict in *The Chrysanthemum and the Sword* explains this commitment in anthropological terms, but her account lacks the immediacy and color of the best participant-observer narrative.[19] Westerners cannot understand the vitality of the Japanese spirit. After detailing the outcomes of various battles, Tsurumi Shunsuke tells us:

> This action [suicide] was seen by the Japanese on the main islands as a proper model for their own behavior should the U.S.A. prove victorious and land in Japan. The Government declared that loyal subjects of the Emperor must prepare themselves for glorious self-destruction for the sake of preserving the national structure. The tenet was that even when all the Japanese, including the Emperor himself, had perished this structure would remain. . . . Very few people in Japan doubted this line of reasoning, and virtually no one, not even social scientists or members of the various religious sects, ventured to criticize it.[20]

The significance of this, lost on many Allied authorities, was that only the emperor could cancel the obligation of every Japanese citizen to give his life for the eternal kingdom. For westerners who find this Masada complex baffling, there are two accounts of revolts of Japanese prisoners of war in Australian and New Zealand camps that convey the Japanese ethos better than any historian's explanation. Both revolts were caused by the unwillingness of the prisoners to continue to live, since they had disgraced themselves, their families, and the emperor by allowing themselves to be taken into custody in the first place; they had failed to commit suicide in a POW camp, and believed (in many cases correctly) that with a mass outbreak, their Australian and New Zealand captors would necessarily turn the machine guns on them. Charlotte Carr-Gregg, an Australian sociologist, in *Japanese Prisoners of War in Revolt,* looks at the suicide wish in the outbreaks at Featherstone and Cowra.[21] Asada Teruhiko, who was a prisoner of war, tells the story of a Cowra prisoner, from capture while unconscious to return to a Japan that would not claim him, in a compelling book, *The Night of a Thousand Suicides.*[22]

These accounts are definitive. The Japanese threat to fight to the last man, woman, and child, with bamboo spears if necessary, should the emperor demand it, was serious.

Some Allied sources could not believe it. Such commitment was not human. A source relied on by Gar Alperovitz, a Combined Chiefs of Staff "Estimate of the Enemy Situation" as of 6 July 1945, says, "Although individual Japanese willingly sacrifice themselves in the service of the nation, we doubt that the nation as a whole is predisposed toward national suicide."[23] Michael Sherry likewise accepts a Joint Chiefs of Staff (JCS) study in April 1945 that states: "There are no indications that the Japanese as a whole share the fanatical Nazi psychology of committing national suicide."[24]

It is difficult to know what sources informed the military researchers. On Saipan, on Okinawa, on every Pacific island soldiers and civilians alike had committed suicide *en masse* when the battle was hopeless. The Chinese, who know something about Japanese motivation and culture, took the prospect of last-ditch fighting, even to massive civilian casualties, seriously. Historian Tien-wei Wu, in a 1994 analysis of the proposed *Enola Gay* exhibit, discussed this matter: "By all accounts, the Japanese were determined to fight the Americans to the end, if they invaded the homeland. That 'one hundred million die together' was not merely a slogan but a true possibility in a country like Japan."[25]

Nakamura Masanori, in his *Japanese Monarchy*, cites with approval Joseph Grew's wartime contention that only orders from the emperor to cease and desist would bring far-flung Japanese armies to lay down their arms.[26] Without those orders, they would fight to extermination.

No one doubted the ferocity of Japanese resistance, increasing as the fighting got closer to the homeland. This ferocity would likely be intensified on 1 November 1945, when U.S. troops in Operation OLYMPIC were due to land on the southernmost Japanese island, Kyushu. This landing, if it did not trigger surrender, was to be followed by CORONET in early 1946 to take the Tokyo area.

In addition to the intensity of fighting on Iwo Jima and Okinawa, other events in 1945 made the invasion of Japan loom as horrendous. The morale problem was highlighted in a front-page *New York Times* story in January 1945 when 6,300 Canadian conscripts, out of a total of 15,600 drafted for overseas duty, went AWOL.[27] Canadians were thought to be as patriotic and battle-ready as Americans, but Canada had been at war two years longer than the United States. Was a similar situation in store when the U.S. Army started heavy postings to the Pacific?

February and March were good months in Europe, but the intensity of the Pacific War increased. Hanson Baldwin discussed the "Let-Down Problem" and the necessity for a conclusive victory over Japan in the *New York Times*. Here was

> . . . one of the greatest problems the country ever has faced. . . . The Army itself will have to cope with a psychological problem of first

magnitude, which may complicate the prodigious military and logistical problem of "redeploying" our forces for the war in the Orient. . . . To Americans, tired like all peoples of bloodletting . . . it might appear the best and easiest course to make a compromise peace with Japan.

But if we do, our sons and our sons' sons will live to regret it . . . as surely as the sun sets, twenty, thirty, fifty years from now, a rearmed and perhaps far more powerful Japan—bent on bloody revenge for her present defeats—will war upon us again.[28]

By March Gen. LeMay was well into his incendiary bombing, and Japanese cities were going up in flames. The 9-10 March assault on Tokyo, which brought more destruction than either of the atomic bombs, gave the Japanese their first serious exposure to terror bombing. But American authorities did not assume that Japan could be bombed into submission; Adm. Chester Nimitz ordered 75 percent of XXI Bomber Command's effort to be directed against airfields of Kyushu and neighboring Shikoku between 17 April and 11 May.[29] This was undertaken not only to hinder the destructive kamikaze attacks on American forces at Okinawa, but also to begin softening up Kyushu for OLYMPIC.

The U.S. Joint Intelligence Committee (JIC) delivered its major analysis of the problem of defeating Japan by blockade and bombardment on 18 April. JIC concluded, as a concession to navy and air force opinion, that air and sea attack would "reduce progressively Japanese will to resist" Allied forces, and would break the Japanese will to continue the war. But while this would inevitably force surrender, the army point of view won out: surrender by siege and bombardment would not happen "within a reasonable length of time." Some JIC analysts estimated that victory by siege and bombardment might take "a great many years."[30]

On 25 April the Joint Chiefs of Staff reviewed a planning document on Pacific strategy that incorporated all intelligence and planning work up to that time. This document endorsed the strategy of early invasion, but tiptoed around the touchy issue of probable casualties. The planning staff stated with some precision that the "average casualty rate per thousand per day for operations in Guadalcanal, Leyte, Attu . . . all of which were amphibious assaults" was 7.45.[31] (This rate was three and one-half times the rate for land warfare in Europe.) But the planners did not multiply the average Pacific casualty rate by the number of troops scheduled for

OLYMPIC, no doubt because the result was frightening: *101,750 casualties in the first month.*

At the same time the JCS was evading this depressing forecast, Gen. Douglas MacArthur's headquarters was beginning to hear chilling information about Japan's ability to fortify Kyushu despite the decimation of its navy and the pounding of LeMay's B-29s. ULTRA decrypts from the Allied military codebreaking operation in Australia on 25 April furnished Gen. Charles Willoughby, MacArthur's intelligence chief, with a first estimate of Japanese strength on Kyushu by the time of the scheduled invasion: ten combat divisions.[32] The Japanese had correctly calculated American invasion plans, which was not difficult: there were only three plausible landing sites on Kyushu, and these sites had top priority in Japanese preparations. From then until August, despite the B-29s and naval encirclement, Kyushu reinforcements grew rapidly. As Edward Drea summarizes the ULTRA findings:

> Japanese reinforcements seemed to blossom with the warm May weather in Kyushu. . . . ULTRA highlighted underground aircraft hangar construction and new, concealed dispersal airfields on Kyushu designed for such operations (June 6/7, 8/9). ULTRA exposed daily the high command's efforts to transform Kyushu into a mighty stronghold. Nowhere could one detect pessimism or defeatism. According to ULTRA, Japan's military leaders were determined to go down fighting.[33]

Knowledge of what the Japanese were planning was not necessary for enterprising reporters to sense the growing menace of Pacific events. Bruce Rae in a major *New York Times* story of 27 May titled, "Okinawa is a Lesson for Invasion of Japan," laid it out starkly: "the invasion of Japan and the fighting that lies ahead after the landing will be without qualification the hardest we have ever been called upon to face." Rae then refers to the skill and tenacity of the Japanese on Okinawa. But "the thing that clinches it is the topography of the main islands of the enemy empire, which is Okinawa magnified and multiplied."[34] Truman read the *Times*.

The morale problem festered. A 1 June 1945 *Times* story quotes Undersecretary of War Robert Patterson discussing the pressure to discharge more soldiers. He was against it: "Hurrying demobilization now will have a grim result if it prolongs the war."[35] Patterson was responding to a proposal by Congressman Andrew May, chairman of the House Military Affairs Committee, to release more soldiers.

Optimists in Washington seized on the fall of Prime Minister Koiso Kuniaki's cabinet on 5 April, and its replacement by that of Adm. Baron Suzuki Kantaro, as a sign that Japan was wearying and beginning to crack. On 9 June Suzuki torpedoed this assumption in a speech to the Diet. After the standard shibboleths about Japan fighting an unwanted defensive war, he concluded that there was only one path for the nation: "to fight to the very end."[36]

On 14 June Truman began to prepare for his first meeting with Winston Churchill and Joseph Stalin. He instructed his chief of staff, Adm. William D. Leahy, to obtain certain information about the Pacific War from the military chiefs. Leahy's instructions to the military leaders are vital to understanding what was important to the president:

> The President today directed me to inform [you] that he wishes to meet with the Chiefs of Staff in the afternoon of the 18th, in his office, to discuss the details of our campaign against Japan.
>
> He expects at this meeting to be thoroughly informed of our intentions and prospects for his discussion with Churchill and Stalin.
>
> He will want information as to the number of men of the Army and ships of the Navy that will be necessary to defeat Japan.
>
> He wants an estimate of the time required and an estimate of the losses in killed and wounded that will result from an invasion of Japan proper.
>
> He wants an estimate of the time and the losses that will result from an effort to defeat Japan by isolation, blockade, and bombardment by sea and air forces.
>
> He desires to be informed as to exactly what we want the Russians to do . . .
>
> It is his intention to make his decisions on the campaign with the purpose of economizing to the maximum extent possible in the loss of American lives.
>
> Economy in the use of time and in money cost is comparatively unimportant.
>
> I suggest that a memorandum discussion of the above noted points be prepared in advance for delivery to the President at the time of the meeting. . . .[37]

If Truman's instructions to Leahy were not sufficient evidence of what mattered to the president, an entry in his diary 16 June reads: "I have to decide Japanese strategy—shall we invade Japan proper or shall we bombard and blockade? This is my hardest decision to date."[38]

As part of his preparation for the meeting, General Marshall requested from MacArthur a casualty estimate for OLYMPIC through the first ninety days. The answer came back from Pacific Headquarters: 105,000 battle and 12,600 non-battle casualties.[39]

Marshall was upset. The casualty matter was so sensitive, and Truman was taking so much heat to get the boys home, that Marshall wired back to MacArthur that this estimate was too high to be acceptable. Did that stern-jawed battle hero stick to his estimates? Not in the least. Here we have hard evidence of Douglas MacArthur's ambition to achieve eternal fame as the commander of the largest amphibious invasion in history: fourteen divisions versus Eisenhower's nine at Normandy. As Drea notes, this history-making prospect "held overwhelming appeal to MacArthur's vanity."[40] Knowing that if OLYMPIC loomed as too costly Truman might cancel it and wait for Japan to starve, MacArthur sent back a cable dismissing the first estimate as "purely academic and routine." MacArthur then said he did not really expect such high casualties. He added, "I most earnestly recommend no change to OLYMPIC."[41]

Here we find not only a vainglorious general fudging the figures, but a statesmanlike and candid chief of staff letting him get away with it.

So MacArthur's original estimate was not presented to the president. Marshall had an estimate, extrapolated from the casualties on Luzon, of 31,000 in the first thirty days. There are several problems with this. Forrest Pogue, Marshall's biographer, notes that this figure did not reflect such things as the kamikaze losses at Okinawa.[42] More important, and entirely ignored by the Hiroshima cultists who make much of this conference, Marshall did not at this time have the ULTRA decrypts that were so devastating a month later. The minutes of the 18 June meeting read: "He [Marshall] said, in answer to the President's question as to what opposition could be expected on Kyushu, that it was estimated at eight Japanese divisions or about 350,000 troops. He said that divisions were still being raised in Japan and that reinforcement from other areas was possible but it was becoming increasingly difficult and painful."[43]

Here Marshall was not conniving in a fraud. At that time 350,000 was close to what ULTRA revealed, and the air force generals were confident that they could shut down any chance of Japan seriously reinforcing Kyushu.

The casualty matter was discussed much more before the meeting was through. Admiral Leahy thought Marshall's estimate too low, and said the Okinawa rate of 35 percent should apply. Nobody worked this out before the president.[44] Admiral King argued that the rate would be lower on Kyushu than on Okinawa, since "there would be much more room for maneuver." King had not studied the relief map of Kyushu.[45]

Truman appeared to be content with Marshall's low estimate, but nonetheless the minutes record Truman saying, "He had hoped that there was a possibility of preventing an Okinawa from one end of Japan to the other."[46]

All these estimates were little better than necromancy. No one at this conference could know that the attempts at air interdiction would fail to the extent of allowing the Japanese to build up the army defending Kyushu to 900,000.[47] No one could know what fighting with their backs to the wall, and on sacred soil for the first time, would do to Japanese ferocity. No one could know how many of the kamikaze planes, kaitens, suicide boats, and other unique devices would get through to U.S. ships. No one could know how effective the satchel charges prepared for lone Japanese soldiers to explode under American vehicles would be. No one could know whether as many things would go wrong with OLYMPIC as went wrong with OVERLORD (Normandy).

Denis Warner and coauthors Peggy Warner and Sadao Seno, experts on kamikazes, in their projection of what might have happened on Kyushu, conclude "Those casualty figures that were tossed about before the White House meeting on 18 June might have been surpassed in a single day. Just a handful of suicide planes caused doubts as to the wisdom of the Lingayen Gulf landing in January. This time the suicide planes would have numbered hundreds, if not the thousands the Japanese planned."[48]

Hiroshima cultists who attempt to show that Truman could not have feared invasion casualties, hence had no good military reason to drop the bomb, make much of the 18 June meeting, and of the fact that Leahy's high estimate drops out of the discussion.[49] But even if the low estimates on 18 June were credible at that time, by 1 August these conjectures were as out of date as bows and arrows.

On 21 June organized resistance on Okinawa was officially over, but alarm at the high casualties continued. Lt. Gen. Simon B. Buckner, commanding U.S. forces until killed in the last days of the battle, had "to defend his conduct of the campaign from rear-area criticism."[50] As Ronald H. Spector describes it in his landmark history, *Eagle Against the Sun*:

> On Kyushu, the Japanese waited. Okinawa—although a complete American victory had the paradoxical effect of discouraging the Americans while inspiring the Japanese. Imperial Navy strategists, reviewing the damage, real and imagined, which the kamikazes had inflicted on American shipping, estimated that 30 to 50 percent of the American invasion fleet could be put out of action prior to landing . . . . Japanese army planners were also encouraged by thoughts of the battle for Okinawa, where less than three divisions, cut off from all support and subject to naval gunfire, had nonetheless held out for over a hundred days against an American force more than twice as strong. They expected the battle for Kyushu "to be fought under conditions incomparably more advantageous to the Japanese."[51]

As one indication of the American mind in June 1945, the *New York Times* index for that month shows eighty-one stories about redeployment and demobilization of American forces. Secretary of State-designate James Byrnes' simmering distrust of the Soviet Union, which Hiroshima cultists largely blame for Truman's "strategy of showdown" and atomic diplomacy, was not the main concern in the White House.

July was the crucial month. ULTRA and MAGIC (the diplomatic codebreaking operation) both fed discouraging information into the Allied decision-making apparatus.

MAGIC carried news of the inhibited activities of the Japanese peace party, operating through Foreign Minister Togo Shigenori and Ambassador Sato Naotake in Moscow. Marshall, Byrnes (who became secretary of state on 3 July), and Truman read the MAGIC intercepts. They were very clear. They did not show a Japan ready to surrender. They showed an *elite* ready to negotiate an armistice, fearful of word getting to the military about what they were doing.[52] Army zealots had controlled the empire since the 1930s. The Emperor was with the peace party, but he too was in danger of being taken into custody by the hotheads.

Even being suspected of wanting to end the war was enough to get one arrested. On 15 April, War Minister Anami Korechika ordered the arrest of 400 suspected peace activists, including Yoshida Shigeru, former ambassador to Great Britain and future prime minister.[53] The overtures to the Soviet Union to mediate an end to the Pacific War began in June, in the utmost secrecy. On 7 July, the emperor instructed Togo to arrange to send Prince Konoye Fumimaro to Moscow bearing a message from the throne. MAGIC picked up these negotiations. A long series of cables between Togo and Sato revealed the elites as increasingly wanting to end the war, but unable to offer the Soviets any idea on what terms. One Togo to Sato message read "Endeavor to obtain the good offices of the Soviet Union in ending the war short of unconditional surrender. . . ."[54]

These messages have been seized upon by Truman bashers to prove that with a slight adjustment of surrender terms, peace was available well before Hiroshima. The truth is that peace would have been available only had the peace party (Marquis Kido Koichi, Togo Shigenori, Yonai Mitumasa, and others) been in control. They were not. All of Gar Alperovitz's claims along this line depend for their plausibility on this verbal sleight of hand: "The one condition the Japanese asked was preservation of 'our form of government'. . . . With the interception of these messages there could no longer be any real doubt as to Japanese intentions."[55] What Japanese? The peace party. But they were not the Japanese who mattered.

Minister of War Anami, Army Chief of Staff Umezu Yoshijiro, Navy Chief of Staff Toyoda Soemu: these were the Japanese in control, and they *never* favored surrender, not after Saipan was lost, not after Iwo Jima was lost, not after the Philippines were lost, not after Okinawa, not even after two atom bombs and a Soviet Declaration of War.[56] They all supported fighting the decisive battle in the homeland, during which the American invaders would take such heavy casualties that the Allies would negotiate an armistice. The cables between Togo and Sato only told the Truman administration what it already knew: the military was in control, and the peace party could not impose terms acceptable to the Allies. Only the emperor's final order subdued Anami.

Anami and supporters insisted up to the end on *four* conditions for a negotiated armistice: no change in the government, no occupation of the home islands, Japanese troops to disarm themselves, and Japan to conduct any war crimes trials. The fox wanted to continue guarding the chicken coop. Revisionists read these cables with one eye closed to the realities of power in Tokyo.

Sato's cablegrams to Tokyo during this period are a study in frustration. The ambassador knew what a perilous situation his country was in, and what was necessary to preserve it. But answers kept coming back with nothing specific, just "Please follow instructions, and tell the Russians the Emperor wants to end the war."

Truman knew what was going on. On 25 July, he wrote in his diary about prospective use of the atomic bomb: "The target will be a purely military one [we will never know whether he really believed this] and we will issue a warning statement asking the Japs to surrender and save lives. *I'm sure they will not do that*, but we will have given them the chance" (italics added).[57]

MAGIC showed the elite scurrying about ineffectually, trying to prevent the ship from sinking; ULTRA showed the generals building up Kyushu defenses. No one reading the two intelligence sources could have believed the barons and marquises were about to face down the generals and admirals.

Truman and entourage left for the Potsdam Conference on 7 July. Much has been made of Truman's closeness to Secretary Byrnes, presumably a relationship influencing Truman's alleged desire to intimidate the Russians by brandishing atomic bombs. Geoffrey Warner reminds us that not only is there no evidence of attempted intimidation on Truman's part, there is good evidence that however close Truman and Byrnes may have seemed on the trip to Potsdam, Byrnes did not have Truman in his pocket.[58] From the president's diary, 7 July: "Had a long talk with my able and conniving Secretary of State. My but he has a keen mind: But all country politicians are alike. They are sure all other politicians are circuitous in their dealings. When they are told the straight truth, unvarnished, it is never believed—an asset *sometimes*."[59]

At Potsdam Truman learned of the success of the atomic device (not yet a bomb) at Alamogordo. In the first excitement of hearing that the tremendous project had largely succeeded, and with renewed promise that the Soviets would soon enter the Pacific War, he wrote in his diary on 18 July: "P.M. [Churchill] and I ate alone. Discussed Manhattan (it is a success). Decided to tell Stalin about it. Stalin had told P.M. of telegram from Jap Emperor asking for peace. Stalin also read his answer to me. It was satisfactory. Believe Japs will fold up before Russia comes in. I am sure they will when Manhattan appears over their homeland."[60]

This was not a considered judgment. Truman's euphoria wore off as his military people told him of new intercepts in the ULTRA series; he came to realize that the Japanese military might be impervious to atomic bombs *and* Soviet armies. As noted earlier, on 25 July, a mere week later, Truman wrote he was sure the Japanese would *not* surrender. And while he knew of the increasing alarm of the Togo-Sato cables, he also knew those two were not running the country, and the emperor had only asked for peace, not offered to surrender.

Also at Potsdam, the British and Americans put together a declaration calling on Japan to surrender, giving a reasonably specific account of what would happen when it did; they then secured Chiang Kai-shek's agreement to the declaration, and published it to the world on 26 July. This declaration will be discussed in chapter three; here it need only be said that Premier Suzuki Kantaro dismissed it with a term translated as "we will ignore it."[61]

While Truman was at Potsdam, MacArthur's people were grinding out intelligence that would be useful to their coming task. G-2 published an "Estimate of the Enemy Situation" every other day. Summary 1202, 19/20 July, had a long section on "Military Aspects of Empire Terrain and Communication." There was, this summary said, a "scarcity of areas suitable for large scale mobile warfare."[62] Japan was compared unfavorably with the Philippines for military operations; it was more hilly, more wooded, with a limited number of suitable landing beaches. All of these factors were disadvantageous to a landing force.

On 20 July, Gen. Carl Spaatz, commanding the Strategic Air Force in the Pacific, received a report from Gen. H.H. Arnold's headquarters about the final targeting decisions for air operations against Japan. Several undated and often unidentified documents were attached to the report, at least two of them describing meetings between the Joint Target Group (JTG) and members of the United States Strategic Bombing Survey (USSBS). The USSBS conferees had returned from Germany, offering advice about what targets had been worthwhile in Europe, and what were likely to be worthwhile in Japan.

It is clear from these documents that the USSBS people thought no bombing campaign could be decisive in the short run: "Based on German experience it would appear to be doubtful that any system of target selection would make possible effects which would have decisive military consequences within a period of four to five months."[63] Translation: it will take more time than that to get Japan to surrender. The preferred targets of the USSBS group: food supply, via nitrogen plants and rice production; and transportation. Urban area attacks rated very low.

The JTG responded with its own priorities. This group agreed that attacks on transportation should rank high; next priority, as a group, would be stores of ammunition, airplane plants, and industrial housing; but "Rice production is not considered a profitable target." The reason for this: *"indigenous food supplies may be very important to the commander charged with occupation"* (italics added).[64] This reason was never credited by USSBS, whose members failed to see into the future of Japan under American control—seventy million people would need to be fed. But there was another evaluation put forward by JTG:

> This program [bombing] must, however, be examined in the light of Japan's present military requirements. Her ground forces are at the present time nowhere actively engaged in such numbers as to impose any serious wastage of either equipment or supplies. It is estimated that Japan has in reserve ammunition equivalent to 1.5 to 2 million tons of steel content which is estimated to equal 350 months of defensive fighting from fixed positions. This is equivalent to all the ammunition Japan could produce in a year under favorable conditions and twice as much as the current estimated rate of production.[65]

So *this* crucial part of the U.S. military did not anticipate surrender due to shortages in the near future. Invasion "in the next few months" seemed likely. The targeting priorities were modified only slightly by USSBS recommendations.

In Moscow, Ambassador Sato was close to despair over the inability of his government to be specific about terms for ending the war. One of his last cables, 27 July, said:

> In presenting a proposal to end such a tremendous undertaking as the present large-scale war, we do not, in the final analysis, have a definite proposition but are only explaining our intention in an indirect way. It is absolutely impossible to cause the Soviet Government to make a move with such a noncommittal attitude on our part.[66]

Not only the Russians, but the listening Americans knew the bankruptcy of the peace initiative of the Japanese *elite*.

Reaction in Tokyo to the Potsdam Declaration was not as hostile as Premier Suzuki's speech seemed to indicate. The vice-minister of foreign affairs, Matsumoto Shunichi, took the lead in arguing to his colleagues that despite the "unconditional" rhetoric, the Allies were offering conditions. They were, Matsumoto thought, the best Japan could get, and should be accepted. Most of the peace party agreed; War Minister Anami and his supporters remained adamantly opposed, which meant that the Japanese *government* was opposed.[67]

ULTRA intercepts now confirmed to MacArthur that attempts to prevent reinforcement of Kyushu were failing. On 28 July, Gen. Charles Willoughby told the chief of staff, Gen. R.K. Sutherland, of the increasing danger:

> The rate and, probable, continuity of Japanese reinforcements into the Kyushu area are changing the tactical and strategic situation sharply. At least six (6) additional major units have been picked up in June/July; it is obvious that they are coming in from adjacent areas over lines of communication, that have apparently not been seriously affected by air strikes. There is a strong likelihood that additional major units will enter the area before target date; we are engaged in a race against time. . . .[68]

Just one day later Willoughby was so exercised that he drafted an amendment to the existing "G-2 Estimate of the Enemy Situation," claiming "This threatening development, if not checked, may grow to a point where we attack on a ratio of (1) to (1) which is not the recipe for victory."[69] But even ULTRA, accurate as it was in revealing Japanese reinforcement on Kyushu, missed a few troops. At the end of fighting, the Japanese had 900,000 soldiers defending Kyushu, with more to come, opposing the 766,700 Americans readying for the invasion.[70]

General Marshall was following the ULTRA decrypts; they jarred him out of his complacent 31,000 thirty-day estimate as given the president on 18 June. Truman claims in a letter dated 12 January 1953 that he had asked Marshall at Potsdam "what it will cost in lives to land on the Tokyo plain and other places in Japan. It was his opinion that such an invasion would cost at a minimum one quarter of a million casualties, and might cost as much as a million, on the American side, with an equal number of the enemy."[71]

Many historians write this estimate off as self-serving, nothing more than wishful reconstruction of a failing memory. Perhaps. But the laughably unrealistic underestimates *put on paper* by casualty-shy military people certainly do not command the high ground of credibility. Marshall may have given such an estimate orally. Truman may have accurately remembered. Those who are so certain that landing on Kyushu would have been a walk (meaning only 31,000 casualties at D plus 30) must engage the ULTRA intelligence, as well as the confident beliefs of the Imperial Japanese Army commanders that they could not only have severely damaged the first wave attack, but beaten it back so convincingly that the United States would have sued for peace.

Edward Drea, who has studied ULTRA decrypts a long time, says, "It seems likely that the wave of reinforcements that ULTRA spotlighted played heavily on Marshall's mind and caused him to revise his earlier casualty projection dramatically upward. Unlike Stimson, Marshall continued to worry about American losses during an invasion of Japan; his concern did not dissipate in the vision of a radioactive cloud over Japan."[72]

However low the political generals put the expected losses on Kyushu, the medics, capable in this situation of need-free perception, told a different story. Chapter 15 of *Medical Service in the Asiatic and Pacific Theaters* contains a table compiled on 31 July 1945 by Lt. Col. D.B. Kendrick. The title of the table is: "Estimated casualties and calculated whole blood requirements, OLYMPIC." The "Total Casualties: X (or D Day) plus 30" figure is 71,341. "X plus 120" is 394,859.[73] Cut these heavily to be conservative. Perhaps Kendrick was a pessimist (he went on to become MacArthur's personal physician). These figures still have more credibility than the 31,000 for X plus 30 passed in front of Truman on 18 June.

There was another pessimistic estimator in Secretary Henry Stimson's office, an expert consultant by the name of W.B. Shockley; he reported to Edward L. Bowles, a high-level scientist close to Stimson who managed to avoid the spotlight. Shockley's main task at the time was "to gather and organize information bearing on the problem of casualties in the Pacific War." One of the sources he consulted was Quincy Wright of the University of Chicago, whose two-volume *A Study of War* was published in 1942. Shockley was disturbed because he had such trouble getting data from various military commands; G-2 was supposed to study casualties, but dealt only with enemy casualties. Based on what Shockley put together, however, we know two things: (1) that he was not casualty-shy, as were MacArthur and the politically sensitive officers; and (2) he blew sky-high the contention that casualty figures for the invasion of Japan of a million or more, and estimates of U.S. *deaths* above the one-half million mark, were postwar inventions of Truman and colleagues. In his report to Bowles of 21 July 1945, Shockley said:

It seems to me most important that the facts relating to [casualties] be surveyed thoroughly and coordinated into a single well integrated picture. Such a study should be available for consideration in connection with the total casualties to be expected in the Japanese war, the rate at which land invasion should be pushed ahead in Japan or held back while attrition by air blockade proceeds, and the relative apportionment of effort between Army Air Forces and the Army Ground Forces and within each Force. The reason why a study of casualties would have such diverse applications is that the big cost to the nation in this war will be dead and disabled Americans. Consequently, in evaluating one plan or another, the expected casualties should be estimated as accurately as possible. . . .

The most basic problem in the Japanese war is the establishment of what is necessary to cause Japan to capitulate. There is a very important historical study which can be made in this connection but apparently has never been made either in the War Department or outside. The object of the study is to determine to what extent the behavior of a nation in a war can be predicted from the behavior of her troops in individual battles. If the study shows that the behavior of nations in all historical cases comparable to Japan's has in fact been invariably consistent with the behavior of troops in battle, then it means that the Japanese dead and ineffectives at the time of defeat will exceed the corresponding number for the Germans. In other words, we shall probably have to kill at least 5 to 10 million Japanese. This might cost us between 1.7 and 4 million casualties including 400,000 to 800,000 killed.[74]

Here we have the social "scientist" mind in its purest form, assuming that one could find anywhere in the history of mankind "cases comparable to Japan's." But however unrealistic his project, and however sympathetic Quincy Wright might have been, Shockley accomplished one thing—he alarmed Stimson about the conceivable losses of his GIs. Stimson's claim to have been told that the invasion might cost over a million casualties was not a postwar invention. It came from his staff.

Robert Messer, one of the more imaginative members of the "Truman knew Japan was ready to surrender" school, points to the "recent discovery" of statements Truman made in a journal he kept at Potsdam, and in letters to his wife, as showing that the president lied publicly about his reasons for dropping the bomb. After Stalin reaffirmed Soviet entry into the Pacific War, Truman noted in a letter of 18 July, "I've gotten what I came for—Stalin goes to war on August 15. . . . I'll say that will end the war a year sooner now, and think of the kids who won't be killed: That is the important thing." Messer claims this statement shows Truman expected that "Soviet entry alone would end the war before an invasion of Japan."[75] This is not a legitimate interpretation. The statement shows only that Truman thought the war would end a year earlier than previously anticipated. There is no warrant for holding that Truman thought Japan was ready to surrender.

By 1 August fear of a bloodbath crested. The "Sixth Army G-2 Estimate of the Enemy Situation, OLYMPIC Operation" is very pessimistic. Numerical strength, terrain advantages, and Japanese fanaticism indicated "that a very strong and ferocious defense will be interposed at the beaches." Caves, tunnels, and pillboxes were much more intensively developed than on Okinawa; on Kyushu, "strong measures are being taken to disperse and conceal aircraft and to accumulate stores of avgas, ammunition, and base ordnance in critical areas."[76]

Was it mere blind bureaucratic routine that caused the JCS on 6 August to request from its planners a scenario for bypassing Kyushu and attacking northern Honshu? Certainly the Joint War Plans Committee took the request seriously. A ninety-six-page plan to accomplish this was ready by 9 August.[77]

This planning process was not scientific, nor were the officers who staffed Marshall's headquarters clairvoyant. Consider a 12 August memo for the chief of staff from Maj. Gen. Clayton Bissell. This was after the two bombs had been dropped, the Soviets were cruising through Manchuria, the Japanese government was partially in the hands of the emperor and the peace party (though Anami and his supporters were not fully agreed to surrender), and the United States' note implying that the emperor could remain head of the government was being considered in Tokyo. Bissell wrote

> Large, well-disciplined, well armed, undefeated Japanese ground forces have a capacity to offer stubborn fanatic resistance to Allied ground operations in the homeland and may inflict heavy Allied casualties . . . Japanese stock piling has established food and munitions in all areas of expected invasion in sufficient quantities to support operations for from about four to six months despite expected serious disruption of Japanese rail, road and water transport systems. . . . *Atomic bombs will not have a decisive effect in the next 30 days.* [italics added][78]

Let it be said that Bissell was right about the capabilities and intentions of the Japanese *military*. What he could not have known was the power and audacity of a hitherto acquiescent emperor, Privy Seal, and nobility.

Even with Hiroshima and Nagasaki, with the Soviet entry, and with an impressive (though outnumbered) American invasion fleet shaping up, surrender barely came off in mid-August. Despite the final submission of War Minister Anami, Army Chief of Staff Umezu, and Navy Chief of Staff Toyoda, who had been the three Supreme Council holdouts, army hotheads got out of control. Dissident forces seized the Imperial Compound the night before the emperor's broadcast, turned the place inside out trying to find the recording of his surrender rescript, assassinated Lt. Gen. Mori Takeshi (commander of the Imperial Guard at the palace), attempted to assassinate Premier Suzuki Kantaro and burned down his house when they found he had escaped, and tried to take over the radio station that was to broadcast the emperor's surrender the next day.[79]

The sticking point in Japanese surrender in August 1945 was *not* the terms of surrender; it was the still unknown ability of the emperor to make a surrender *of any kind* hold.

John Dower has the ultimate answer to those who tell us now that peace was there to be had in 1944 and early 1945 if we had only modified the unconditional surrender rhetoric, and signaled acceptance of the emperor: "The suggestion that there may have been serious lost opportunities for a peace settlement in 1944 or early 1945 remains almost unbelievable, and the small murmurs about peace which Iriye [in his rose-tinted book *Power and Culture*] seizes upon seem as candles set against an inferno of hate."[80]

The inferno of hate was stilled only by the inferno of the atom.

•　　　•　　　•

The preponderance of evidence shows that *at the time of decision* the Truman administration believed, with good reason, that invasion plans threatened an unacceptable loss of life, to Japanese as much as to Americans. Hiroshima cultists deny this and go beyond it to claim that whatever Truman thought, postwar investigation showed Kyushu defenses to have been weak, and OLYMPIC if it had gone forward would not have been traumatic. A major theme of Hiroshima cultist's rhetoric is, "Even if Truman did think an invasion would be costly, he was wrong, hence dropping the bomb was wrong."

Let us look briefly at what postwar investigators learned about the prospects for OLYMPIC. While wartime estimates of the cost in casualties of invading Kyushu were all over the lot, postwar estimates were not so scattered. The majority of studies concluded that the invasion would have been costly, hence Truman was right to fear it.

One document, however, disputes this conclusion, and has achieved notoriety through its "discovery" by Gar Alperovitz. In a *New York Times* op-ed story of 3 August 1989, titled "Did We Have to Drop the Bomb?", Alperovitz describes this "secret U.S. intelligence study" as if he had found the Rosetta stone.[81] Five years later, in a similar story in the *Washington Post*, he was still impressed with this "official study."[82]

The truth is that this document had never been lost or misplaced, and when it was declassified in 1977, it was available for all to see.[83] But it is not a study of why Japan surrendered nor of what casualties the U.S. would have sustained had it invaded Kyushu. It is a puff piece by Col. R.F. Ennis, chief, Intelligence Group, War Department Operations Division. Ennis's superior told him on 29 January 1946 to study how the typhoon that struck Japan in October 1945 would have affected OLYMPIC had that invasion gone forward.[84]

Two of Ennis's six pages discuss how the typhoon might have affected the American forces (not much). The third discusses how it would have affected the Japanese defenders (also not much). It is not clear what research Ennis did for this section; he may have debriefed officers returning from Asia and passing through the Pentagon.

But then Ennis has two pages dealing with "Growth of Surrender Psychology," and a page dealing with "Development in Event Operation OLYMPIC Proved Necessary." Here Ennis is simply misinformed. Ennis alleges that the emperor told a cabinet meeting 20 June that Japan should have a plan to end the war at once, and "As a result of this statement by the emperor, Premier Suzuki decided to stop the war." There was no cabinet meeting that day.[85] Suzuki did not see the emperor; Togo and Kido did. Kido persuaded the emperor to call a meeting of the Supreme Council for the Direction of the War in two days. At this 22 June meeting, the emperor questioned previous decisions to fight to the end, suggested that there might be other means of coping with the current crisis, and solicited opinions from the Council members. Togo then suggested that an envoy be sent to Moscow to obtain Russia's help in ending the war. War Minister Anami and Army Chief of Staff Umezu disagreed, the emperor rebuked them, and the Emperor left the room. Nothing like Ennis's scenario happened.

Ennis also says, "Investigation shows that there was little mention of the use of the atomic bomb by the United States in the discussions [of the Japanese Cabinet and Supreme Council] leading up to the 9 August decision."[86] This stands to reason. There could have been no mention of the bomb until the United States dropped the first one 6 August. By 7 August it was on every lip. Less imaginative, but equally fallacious, is Ennis' claim, emphasized by Alperovitz, that "The war would almost certainly have terminated when Russia entered the war against Japan." There is no warrant for this (see the discussion in chapter four). The Ennis study is worthless.

The most recent study of invasion plans is Ray Skates' 1994 book, *The Invasion of Japan: Alternative to the Bomb*. Skates has used most of the significant wartime American planning and intelligence documents to assess the decision to use the bomb rather than invade, but he neglects the massive body of United States Strategic Bombing Survey and Far East Command interrogations. His casualty estimate for OLYMPIC is 60,000 to 75,000 with 15,000 to 20,000 deaths; this is higher than the 18 June estimates, and gives little support to the Hiroshima cultists.[87] Where he does support those who believe the bomb was unnecessary is in his treatment of unconditional surrender; for Skates *this* was the sticking point that prolonged the war. Since the next chapter deals with that topic, it will not be discussed here.

Of the systematic investigations of Kyushu defenses conducted by official bodies after the war, the only one to offer significant comfort to the "easy invasion" camp is that conducted by the Ninth Army Corps. Ponderously titled "Report of Reconnaissance and Survey of Japanese Dispositions in IX Corps Zone of Operations on Southern Kyushu Operation Olympic (Reconnaissance Made 3-5 December 1945)," it suffers from the brevity of the investigation. Ninth Corps investigators knew what they were after, however, and went directly to the sources. The report is better organized than most. Terrain, kamikaze, and other desperate measures favored the defense, but the Japanese were short on weapons, vehicles, and communication. The conclusion: "Summarily, the soundness of the Operation Plan [for] IX Corps dated 12 August 1945 was confirmed."[88] This is a minority opinion.

Supporting the belief that Japanese forces would have decimated the first wave of a U.S. landing is the testimony of almost every Japanese officer involved in the defense of Kyushu who was interrogated after the war. None claimed that Japan could have won the war; many of them believed that they could have done so much damage that the United States would have given up the invasion. The consensus was that they would have repulsed the first wave of attackers, whereupon they could have negotiated a favorable peace. "Favorable peace" in this context is what Anami and the two service chiefs demanded even after the atomic bombs and Soviet intervention: retention of the emperor (which Truman obliquely approved), no occupation, self-disarmament of Japanese forces, and war crimes trials conducted only by Japanese.

This unanimity from Japanese defense commanders is striking. Navy and air commanders presided over mere remnants of their forces, but the Japanese spirit, and their suicide devices, still gave them hope. The army, short as it was of fuel, was almost manic because of its powerful defense of Okinawa. Naturally all this Japanese testimony can be impeached. Pride and patriotism would mitigate against confessions of weakness. But it cannot be written off entirely; the witnesses stood to face war crimes trials that would have gone easy on those who believed that Japan should have surrendered early, not those who thought Japan had a fighting chance of bloodying another American amphibious force.

But the testimony of competent American investigators after the war cannot be so impeached. There were at least a half dozen who had no vested interest in their conclusions, no need to justify atomic weapons, no reputation at stake; and they were firmly convinced that OLYMPIC would have been the disaster that Truman wanted so desperately to avoid.

One significant perspective comes from an officer who may never have been in the Pacific at all. Col. S.L. Weld was responsible for training and equipping U.S. divisions redeployed from Europe prior to departure for Japan. An eight-week period was regarded as minimum training for the quite different task in the Pacific. The timetable for such training had always been tight; the Battle of the Bulge had delayed conclusion of the war in Europe. On 7 August 1945 the War Department announced new readiness dates which precluded any retraining for two divisions; another would have had only twenty days, and a fourth only nine days.

Weld observed, "This situation was particularly disturbing in view of the fact that the scheduled operation was amphibious, and neither division had had amphibious training."[89] Robert R. Palmer and coauthors, in *The Procurement and Training of Ground Combat Troops*, conclude:

> Thus the course of events during the months between V-E Day and V-J Day had been such as to make the prospects of redeployment training most unfavorable. Personnel turnover and other difficulties had been so formidable, indeed, that a key officer [Weld] in the G-3 Section of Headquarters, Army Ground Forces, was later constrained to remark: "The capitulation of Hirohito on 14 August saved our necks. With things being as they were it would have been absolutely impossible for us to have sent well-trained teams to the Pacific for participation in the scheduled invasion of Japan."[90]

By far the most probative postwar investigation of Kyushu defenses was that of Edmund J. Winslett, officer in charge of Sixth Army photographic intelligence, preparatory to OLYMPIC. Winslett began development of tactical intelligence for this operation in early 1945. Immediately after the war he was able to visit all the sites covered by his operation; the sixteen-page text of his report, "Defenses of Southern Kyushu," was presented at the United States Army Military History Institute, Carlisle Barracks, 3 June 1946.

There is no equivocation in Winslett's report; Southern Kyushu was fortified and supplied amazingly. Here is his description of one landing site, the area around Kagoshima:

> I travelled by jeep from Kagoshima, to Ibusuki, inspected the entire installation. Here is what was found. The road is defended by the same general plan as was Nakurazaki beach with the additional safeguards of hundreds of caves, artillery ports in the cliffs and prepared installations to concentrate both heavy and light fire on the road and paralleling railroad. I haven't the time to go into detail on the maze of caves, their completeness and complicated network of communication passageways. Underground installations were not confined to supply and ammunition, they had caves for everything, C.P.'s mess and housing, vehicles and even farmers had their safety caves. This seaplane plant was now being devoted to the manufacture of the Japanese version of the DUWKS, there were six among the burned

remains of the original plant and the parts for many hundreds of them were stored in the caves in the overhanging cliff. . . . Inside the burned plant were many concrete individual rifle strongpoints. The plan was easy to understand, a fight right in thru the plants, to the death.[91]

After eleven pages of such descriptions, his conclusion: "After a personal survey of the areas in which our invasion landings were scheduled to take place, I am convinced that the greatest battle the American Armies have ever won was the one which was never fought—the INVASION OF KYUSHU."[92]

Hiroshima cultists who solicit our agreement to the proposition that Japan was a shaky derelict waiting to be pushed over when Truman dropped atomic bombs must come to grips with Winslett.

A second highly credible analysis was completed by the organization that would have landed at Kushikino had the invasion gone forward, and which was put in occupation of Kyushu after the surrender. This is a balanced thirty-nine-page report, done by Headquarters, Fifth Marine Amphibious Corps, dated 30 November 1945. It acknowledged weaknesses of the defenders (fortification not all completed, supplies inadequate) as well as strengths (12,725 kamikaze planes available, with adequate fuel; great terrain advantages). It concludes, "In theory, the Japanese plan of defense was conceived to be and probably would have been, in the initial phases, a costly one for the invasion forces."[93] The invasion would have succeeded only after "gradual annihilation" of the defenders.

The British had a "Combined Operations Observers" team on Kyushu by November; its extensive report was made on 4 April 1946. This document is descriptive, with little evaluation. It emphasizes the "no retreat under any circumstances" order for the beachhead defenders, and their dependence on lunge-mines and shoulder-pack mines—all suicide tactics.[94]

Headquarters Sixth Army furnished a twenty-three-page report, "Japanese Plans for the Defense of Kyushu," on 31 December 1945. It is based entirely on questioning of Japanese military personnel, is nonevaluative, and hence adds little to the testimony compiled by USSBS and Far East Command. The Japanese tapped by Sixth Army were no less confident of holding the invasion beaches, at least through the first wave, than the ranking officers interviewed in Tokyo.[95]

There were also reconstructions of the probable invasion scene by individuals. One of the most alarmist, by Lt. Comdr. Philip

Gustafson, USNR, appeared in the *Saturday Evening Post* 5 January 1946. "What If We Had Invaded Japan?" takes its casualty projections from Gen. Charles Willoughby; they are upwards of a million.[96] This represents casualties not only of OLYMPIC, but of CORONET, on the Tokyo Plain, scheduled for March 1946. Gustafson's main contribution is in a report of a tour of the underground defense network in the Tokyo area, and in extensive discussions of the kamikaze program with two of its mid-level procurers. These two militarists seemed to see nothing wrong with encouraging young men to fly to certain death, which bothered Gustafson.

A more scholarly study was written in 1965 by K. Jack Bauer, an assistant to Samuel Eliot Morison during the writing of the *History of U.S. Naval Operations in World War II*; and Alvin D. Coox, historian at San Diego State College and collaborator with Hayashi Saburo on the excellent war history *Kogun*. The perspective of twenty years enabled these two scholars to produce a narrative that is both credible and moving—"Olympic-Ketsu-Go."

Two quotations from Bauer capture the fantastic, but true, devotion of the Japanese bitter-enders as well as the thought process of the emperor, when he called the whole thing off. The bitter-enders, unnamed, believed that:

> As late as surrender time—even after the A-bombs had been dropped—a staff lieutenant colonel, related to the War Minister himself, was fervently convinced that even if the whole Japanese race were all but wiped out, its determination to preserve the National Polity would be forever recorded in the annals of man; whereas a people who sacrificed their will upon the altar of physical existence could never deserve resurrection. It would be useless for the people to survive the war, anyhow, if the structure of the State itself were destroyed. It was better to die than to seek ignominious "safety," . . . Dignity and practicality demanded Japanese resistance to the end; certain victory might yet be snatched from uncertain defeat. . . . Eternal life was to be sought in death.[97]

Fortunately, the emperor, whatever his complicity in Japan's early aggressions, at the last Imperial Conference saw things more clearly:

> He was profoundly troubled, continued the Emperor. What would happen if Japan plunged into decisive battle under such circumstances?

The entire race would be obliterated, and this would be a betrayal of the trust of ancestors and the duty toward posterity, lest Japan never again rise. Continuation of the war, then, could only serve to cripple Japan, extinguish civilization, and bring misfortune to mankind.

The Japanese Emperor's decision to end the war, under enormous external and internal pressure, obviated the American landings and the hemorrhage that was bound to occur soon on the beaches of Miyazake, Satsuma, and Ariake. Not only would five U.S. ground divisions, etc., be saved from the destruction at sea which the Japanese resolutely promised them, but untold thousands of Japanese would not die either—such as the squadrons of Kamikaze pilots and sailors with one-way tickets to the shrine of heroes at Yasukuni; or the women and children clutching pitiful staves and bamboo spears. The Japanese themselves have called the ending of the war a form of merciful euthanasia, and thank their gods that the nightmare operations OLYMPIC and CORONET never had to be invoked.[98]

Other speculations about OLYMPIC and its probable results add little to those mentioned here. This non-battle is still being argued about, but time has not diminished the consensus of 1945-46 that American forces would have won out, with losses that would have horrified Harry Truman, and would have permanently embittered an American public already bitterly anti-Japanese.

Matsumoto Keisuke, lt. col. in the Japanese Self-Defense Forces, briefed the U.S. -Japan Military History Exchange Conference on 25 October 1987. His topic: "Preparations for Decisive Battle in Southern Kyushu in Great East Asia War." The U.S. forces, Matsumoto said, would have overwhelmed the spartan Japanese troops. But "if the war had not ended, spectacular and brilliant battles would still have been fought by the Japanese forces."[99]

•   •   •

Harry Truman ordered the bombing of Hiroshima and Nagasaki primarily to end the war as soon as possible and save lives. This conclusion is compelled by the evidence, and yet there are challenges to this motivation. The most powerful challenge is based on the belief that atomic bombs were dropped on Japan, and nowhere else, because of American racism. This belief will be discussed further in chapter seven; here a summary of the argument against it will suffice.

There are two intractable facts that destroy this argument: (1) Hiroshima cultists cannot challenge the timetable that made the first bomb available only after Germany had surrendered, leaving Japan as the sole Axis power yet to be overwhelmed. What evidence anywhere implies that the United States would not have used atomic weapons on Germany had it been still a belligerent, when the bombs were developed precisely out of fear Germany would get them first, and when the Allies obliterated Dresden and several other towns as thoroughly as the atom destroyed Hiroshima and Nagasaki? (2) The directive issued to Col. Paul Tibbets in September 1944 instructed him to train *two* bomber groups to make simultaneous drops on Germany and Japan.[100] This also is unanswerable.

Japan's sense of victimization is so deeply rooted that the racism argument cannot be successfully countered in that country. There is no justification for its acceptance elsewhere.

Then there is the atomic diplomacy argument, the main stock in trade of some American Hiroshima cultists: Truman dropped the bomb to intimidate the Soviet Union. This possesses a kernel of truth. Anticommunism and anti-Sovietism had burgeoned in 1920s America, receded during the war, and began growing in 1944 as the Russians occupied Eastern Europe. President Truman, James Byrnes, Ambassador Averell Harriman, and a few others worried about the extension of Soviet power, and welcomed the clout that possession of nuclear weapons gave the United States. But uneasiness about the Soviets in the summer of 1945 was not a full-blown cold war. Checkmating Soviet moves did not dominate the Truman White House until much later. The dominant (and warranted) opinion of American historians, as J. Samuel Walker noted in 1990, is that the bomb was used primarily for military reasons.[101]

Most Hiroshima cultists realize the flimsiness of their arguments *for* atomic diplomacy, and seek to buttress them by claiming that Truman could have ended the war simply by guaranteeing the emperor (softening the unconditional surrender rhetoric); or by waiting a week or two until the Soviet Union entered the war; or by tightening the siege until Japan simply collapsed. These counterfactual arguments cannot be sustained, and will be discussed in chapter two.

There is a bureaucratic answer to the question, "Why did Truman drop the bomb?" It is best developed by Stanley Goldberg, Gen.

Leslie Groves' biographer, in a paper at the American Historical Association convention in January 1995. Goldberg considers the conventional explanation for using the bomb, to shorten the war and save lives; he also considers the atomic diplomacy theory. He does not find these incompatible; both could have been operative:

> But more important than that, on the basis of my work, I am convinced that both of these motivations, while evident, are far less important than three others:
>
> 1) Momentum (no one ever said "stop, it is not needed."), 2) Protection of the reputations of the civilian and military leadership of the project, and 3) The personal ambitions of some, especially of General Leslie R. Groves. These three factors were at play, almost from the beginning, by which I mean the spring of 1941, when Vannevar Bush, who was essentially FDR's scientific advisor, was struggling with the question of whether or not to initiate an all-out, crash program to try to build an atomic bomb.[102]

As this all-out Manhattan Project gathered momentum, secretly absorbed money and resources, and by 1944 seemed unlikely to produce a bomb before Germany surrendered, the project's managers and supporters began to worry. Suppose it all came to naught? Inquisitive congressional committees were told that after the war, all would be explained. Goldberg's analysis:

> But as the costs mounted and the mystery deepened, Bush, Conant, Secretary of War Henry Stimson and Under Secretary of War Robert Patterson become more and more nervous. Several times late in the war, Stimson or Patterson would preface notes to each other concerning Manhattan Project business with jokes about how, if the Project were not successful, they would spend the rest of their lives in Leavenworth, or worse, testifying before Congress.[103]

Goldberg then leads us through the final hectic moments before Hiroshima and Nagasaki. Vast expenditures at Oak Ridge had to be justified by using a uranium bomb. Even vaster expenditures at Hanford had to be justified by using a plutonium bomb. Thus, "What the evidence does suggest to me is that we were determined to use the atomic bomb on Japan before we gave them the chance to surrender."[104] The existence of the atom bombs delayed the end of the war!

This implies a degree of mendacity on Truman's part that is hard to credit. It implies that the Potsdam Declaration was phony, that had Suzuki signalled acceptance rather than the unfortunate word *mokusatsu* the war would have gone on anyway, and that Truman's expressed desire to avoid casualties was not quite sincere. It also implies that Truman was too soft to handle a congressional investigation of the $2 billion Manhattan expenditure. Of course there would have been an investigation, but Truman's hands were clean, and he was feisty enough to have told congressional inquisitors to "come out to New Mexico, we'll show you that we *do* have a powerful new weapon that was worth the money." In the euphoria of the end of the war, this would have worked, just as the final indirect retention of the emperor worked despite overwhelming public disapproval.[105]

Harry Truman was a decent and considerate person. Sometimes he blew off steam. Sometimes he made unwise decisions (such as approving the crash program to build H-bombs in 1950), but the Hiroshima decision was not one of them, and does not deserve Martin Sherwin's incautious charge that Truman's exultation about the bomb's success, "This is the greatest thing in history," was a "vile remark."[106] Chapter six will discuss what was *really* vile about the Pacific War. Truman was arguably the most honest and candid of American presidents since 1932. None of the major Truman biographers find him to be mendacious; nor do they believe anti-Soviet motives or racism dominated the 1945 decisions.

Atomic diplomacy and other cultist variants purport to show a White House fixated on Russia, or strongly racist, or dominated by bureaucrats. One cannot quarrel with the claim that many bureaucratic and personal motives of the makers of the bomb were brought to bear upon the president; these analyses do not, however, remove the pressure point of *decision*, which lay with the president. He ordered the dropping of the first bombs "as available" as surely as he ordered cancellation of the third. And the White House was fixated on securing Japan's surrender, on terms that would obviate recrudescence of militarism, as quickly and with as few casualties as possible.

2

Was Japan Ready to Surrender?

The most important foundation for attacks on Harry Truman's use of atomic bombs against Japan is the claim that conventional bombing and naval blockade had brought Japan to the point of surrender by the summer of 1945, and that the Allies could just sit tight and wait. Neither atomic bombs, Soviet entry into the war, nor invasion were necessary. This "early surrender" hypothesis comes from publications of the United States Strategic Bombing Survey (USSBS). The USSBS was directed in Japan, and its official reports edited and controlled by Paul H. Nitze.

USSBS began as an effort by strategic bombing advocates to establish their craft as the ultimate arbiter of all future wars. "After-action" reports are common military activities; what set USSBS off from the garden variety of after-action reports, according to David MacIsaac, was "its evolution into a Presidential Commission possessed of extraordinary powers and directed by civilians rather than soldiers."[1] And, one might add, by the magnitude of the desolation it was to survey, and the later prominence of its personnel.

On 9 September 1944, President Roosevelt directed the establishment of a USSBS to measure as precisely as possible the effectiveness of strategic bombing in defeating Germany. Franklin D'Olier, president of the Prudential Insurance Company, was recruited to head the survey; he was to have a civilian board of directors and extensive staff support from the military. The civilian directors included some whose later careers were prominent: George Ball, John Kenneth Galbraith, and Paul Nitze.[2]

The survey's first task was to follow Eisenhower's armies into Europe. This was a congenial operation for many of the Survey's Eurocentric members and directors. Galbraith's account of his exploits, particularly the interviews he, Ball, and Nitze conducted with Albert Speer, is lyrical.[3] Inevitably the civilian investigators gave less credit for victory to the strategic bombers than the air force claimed. Galbraith's Overall Economic Effects Division was particularly unimpressed with bombing damage to industry. Only when massive bombing of transportation and petroleum facilities began in mid-1944 was the operation held to be cost-effective.

In June 1945, Nitze, Ball, and Maj. Gen. Orvil A. Anderson, head of air force personnel working for the survey, were brought from Europe to Washington to advise on the most effective bombing plan for Japan. No final reports had been written on their European findings, but as Nitze put it, "we had accumulated sufficient information to draw tentative conclusions."[4] Nitze's later account of his conferences with the Joint Target Group (JTG) is crucial to an understanding of the explosive USSBS publications a year later:

> A concentrated air attack on the essential lines of transportation, including railroads . . . would isolate the Japanese home islands from one another and fragment the enemy's base of operations. I believed that interdiction of the lines of transportation would be sufficiently effective so that additional bombing of urban industrial areas would not be necessary. My plan of air attack on Japan was approved but not my estimate of when it would cause Japan's capitulation. . . . [Fred Searles and I] concluded that even without the atomic bomb, Japan was likely to surrender in a matter of months. My own view was that Japan would capitulate by November 1945. However, the Joint Chiefs saw matters differently. The upshot was that they unanimously recommended that plans go forward for an early invasion of the Japanese home islands. President Harry S. Truman. . . was then left with the choice of using the atomic bomb against Hiroshima and Nagasaki, or of authorizing the attack against Kyushu and the Tokyo Plain. He opted for the atomic bomb. . . .[5]

On 15 August 1945, President Truman asked D'Olier to continue USSBS operations in the Pacific. The authorization this time was broader, and since the navy had played a major role in bombing Japan, the Pacific group was to include navy as well as army air forces personnel. In addition, USSBS was to study more than just the effects of strategic bombing: Truman's letter to D'Olier instructed him to consider postwar military planning.[6] Then there occurred what is now called "mission creep"; USSBS attempted to evaluate the unique impact of atomic bombs, investigate why the Japanese attacked Pearl Harbor, and why they ultimately surrendered.

With the war over, D'Olier had trouble persuading survey employees to transfer to the Pacific. Of the civilian directors, only Nitze was willing to take a major responsibility for the Pacific Survey; he was in effect CEO. D'Olier put in a perfunctory appearance. Galbraith came over to Japan for a month.

Paul Nitze welcomed the chance to give the world its first official and comprehensive evaluation of atom bombs, and he arrived in Japan with some opinions already formed. In addition to his belief that Japan would surrender by November without the bombs, he was ambivalent about the bomb itself. As Strobe Talbott puts it in his biography of Nitze:

> By the time he arrived at Hiroshima and Nagasaki, Nitze was already an experienced observer of what bombs could do. He had seen places in Germany where more people were killed by conventional explosives than by the A-bombs. . . . Nitze saw it as his task to demystify the bomb, to treat it as another weapon rather than the Absolute Weapon. While others believed that nuclear weaponry was truly something new under the sun, Nitze believed that the measurements of the Survey at Hiroshima and Nagasaki showed the effects to be roughly the equivalent of an incendiary bombing raid by 220 B-29s.[7]

It was a belief he never changed: the United States should try to avoid nuclear war, but if it came, it would not be Armageddon.[8]

Nitze was in Japan from 27 September until 4 December. For some of this time he had 1,000 people working for him. In December, most survey employees returned to Washington, D. C., where they processed their data and wrote reports. There were dozens of reports from various divisions of the survey, but only three had the imprimatur of the chairman's office (and hence of Nitze): *Summary Report (Pacific War), Japan's Struggle to End the War*, and *The Effects of Atomic Bombs on Hiroshima and Nagasaki*.

These reports, and most of the documents supporting them, are now in USSBS files (National Archives microfilms of these papers, M1654 and M1655, run to 514 rolls). By 1991, they all appeared to be declassified. Most of the documents concern such things as production, shipping, armed force strength, and photos of bombed sites. These data are probably as accurate as could be expected when agents of a foreign enemy swarm over a defeated nation trying to find out in two months what made that alien culture tick, and what happened to it under siege. But Nitze and his crew asked and answered questions about Japan's motives and intentions, much more convoluted matters. And it was in the official reports from the chairman's office that Nitze was able to get back at the JCS, and Truman, and their wrongheaded preference for invasion or nuclear weapons. Two of the three reports from the chairman's office claim that the atomic bombs had not been necessary to secure Japan's surrender. The most dogmatic statement of this counterfactual proposition appears in both the *Summary Report* and *Japan's Struggle*:

> Based on a detailed investigation of all the facts, and supported by the testimony of the surviving Japanese leaders involved, it is the Survey's opinion that certainly prior to December 31, 1945, and in all probability prior to November 1, 1945, Japan would have surrendered even if the atomic bombs had not been dropped, even if Russia had not entered the war, and even if no invasion had been planned or contemplated.[9]

Here is a counterfactual proposition of breathtaking scope. It was used by critics of Truman's decision to prove that anti-Soviet politics or racism, rather than military necessity, motivated him. Truman could then easily be indicted as trigger-happy, indifferent to civilian casualties, or using the bomb only to intimidate the Soviet Union. And this "all the facts" USSBS rhetoric, coming from a presumably nonpartisan, objective fact-finding commission, effectively skewered Truman, General Marshall, and all the military leaders who had contemplated invasion and had unleashed the atom.

One would think that when confronted with such an extreme claim students of the bomb decision would probe the warrant for it. What serious investigator has ever felt that he had "all the facts" about any matter so complicated as the Japanese decision to surrender? It is absurd on the face of it to claim that "detailed investigation of all the facts" could have been made in a mere two months, especially in a culture alien to the investigators. But such elementary cautions did not inhibit Truman's critics. Gar Alperovitz, Hanson Baldwin, P. M. S. Blackett, Paul Boyer, Gregg Herken, Paul Keckskemeti, Robert Messer, Leon Sigal, the authors of a planned Smithsonian National Air and Space Museum exhibit on the end of World War II, and many others swallow this conclusion of the USSBS whole.[10] I have found only three writers on the end of the

Pacific War, Barton Bernstein, Robert Butow, and William L. O'Neill who overtly question the credibility of USSBS.[11]

Of course Nitze's crew did not gather all the facts. Subsequent investigation by Far East Command's Intelligence Section, by the fourteen members of the (Japanese) Pacific War Research Society, by a score of independent scholars and journalists, and by the staff of the International Military Tribunal for the Far East produced tens of thousands of pages of information, including more extensive and revealing interrogations of Japanese principals than USSBS obtained. And most of what USSBS obtained was not fact in any accepted sense, but only raw data that demanded interpretation. For example, it obtained data about Japan's steel production. Relating this to when Japan would have surrendered if there had been no bomb, no Soviet entry, no planned invasion, is a highly speculative business.

Nitze's position, as he explained it to me in January 1994, is consistent and plausible. Invasion would have been disastrous: "We weren't going to accomplish a damn thing by a ground invasion. These fellows were going to fight to the last man and if we were against that kind of thing, fighting to the last man on the ground, I thought the estimate of 500,000 U.S. casualties was a gross underestimate." Bombing of urban areas was unnecessary; this was the position Nitze took in the Target Planning in June 1945. But "Blockade was having an effect. People were starving in Japan. . . . They couldn't even ship between islands. They would soon run out of food. This would cause the Emperor to work for peace." And when starvation really hurt, they would call it quits: "Even the military don't like to see all their people starve to death."[12]

Plausible, this, but there are problems. How could the specificity of the dates of surrender be warranted? Of course Japan would surrender *sometime* before the country was completely destroyed, unless a Masada complex were overpowering.[13] But when? And how long would starvation take?

Starvation as a cause of surrender is hard to evaluate. Hundreds of Japanese soldiers on isolated Pacific islands starved rather than surrender. As to the home islands, USSBS quotes Hoshino Naoki, who had been chief cabinet secretary during the Tojo government, as saying that bombing Japan's rail lines instead of cities would have made resistance difficult: "It would simply have been a question as to how long it would have taken the Japanese people to starve."[14] But he qualifies this: "Of course, fighting might have continued, but it would have been meaningless."

The best discussion of Japanese nutrition levels is in Thomas R. H. Havens's, *Valley of Darkness*. He notes that in 1945 the Japanese people "took in just 1,793 calories a day. . . yet even then the amount of protein people were eating held up reasonably well."[15] And by way of summary, "To the very end people managed to find food, however sparse or untasty." Further observation about the food situation comes from Yoshida Shigeru, prime minister 1946-47. Food was short in 1946, he says: "Here again, however, the American Occupation forces were most helpful, enabling us to tide over the worst periods with the aid of the imported food they released. . . and also the food stored in different parts of the country during the war—stocks that most fortunately proved to be far more abundant than was expected."[16]

A similar observation is made by Herbert Passin, a member of the occupation: "During the last year or so of the war, the Japanese military had stored away several years' supply of food, clothing, raw materials, equipment, and funds in its arsenals, caves, and other hiding places."[17] Surrender by starvation is at best an iffy business here. Some people did starve. But as William L. O'Neill points out, there was no way to tell how long a blockade would take; surrender was a political rather than a resource problem.[18]

Both Nitze and revisionist writers assume that tightening the blockade around Japan until enough people starved to impel Gen. Anami Korechika and his military diehards to surrender would have been a morally preferable way to end the war. Many ethicists doubt this conclusion. Whatever assumptions are made about the starvation level necessary in Japan's case (one million deaths? two million? ten million?), it is still true that starvation is a horrible way to die, and that the weaker individuals—infants, the elderly, the ill—bear the brunt of it. And the *official* position of the Japanese state was that a hundred million would willingly die for the emperor. The virtue of the starvation scenario must be argued, not assumed. Nishi Toshio quotes General MacArthur saying what may be an exaggeration, but with more than a kernel of truth: "No weapon, not even the atomic bomb, is as deadly in its final effect as economic warfare. The atomic bomb kills by the thousands, starvation by the millions."[19] Spencer Weart also deplores starvation: "It would not necessarily have been the kindest way to end the war; a blockaded nation feeds its soldiers while its old men, women and children die lingering deaths."[20] Horrible as the 200,000 deaths from atomic bombs were, they do not automatically outweigh millions of deaths from starvation.

Bombardment of Japanese rice-growing areas, and use of herbicides to bring starvation were discussed in the USSBS-JTG conferences. One objection to this strategy brought by JTG was well-taken: "Japanese rice production is not considered a profitable target in view of currently accepted strategy. It is felt that indigenous food supplies may be very important to the commander charged with occupation."[21] JTG was assuredly right. There was little conspicuous foresight from military offices, but this was one instance.

In USSBS publications, however, Nitze does not emphasize starvation. Page one of *Japan's Struggle* tells us how they know there would be early surrender: "The evidence is chiefly in the testimony obtained by Survey interrogation of the Army, Navy, Government, and Imperial household leaders who participated or were influential in the struggle within Japan over whether to continue the war to or accept surrender."[22] This claim can be subjected to careful scrutiny.

Such scrutiny should include the competence and bias of both interrogators and witnesses. Most of the interrogators were military figures with no special skills except martial arts; few were Japanese language specialists. USSBS did, however, obtain the services of a large number of native Japanese speakers (Nisei, and Caucasians raised in Japan) and academics and businessmen who had lived there to act as translators and interpreters. Biases of the American interrogators were obvious: army air force personnel wanted to hear that conventional bombing brought about surrender, navy officers that surrender was caused by the sea blockade and naval aviation. This means that when a Japanese respondent claimed that atom bombs were key factors in ending the war, this was prejudicial to that respondent and hence highly credible.

The most likely informant bias was to claim support for an early peace, or to have been against the war from the beginning. Admitting support for the war from the beginning and the desire to fight to the bitter end could hurt the informant in the eyes of his captors, and also in war crimes trials. Thus those who admitted to belligerence were putting themselves in jeopardy, and their testimony is reluctant and highly credible. An additional bias was to exonerate the emperor; none of those interrogated by USSBS depicted the emperor as supporting the Japanese military.

One liability of all investigations of the origin, conduct, and conclusion of the Pacific War was the scarcity of Japanese documents. Between the emperor's surrender rescript and American occupation of Japanese-held territories, there was an orgy of document destruction. Fortunately the diary of Marquis Kido Koichi, lord privy seal, has not been seriously impeached, and thus sheds much light on the end of the war.

Generally, the testimony taken by USSBS seems to be credible. How this testimony was processed by USSBS, especially by the final editor in the official reports from the chairman's office, is another matter.

The influentials whose testimony might have given some kind of warrant to the early surrender hypothesis number about four dozen. Despite its massive program, USSBS interrogated less than half of them.[23] The record shows that Nitze himself interrogated, or attended the interrogations of, ten Japanese.

His first session was the 1 October questioning of Tatebayashi Mikio, chief of the Civilian Defense Bureau, Ministry of Home Affairs.[24] Tatebayashi was not a prime player in the surrender drama. He knew about air raid warning systems and civilian defense programs instituted after the Doolittle Raids of April 1942, but it is not clear why he drew Nitze and Maj. Gen. Grandison Gardner to his questioning. He said nothing about any of the big questions: why Japan went to war, why it surrendered, or how atomic bombs affected the surrender decision.

On 4 October Nitze sat in on the interrogation of Araki Matsuo, chief of the Electrical Power Bureau, Ministry of Industry and Commerce.[25] The product of this interview could have been received and summarized for transmission to top echelons of USSBS by a bright sergeant. Araki brought four charts showing the structure of the industry and government regulation thereof. On declaring war, quitting war, atomic bombs, there was nothing.

On 5 October, Nitze and Gardner joined Adm. Ralph Ofstie in questioning a more important official, Adm. Toyoda Teijiro—navy minister 1940-1941, then foreign minister for five months, chairman of Japan Steel until March 1945, then minister of munitions.[26] Toyoda Teijiro (not to be confused with Toyoda Soemu, interviewed later) was important enough for Nitze to sit in on a second interrogation on 9 October.

This first interrogation covered many military and economic matters, but there was no support of Nitze's early surrender hypothesis. When Nitze came back to the 9 October interrogation of Toyoda Teijiro, the transcript notes, "The meeting was largely taken up with arrangements to make available all the records of the munitions industry. . . . "[27] There was nothing about war or peace decisions.

On 6 October, Nitze and Gardner interrogated Shiina Etsusaburo.[28] He was a businessman with experience in Europe and Manchukuo who became head of the Japanese Total Mobilization Bureau in 1943. It is possible that his uninspired rendering of Japanese wartime mobilization was enlightening for his high-ranking interrogators, but not likely.

Abe Genki was interrogated on 10 October with Nitze and Gardner again sitting in.[29] Abe was minister of Home Affairs in the Suzuki cabinet from April to August 1945. The surviving text of this interrogation is all about civil defense; there could have been nothing of value to Nitze in this record.

The last recorded interrogation for Nitze in October was on the 15th, of Lt. Gen. Yoshizumi Masao, chief of the Military Preparedness and Equipment Bureau from April 1942 to March 1945.[30] Nitze learned more than he could have wanted to know about how requisition, supply, hierarchy, interservice conflicts, and transportation failures were handled by the Japanese. Yoshizumi's summary was at least succinct: "They [his bureau] were faced with an insoluble problem." There is no talk of starting or ending wars.

Thus halfway through his time in Japan, Nitze had personally uncovered no confirmation whatsoever of his early surrender proposition; but he had not interviewed any leaders of the peace group, and only two second-level militarists. He then took leave of interviewing until 8 November.

On that date, Admiral Ofstie, Paul Baran (a protégé of John Kenneth Galbraith) and Lt. Comdr. G.N. Spinks interrogated Nomura Kichisaburo, who was both admiral and ambassador, with Nitze and others sitting in. This was the first top echelon witness to come within Nitze's purview. Nomura had been naval attache in the United States 1916-18, and came back as ambassador in 1941 to negotiate with Secretary Cordell Hull until Pearl Harbor; he was then interned, and returned to Japan in July 1942. He was appointed to the Privy Council in May 1945. This interrogation was a marathon session. The three interrogators elicited from the aging Admiral a short course on the events of the Pacific War. For the first three hours or so, Ofstie and Baran alternated in asking Nomura about the outbreak and first two years of the fighting.

When Lt. Comdr. Spinks took over, he turned to the fall of the Tojo cabinet and the beginnings of the peace movement. Nomura believed that the people were willing to die fighting, that "it was the destiny of our country to continue this very unwise war to the very end." Soviet entry into the war and atomic bombs were not major factors in his mind, but they did contribute to popular unease. Before the Suzuki cabinet came in, and the damage to Japanese cities and industries became apparent, the war could not have been stopped: "They [the people] had never been told the truth about the situation and there would have been civil war in Japan among the people."[31] There were no direct answers from Nomura to Nitze's concerns.

The next day, 9 November, was a high point for the survey. Chairman Franklin D'Olier was in Tokyo, one of the most renowned Japanese leaders was to be interrogated, and D'Olier himself joined Nitze, Galbraith, and Baran in questioning the witness.[32] The witness was Prince Konoye Fumimaro, three-time premier of Japan, former president of the Privy Council, the strong anticommunist leader who took Japan into the alliance with Hitler. In 1944 and 1945 Konoye had worked with the peace party to end the war.

This interrogation, like that of Nomura, covered a wide range of Japanese activity during the previous two decades. Konoye, however, was more intent on self-exculpation than was Nomura. One thing he was not intent on: providing Paul Nitze with evidence to support his early surrender hypothesis. Frame 0503 of the transcript shows the interrogator drawing from Konoye the statement that the main obstacle to ending the war was opposition in the army. He claimed that even in July 1945, had the emperor tried to end the war, there would have been an uprising. Only in August was there a "decrease in the risk of disorders in the event of an Imperial rescript." And what factors contributed to the improved situation in August? Konoye did not hesitate: "The big thing was the deterioration of the war effort; then with the entry of Russia in the war, and the dropping of the atomic bomb, it did a lot to prepare the way for the next move."

Were this not plain enough, the transcript has this exchange:

Q. How much longer do you think the war might have continued had the atom bomb not been dropped?
A. It is a little hard for me to figure that out.
Q. What would your best estimate be?
A. Probably it would have lasted all this year.
Q. It would not have been terminated prior to November 1—is that correct?
A. Probably would have lasted beyond that.

The questioner was not happy with this answer, and worried the matter for two more pages. The final discussion:

Q. Could Japan have continued to fight with these increasing attacks of the B-29's?

A. There was bound to be a limit as to what she could do.

Q. Yet you said if it weren't for the Emperor's statement [surrender rescript] they would be fighting today, did you not?

A. Of course, that was a conditional statement. There was a limit to what they could do. They would do what they could.

Q. Hadn't they almost reached the limit?

A. Of course, they were nearing the limit, but the army would not admit it. They wouldn't admit they were near the end.

Q. Would they not have been forced to surrender, therefore, even if Russia had not come in or even though we had not dropped the atomic bomb?

A. The army had dug themselves caves in the mountains and their idea of fighting on was fighting from every little hole or rock in the mountains.

Konoye had more to say. He thought the emperor would intervene to prevent this last-ditch stand, but did not say when. He was candid about the class interest motivating the peace party: "These were all of the upper rank of men—of higher classes of men who carried on such activities. As far as I know, there was none of the lower ranks. . . . They were afraid of a revolution—a sort of communistic revolution."[33]

And Konoye made abundantly clear that for this elite group, "The really big thing was to overcome the army." Most revisionist discussions of the end of the war ignore this factor, assuming that the emperor could have ended the war by an order long before August 1945. This is another hypothesis of dubious merit. The incidence of insubordination by junior officers and of assassination of government leaders by military fanatics in Japan—government by assassination—was too great for any peace advocate to feel personally secure in promoting his beliefs, or to feel confident that the emperor would not be captured and utilized by insurgents.[34] Every peace activist interviewed after the war mentioned this fear of assassination should his beliefs become known. Konoye was not paranoid in this respect.

While Nitze got no satisfaction from Konoye, his luck was better the next day. On 10 November, Marquis Kido Koichi, Lord Keeper of the Privy Seal and a prime mover in the peace faction, came before the illustrious group: D'Olier, Nitze, Galbraith, Baran, General Gardner, and four other American officers. Kido was close to Hirohito and saw the peace process from within the palace. Presumably much of the questioning during this interrogation also was conducted by Nitze: what would have happened without the Russians and the bomb was a frequent topic.

At first, Kido would not accommodate Nitze's position. The main obstacle to surrender was the army's determination to continue the fight, though Kido thought Minister of War Anami really wanted peace. And the bomb? "The atomic bomb had a strong effect upon bringing those—for want of a better term I would use 'fence sitters'—to the view that the war must be stopped. . . . To answer the question which of the two—the entry of Russia and the dropping of the atomic bombs—had the greatest effect on the army I can not say."

There was more discussion of the role of the cabinet in the surrender and of the problem of securing army compliance. Then the interrogator went directly to his main point:

Q. In the event that atomic bombs had not been dropped and Russia had not entered the war, how long in your opinion might the war have continued?

A. As I have stated, our decision to seek a way out of this war was made in early June before any bomb had been dropped and Russia had not yet entered the war. It was already our decision.

Q. The dropping of the atomic bombs and the entry of Russia into the war apparently did speed the agreement of the services ministries to end the war. What we would like to get is the degree to which this was speeded up.

A. It was not the time factor. It was the fact that it made the task easier to bring the war to a close by silencing those who would advocate the continuation of the war. If there had been no dropping of the atomic bomb or entry of the Soviet Union into the war, I am inclined to be very doubtful whether the policy to bring the war to a close would have progressed as smoothly. A rather large-scale outbreak within the armed forces could easily be imagined.

Q. Is it proper then to interpret it as being your opinion that the war might have been over in any case prior to November 1st even without the entry of Russia and the dropping of the atomic bombs?

A. I personally think that the war would have ended prior to November 1, as every possible effort was being exhausted to terminate the war.[35]

Here was the first, *and only*, affirmation of the early surrender hypothesis by one of Japan's wartime leaders. It took a bit of badgering and just a hint of suggestion; but Kido said it. He also said the effect of the atomic bombs was much greater than conventional bombing; Nitze did not want to hear that. But this was not the last word from Kido.

Kido said many things that were not included in USSBS's "all the facts." Arnold Brackman tabulates Kido's outpourings in *The Other Nuremberg*: "His diaries contained 5,920 entries; his interrogations at Sugamo filled 775 pages. . . . Kido's American counsel . . . put his client directly on the stand. Kido's week-long odyssey opened with his reading a 297-page deposition."[36] Nowhere in all this testimony can one find even a hint at a belief in early surrender without the bomb and Soviet entry.

And on the witness stand 16 October 1947 at the Tokyo War Crimes Trial (International Military Tribunal for the Far East, or IMTFE), under questioning by an interrogator not possessed of USSBS biases, Kido made a statement contradicting what he had told the survey. He identified the Nagasaki bomb as a "great shock to the nation, together with the Soviet Union's participation in the Pacific War. . . . I thought there would be no course left but to broadcast an Imperial rescript to the nation . . . terminating the war."[37] And free of USSBS badgering, he clearly indicated that he did not believe the war would have ended before invasion: "It is my inward satisfaction that *I was instrumental* in saving another twenty million of my innocent compatriots from war ravages and also the Americans tens of thousands of casualties, which would have been caused had Japan gone on fighting to the bitter end. . . ." (italics added).[38] If he kept Japan from fighting to the bitter end, he could not have believed in Nitze's early surrender hypothesis.

Nitze appeared at the interrogation of one other Japanese leader: Toyoda Soemu, admiral, former chief of Naval General Staff and hence a member of the Supreme War Guidance Council in 1945. On 13 and 14 November Toyoda appeared before interrogators Admiral Ofstie, Maj. Gen. Orvil Anderson, and Lt. Comdr. Walter Wilds, with Nitze sitting in. Toyoda had been one of three dissenters when Premier Suzuki tried to get agreement on surrender in

July; at the interrogation, however, he told USSBS that *all* members of the Supreme War Guidance Council had favored peace. He, War Minister Anami Korechika, and Army Chief of Staff Umezu Yoshijiro had merely wanted to obtain better terms than those the Potsdam Proclamation offered. American interrogators, who frequently cross-examined their Japanese witnesses roughly, gave no indication of skepticism with Toyoda. Yet he had opposed surrender even when the American terms allowed retention of the emperor.

The discussion was mostly about naval battles and tactics, but Wilds and Anderson asked him about surrender. One specific question dealt with the atomic bomb and Russia:

> Q. At what time during the course of the war would the Navy have accepted an Imperial rescript terminating the war?
>
> A. That is very difficult to answer because even on the 15th (August) when the Imperial rescript to terminate the war was actually issued, even then we found it difficult to hold down the front-line forces who were all "raring to go," and it was very difficult to hold them back. I do not think it would be accurate to look upon use of the Atomic bomb and the entry and participation of Soviet Russia into the war as a direct cause of termination of the war, but I think that those two factors did enable us to bring the war to a termination without creating too great chaos in Japan.[39]

Toyoda's position on the morale of the Japanese people under bombing was no help to the early surrender hypothesis. He told USSBS that "The effect on the people's morale was not as great as we had feared . . . there was no idea that we must give up the war to avoid even a single additional day of bombing." General Anderson pressed him further on this; the air force wanted to prove conventional bombing had done the most to bring Japan to its knees. Toyoda did not budge. He admitted that "if the air raids were to continue for months . . . it would be impossible for us to continue the war," but he had voted to continue the war in August.[40]

These were the interrogation sessions that might have provided Nitze with *first-hand* testimony supporting the early surrender hypothesis. Unfortunately, it is not there, except for the one constrained statement by Kido.

USSBS interviewed a dozen other high-ranking Japanese; their testimony overwhelmingly indicated that Japan was not about to surrender before the bomb. None claimed the war would have come to an early end.[41] Following is the relevant testimony that Nitze had in his files and should have factored into his conclusion.

Lt. Gen. Endo Saburo, chief of the Cabinet Bureau of Research, was interrogated 7 November. Endo was a soldier's soldier, and delighted in emphasizing Japanese fighting spirit to the seven Americans present. The Japanese, he said, were fighting for a righteous cause, and "winning" was not the big thing. After noting that neither Napoleon nor Hitler had won their wars he said "Whether we win the war or lose the war was not the primary purpose. Therefore, I told my men that they could fight without worrying whether they would actually win the war . . . they should be willing to die gladly, knowing that it was unavoidable and that they were doing the right thing."[42] Endo gave no specific statement on when Japan would have surrendered, but gave abundant evidence of the Masada attitude.

Funada Atsuyasu, secretary of the Board of Information and former Foreign Office official, was interviewed 12 December. According to Funada, the Suzuki cabinet wanted to surrender, but "the die-hards among the military still held out. The hopes of the die-hards were dashed to pieces by participation in the war by Russia and the atomic bomb. Both of these gave good material to the peace group."[43]

On 8 December, Field Marshal Hata Shunroku, commanding general of the Second General Army (Hiroshima) in 1945, was interrogated. Here was another bitter-ender. He stressed to his troops that Japan would win the final decisive battle of the homeland. They would dig in deeply to survive preliminary bombing: "We intended to stand and fight on the beaches. . . . However, when the atom bomb was dropped on Hiroshima, I believed there is nothing more we can do, we might as well give up."[44]

Baron Hiranuma Kiichiro, president of Privy Council, had been wounded by an assassin in 1941, and was one of the most important of the elder statesmen who engineered the surrender. He was interrogated 20 and 23 November. Hiranuma claimed to be one of several Japanese leaders who advocated immediate acceptance of the Potsdam Proclamation. As to causes of surrender, "The biggest factor . . . there came the atomic bomb, so that the country was faced with terrible destructive powers and Japan's ability to wage war was really at an end."[45]

On 2 November, USSBS interrogated Lt. Gen. Kawabe Torashiro, deputy chief, Imperial General HQ, and director of kamikaze operations in the Philippine and Okinawa battles. A fire-breathing supporter of war to the death, Kawabe intended to fly a kamikaze mission himself when the invasion came. He believed his forces had effectively concealed sufficient numbers of kamikaze planes near easily repaired runways to evade and withstand any American bombardment: "We believed probably we would lose the war and we knew we could never win the war; but we never gave up the idea of continuing the fight, using whatever [kamikaze] planes we could manufacture, and we intended to continue to fight unto the very end and make a showdown fight of it."[46]

Fleet Admiral Nagano Osami, who had been chief of Naval General Staff at the time of the Pearl Harbor attack, and was supreme naval advisor to the emperor at the end of the war, was interrogated 30 November. Most of this interrogation concerned the beginning of the war, but Admiral Ofstie, the questioner, did get around to the vital question: "Admiral, could the war have been brought to a close, in your opinion . . . without the entry of Russia into the war and without the employment of either Atom bomb?" Nagano acknowledged that even without these two events, Japan could not win, but "Speaking very frankly, I think we would have been able to extend the war for a considerable time at considerable sacrifice on your part. . . ."[47]

The chief cabinet secretary at the time of surrender was Sakomizu Hisatsume, one of the peace activists; his interrogation on 11 December is one of the most interesting in the whole USSBS series. David B. Truman was in charge, and approached the surrender by asking Sakomizu what he thought when news of the Hiroshima bomb arrived:

> A. When this news came on the morning of the 7th I called the Prime Minister on the phone and reported the announcement. Everyone in the government and even in the military knew that if the announcement were true, no country could carry on a war. Without the atomic bomb it would be impossible for any country to defend itself against a nation which had the weapon. The chance had come to end the war. It was not necessary to blame the military side, the manufacturing people, or anyone else—just the atomic bomb. It was a good excuse. Someone said that the atomic bomb was the kamikaze to save Japan.
>
> Q. How long do you think the war would have continued if the atomic bomb had not been used?

A. We had already asked the Russians to intercede, and we could expect that they would eventually give us some answer. If it had been unfavorable there was just one way to bring peace and that was to broadcast directly to the United States. But it would have been difficult to find a good chance to do so. I think you can understand. Suzuki tried to find a chance to stop the war and the atom bomb gave him that chance.[48]

Most of Truman's critics assert that the atom bombs "changed no minds" in Japan. The claim is false, and also irrelevant. The bomb created a situation in which the peace party and emperor could prevail.

Adm. Baron Suzuki Kantaro, premier at the time of the surrender, was interrogated 26 December. Here, of all people, was the witness who might have been able to dislodge any lingering support for the early surrender hypothesis. Unfortunately the civilian leadership of USSBS was back in Washington. Gens. Anderson and Gardner and civilians Paul Baran and Burton Fisher asked the questions. Suzuki was responsive, even to questions about his instructions from the emperor. About his plight when he became premier (7 April 1945) Suzuki said:

> It seemed to me unavoidable that in the long run Japan would be almost destroyed by air attack so that merely on the basis of the B-29s alone I was convinced that Japan should sue for peace. On top of the B-29 raids came the Atomic bomb, immediately after the Potsdam Declaration, which was just one additional reason for giving in and was a very good one and gave us the opportune moment to make open negotiations for peace. I myself on the basis of the B-29 raids felt that the cause was hopeless. The Supreme War Council, up to the time the Atomic Bomb was dropped, did not believe that Japan could be beaten by air attack alone. They also believed that the United States would land and not attempt to bomb Japan out of the war. On the other hand there were many prominent people who did believe that the United States could win the war by just bombing alone. However the Supreme War Council, not believing that, had proceeded with the one plan of fighting a decisive battle at the landing point and was making every possible preparation to meet such a landing. They proceeded with that plan until the Atomic Bomb was dropped, after which they believed the United States would no longer attempt to land when it had such a superior weapon—so at that point they decided that it would be best to sue for peace.[49]

No clearer, nor more probative, statement exists giving the reason why Japan surrendered when it did.

Maj. Gen. Takashima Tatsuhiko, chief of staff of the Twelfth Area Army defending the Kanto Plain, was interrogated 24 November. This interrogation is a forecast of Armageddon. Takashima knew every detail of the plan by which his army confidently expected to drive MacArthur out of Honshu with intolerable casualties. Was it mere braggadocio? It is difficult to imagine the motive for such a performance. His description of the fortifications of the Kanto Plain fully justifies MacArthur's projection of heavy casualties there, as compared with relatively light casualties on Kyushu. Here was a leader full of bushido and self-confidence, who obviously believed he had been sold out by cowardly civilians:

Q. How were these troops protected in their positions on the coast?

A. The majority of them were in caves. In a local area, they were of the fox-hole type. By August we had communications trenches between squads. We intended to have them between platoons by November. The best caves could withstand a hit by one- or two-ton bombs. By August the total length of under-cover emplacements equalled the length of the shore line in the area.

Q. What is your estimate of the success you would have had, if we had attacked as you estimated?

A. I think we would have been successful and won. We would have succeeded in driving you off the beaches.

Q. Did the dropping of the atomic bombs change your mind in any way?

A. No. There was no change in our plans. Its greatest effect was on civilians. It did not affect the army. Our men were dug in deeply enough to protect themselves. There was only one area where we couldn't get under cement.[50]

This startling interrogation was conducted by two American colonels and a captain. No high-ranking member of the survey was present. Takashima belittled atomic bombs, but there can be no doubt that surrender was the last thing on his agenda.

Rear Adm. Takata Toshitane, air specialist on the Naval General Staff, was interrogated twice. On 1 November the talk was technical and dealt with campaigns from Midway to Okinawa. The next day he was interviewed by Alexander de Seversky, a representative of the secretary of war. Had Takata realized the war was lost when the

Americans took Saipan and could then bomb Japan? Yes he realized then that the bombers could destroy Japan's industrial capacity, "but our hope was that, if we could destroy the invasion fleet when it came to actually land in Japan—although Japan could not win the war—it could hold out indefinitely for any number of years. . . ."[51]

On 15 November, Rear Adm. Tomioka Sadatoshi, operations officer of the Naval General Staff from November 1944, was interrogated. Tomioka was conversant with Japanese intelligence and planning, and heavily involved in the defenses of Iwo Jima, Okinawa, and Kyushu. After the fall of Saipan, he did not think that Japan would win the war: "Our only hope was that we could discourage you by inflicting great damage on your forces. We estimated that we would destroy 30-40% of the initial assaulting forces when you hit the homeland." He expected the invasion of Kyushu in July or early August 1945, since "We felt that your home front pressure would require you to move fast and try to end the war as quickly as possible. . . . You couldn't bomb us into submission, I thought, and therefore you would have to land on the home islands."[52] No hint of early surrender here.

Lt. Gen. Wakamatsu Tadakazu, chief of staff of the Second General Army (Hiroshima) until July 1945, then vice-minister of war, was interrogated 7 November. He was candid about Japan's liabilities in 1945: "Japan expected to repel only the first wave of the invasion. They had no hopes of repelling the second and third waves, but planned to retreat to the mountainous section . . . and not surrender."[53]

Early surrender? With no atom bombs, no Russians, no invasion? Careful inspection of the "testimony of the surviving Japanese leaders involved"—even that incomplete sample available to USSBS during its two short months in 1945—shows only Kido supporting Nitze, everyone else stating that Japan would have fought on indefinitely. When would Japan have surrendered without the bomb and the Russians? The *only* credible answer is that given by Robert Butow when Freeman Dyson asked him about it: "The Japanese leaders themselves do not know the answer to that question."[54]

USSBS conclusions suffer not just from Nitze's preconceived opinions about early surrender, but from the worst features of instant history. There was no time for thoughtful investigators familiar with Japanese history to formulate really probing questions, or to assimilate what was learned in early interviews and use it to sharpen later ones.

Nor was USSBS exempt from the organizational politics that exist in any group; in this case, naval and air forces were at each other's throats, leading witnesses into identifying sea power or air power as decisive, each trying to improve its status in postwar budget and power allocations. Paul Nitze presided over this turbulence as effectively as one could wish, but the bitterness and back-stabbing could not be suppressed.

Dissident opinions were suppressed, however, at least until Nitze left the survey in the summer of 1946. Minor reports finished after that time did not conform faithfully to the party line. One writer in the Urban Affairs Division was particularly deviant. Urban Affairs had commissioned a committee of Tokyo Imperial University, headed by Dean of the Faculty C. Maiide, to make a report on bomb damage to urban areas. Maiide's committee summarized the statistics on damage to Japan's urban areas and noted that though the people still hoped Japan would win "the decisive battles in Japan proper," their leaders had lost heart. The reason, as stated in *The Effects of Air Attack on Japanese Urban Economy*, March 1947, was this: "Particularly, the debut of atomic bombs in the Pacific War theater was decisive."[55] The writer of this demeaning line obviously did not have rank to take his opinions to the top; Admiral Ralph A. Ofstie did.

Ofstie, top naval officer on the Pacific survey, was so agitated by a report submitted to Nitze by his air force counterpart, Maj. Gen. Orvil Anderson, that he exploded: "The volume presents a completely inaccurate and entirely biased account of our war with Japan which is of absolutely no historical value, consistently misrepresents facts, and indeed, often ignores facts and employs falsehoods. From this light treatment of the Pacific war, the authors have arrived at a series of biased conclusions which . . . impose a threat to our future security."[56] Ofstie's purple prose goes on for several paragraphs. Feeling was so bitter that David MacIsaac subtitles one of his chapters "The Great Anderson-Navy War."[57] Fortunately, the worst excesses of this rivalry broke out after the publication of the three official reports of the chairman's office, but it had affected the conduct of inquiry from the start.

Military experience and linguistic competence may have been available in good measure to the USSBS, but there was one deficiency. MacIsaac is surely right in observing that one of the specialties

. . . lacking in the inner councils of the Survey's top level was that of
the historian. That they should have their historian, someone to keep
a record [of USSBS activities], they had no doubt. But that they should
have one or two of the country's most noted historians working with
them in an *advisory* capacity never entered their heads. It seems evident that the very nature of their task required the presence of an historian noted for his ability to ask tough questions of the evidence.
[italics original][58]

MacIsaac suggests someone such as William L. Langer or Carl
Becker. Such an historian would no doubt have noted the discrep-
ancy between the interrogation results and Nitze's counterfactual.

But the presence of a Langer or Becker would not have lessened
the frantic pace of the investigation in Japan. Calm deliberation was
never in the cards. James Beveridge, the survey's in-house historian,
reports that at the 28 November staff conference in Tokyo just before
Nitze returned to the United States, "Mr. Nitze congratulated the
whole group on the conduct of what he called the fastest moving,
hardest-hitting post-war organization on record."[59]

That speed and power were not conducive to successful interrogation and evaluation has escaped the consumers of USSBS intelligence. There is no room here for an extensive review of the data
USSBS did *not* gather, but one example is suggestive. The Historical
Division, Military Intelligence Section of the Far East Command,
U.S. Army, on 23 December 1949 interrogated Lt. Col. Inaba Masao,
chief of the Budget Branch, Military Affairs Bureau, Japanese War
Ministry, in 1945.[60] Inaba was active in the group determined to
"fight on with unshakable determination" even as the cabinet was
wrestling with terms of surrender on 11 August. This group
usurped the authority of War Minister Anami Korechika and published a fire-breathing proclamation in the newspapers calling on all
Japanese to "eat grass, swallow dirt, and lie in the fields" if necessary to destroy the arrogant enemy.[61]

Inaba was clearly not toadying to his inquisitors when he was
interrogated. In response to a question about the attitude of the
imperial family in August, he said:

he thought the members of the imperial family had become too nervous, especially after the appearance of the atomic bomb. It appeared
that the Empress Dowager had wished to have a strong aerial shelter

constructed in the OMIYA Palace but the Army did not approve of the idea. A sturdy aerial shelter had been constructed already in the Imperial Palace. The Army wished her to use this in time of emergency, since it was located close to the OMIYA Palace. However, it appeared that this incurred her displeasure. Prince MIKASA was also extremely nervous, and rebuked the War Minister, or did various other things. Anyway, the members of the Imperial Family appeared to have been shaken extremely by the atomic bomb. We presumed these facts greatly influenced the minds of the advocates of peace.[62]

Here is a mind-boggling possibility: the war ended when it did because of the fearfulness of the imperial family.

This is one of the few negative comments about the imperial family in the whole series of interrogations. The reason for Inaba's deviance can only be guessed at. His testimony strongly supports the orthodox position that the bomb was a motivating shock contributing to surrender.[63] Had USSBS done anything approximating a thorough job, it would have taken Inaba's testimony and might have acknowledged it.

But not necessarily. The most consequential of the Pacific Survey's publications, *Japan's Struggle to End the War*, says nothing of the attempted coup d'etat by Inaba and five other junior military officers on the evening of 14-15 August, the night before the emperor's surrender rescript was broadcast. This is an amazing omission. Robert Butow devotes a sixteen-page chapter to the insurrection. *Japan's Longest Day* is primarily about that specific event. One can understand its omission from *Japan's Struggle* only by assuming that the attempted coup demonstrates such fanatical resistance to surrender that Nitze's conclusion becomes unbelievable.

As recounted in chapter one, even as late as 14 August, dissident forces seized the Imperial Compound and went on a rampage of assassinations, attempted assassinations, and arson. There were other rebellions even after the emperor's broadcast. Surrender, in August 1945, barely came off. It was not just around the corner absent Hiroshima, Nagasaki, and a rumored third atomic bomb due on Tokyo.[64]

In addition to ignoring the final convulsion, *Japan's Struggle* contains errors that more time, greater care, and less bias would have prevented. All of these errors support the early surrender hypothesis. *Japan's Struggle* says that when Tojo Hidecki fell and Koiso Kuniaki replaced him in July 1944, "Koiso received an Imperial admonition to give Japan's situation a 'fundamental reconsideration' looking to the termination of the war;" Robert Butow refutes this.[65] *Japan's Struggle* states that "The Emperor on his own initiative in February 1945 had a series of interviews with the senior statesmen whose consensus was that Japan faced certain defeat and should seek peace at once." Grand Chamberlain Fujita's notes, taken at these interviews, show these claims to be false.[66]

Japan's Struggle says that Prince Konoye told the survey that he had secret instructions from the emperor in July 1945 to negotiate through the Russians for "peace at any price." No such statement appears in the transcripts of Konoye interviews, and the testimony of Foreign Minister Togo contradicts it.[67] *Japan's Struggle* says that in April 1945 when Suzuki was made prime minister, the emperor told him to make peace at any price, and that this was known to all members of his cabinet. This is wholly false.[68]

Japan's Struggle admits that the atomic bombs shortened the war and expedited the peace, but the basic thrust of the document faithfully reflects Nitze's pre-investigation opinion. Conventional bombing and naval blockade are alleged to have set in motion an irrevocable course toward surrender. Starvation was the thing; atomic spectacles were irrelevant.

Nitze's pre-investigation opinion meshed conveniently with the biases of army air forces personnel at the time. Hap Arnold and others made every effort to secure an independent U.S. Air Force, equal to army and navy (or perhaps superior to its competitors for the budget dollar). This was thought to be a distinct possibility after the war. The specific goal was a seventy-group air force.[69] Atomic bombs were seen as an obstacle to this level of air strength. If one bomb carried by one plane could wipe out a city the size of Hiroshima, what need for seventy groups? Their fliers would be out of business. This goal changed, in a year or two; the U.S. Air Force came to want seventy groups with nuclear armed planes predominating.

Perhaps more debilitating than these biases and errors was the failure of USSBS to obtain and use the massive *pre-surrender* intelligence gathered by *ULTRA*. Whatever testimony USSBS took after the war, however desolate the bombed-out landscape, the most probative evidence of Japanese intentions and capabilities during the last months of the war is in these intercepted communications.

The feeble and vague attempts of the Japanese peace party to negotiate a favorable armistice through Moscow are well known.

The belligerent and successful efforts of the Japanese military to prepare for the "decisive battle of the homeland" lay buried in the decrypted cable traffic. There were no distortions of special pleading or memory lapse here. There was only evidence of Japanese determination to fight on, sufficient to alarm MacArthur's intelligence chief, General Willoughby, and to justify a substantial increase in casualty estimates.[70]

The accepted belief in American commands was that air power could shut off reinforcement of Kyushu, and Gen. Curtis LeMay's bombers had been working at this for months. Japan was thought to be all but prostrate; USSBS cites exhaustively the surveys by members of the peace party showing that Japan could not continue the war, that it had to accept Allied terms.[71] Willoughby saw a different reality: "we are engaged in a race against time."[72]

USSBS claims victory was just waiting to drop into Allied laps.

USSBS, fascinated with interviewing Japanese grandees, was determined to show that conventional strategic bombing (with *some* help from the navy) had brought Japan down. It concocted a scenario in which "Japan's Decision to Surrender" simply took a little time. The peace party had to beat down the militarists. It would have happened soon, atom or no.

There is no basis for this scenario. No one can ever know how long the war would have gone on.

3

Was the Policy of Unconditional Surrender Justified?

Almost as important in the theology of Hiroshima cultists as the atomic diplomacy and racism doctrines is the claim that the unconditional surrender policy kept Japan from capitulating. Had this policy been repudiated, we are told, the bombs would not have been necessary. This approach enables cultists to attack Franklin Roosevelt as well as Harry Truman.

Some even extend their disapprobation to Winston Churchill, and Churchill biographer John Charmley now wants us to believe that Churchill's rejection of appeasement and insistence on bitter-end opposition to Hitler were equally wrongheaded.[1] Mr. Charmley will not be defended here; I intend only to inspect Roosevelt's reasons for insisting on unconditional surrender, and to establish that Truman's stance on that doctrine was not fanatical. In doing this, I shall contend the following: (1) Truman had no good reason to believe that the only tolerable modification of unconditional surrender, permitting retention of the emperor, would have led to early Japanese capitulation and (2) that the Potsdam Declaration defined surrender in a fashion acceptable to the Japanese peace forces. The Potsdam specification of what unconditional surrender meant, coupled with Hiroshima, Soviet entry, and Nagasaki, brought the end of the war.

Two of the most vigorous attacks on unconditional surrender are British. Lord Hankey, secretary of the Versailles Peace Conference in 1919 and then for twenty years secretary to the British cabinet, after an inaccurate account of the doctrine's development in World War II, says that "the results were deplorable, and whoever was responsible, a snap decision on such a far reaching subject was one of the gravest errors of the war."[2] Elizabeth Anscombe, the British philosopher who campaigned to dissuade Oxford University from giving an honorary degree to Mr. Truman because of Hiroshima, is even more negative: "It was the insistence on unconditional surrender that was the root of all evil. The connection between such a demand and the need to use the most ferocious methods of warfare will be obvious."[3] Historian Herbert Butterfield, in an address at Chatham House 19 June 1951, is less colorful but equally derogatory of unlimited aims in war, of wars to end war, or of wars of right versus wrong. He does not mention the unconditional surrender slogan, but it is clearly the object of his disapproval: "It is argued that if you are quarrelling about Alsace you had better say that you are quarrelling about Alsace, and not that you are fighting for righteousness; for in the one case you can transact business when you are tired of fighting, while in the other case you are dedicated to a war of destruction." Nor, says Butterfield, should you "awaken the moral indignation of the people" in a war, since then you cannot withdraw from the war when it is possible to do so.[4]

Of course there were also American opponents of unconditional surrender; Anne Armstrong was one of the most vigorous. After interviewing a number of German generals, she says that doctrine was the root of the failure of the anti-Nazi movement to overthrow Hitler in 1944; Manstein, Guderian, and Jodl "gave as explicit reasons for their refusal to cooperate with the plot" the fact that the alternative to Hitler was unconditional surrender.[5]

Hanson Baldwin, prominent American writer on military affairs, called the doctrine "perhaps the biggest political mistake of the war."[6]

Unconditional surrender was not the invention of President Roosevelt, sprung on an unsuspecting world at the Casablanca Conference. One of the few who have traced the phrase back through history is Lord Hankey: he found it in Polybius, where Carthaginian envoys agreed in 150 B.C.E. to a Roman demand for unconditional surrender. The Romans then set as their terms surrender of all territory, people, and buildings. The Roman Senate softened these terms at first, demanding only 300 hostages. But the terms stiffened, demanding evacuation of the entire population to a site ten miles from the sea. Carthage resisted, a bitter war ensued, and in 146 B.C.E. Carthage was destroyed. Hankey observes that such tragedies "nearly always follow from such extortionate demands."[7]

Before World War II, foreign wars in which the United States was involved ended in negotiated armistices. The unconditional surrender phrase entered the American lexicon in the Civil War: Ulysses S. Grant demanded unconditional surrender of the Confederate troops at Fort Donelson, and the Williams Resolution of 1865 required "the unconditional submission of those who have rebelled against us."[8] Roosevelt referred inaccurately to the Civil War events both at Casablanca and at a later news conference in Hawaii, but the real origin of his devotion to unconditional surrender was his experience during and after World War I.

Roosevelt was an active participant in the settlement of World War I. He was assistant secretary of the navy from 1913 to 1920, when he absorbed the "big stick" philosophy of his cousin Theodore Roosevelt, disagreeing with Woodrow Wilson's 1917 "peace without victory" speech. As Earl Pomeroy shows in his article, "Sentiment for a Strong Peace, 1917-1919," the Wilsonian program, with its Fourteen Points, did not have widespread support. Theodore Roosevelt, Henry Cabot Lodge, William Howard Taft, and other prominent politicians wanted a hard peace, and American military leaders were of a like mind.[9]

Gen. John Pershing was perhaps the most adamant of those demanding the complete destruction of German armies. His pressure on President Wilson was partially effective, and Wilson told the Germans on 23 October 1918 that the United States would deal with the "military masters and the monarchial autocrats of Germany" only on the basis of surrender. But the Allies nonetheless granted an armistice. Pershing, in his memoirs, complained that "Instead of requiring the German forces to retire at once, leaving material, arms and equipment behind, the Armistice terms permitted them to march back to their homeland with colors flying and bands playing, posing as the victims of political conditions. . . . The surrender of the German armies would have been an advantage to the Allies in the enforcement of peace terms and would have been a greater deterrent against possible future German aggression."[10]

Laurence Stallings, in his study of World War I, repeated some of Pershing's more colorful language: "Foch . . . wanted the Germans on the ropes when he, as referee, would stop the bout, but Pershing wanted the German champion stretched cold on the canvas for the count of ten. . . . At Paris, there was a meeting of the Allied Supreme War Council, three members keeping it secret from the fourth [Wilson]. Clemenceau and Lloyd George and Orlando quietly steamed the stamp from a fresh deck and began to mark the cards."[11] Wilson was out of it. And as Pershing told a friend in 1923,

"They never knew they were beaten in Berlin. It will all have to be done all over again."[12]

Franklin Roosevelt was thoroughly in sympathy with Pershing. As acting secretary of the navy in 1918, he dealt with the disposition of the German fleet. Against heavy opposition he recommended that the fleet be surrendered rather than simply interned. He convinced Wilson to back him, and the armistice so provided. But it was a minor success.[13] There should have been no armistice until the Germans were forced back to their own soil, visibly defeated, completely foreclosed from a future claim that they did not lose the war on the battlefield.

General Pershing's eighty-third birthday was 13 September 1943; American forces were then struggling in their ill-fated invasion of Italy. Roosevelt sent Pershing a birthday greeting: "Today brings forcibly to mind that you wanted to go through to Berlin in 1918."[14]

Roosevelt did not impose the doctrine on unwilling subordinates. It also bubbled up from below. The best account of how it developed during World War II comes from Iokibe Makoto, professor of history at Kobe University, in an article in the *Japanese Journal of American Studies*. As Iokibe tells us, the influential Council on Foreign Relations began studying postwar policy as soon as the war broke out. On 8 April 1942, Grayson Kirk, then professor of government at Columbia University, presented a paper, "The Armistice Negotiations, 1918," to a meeting of the CFR in New York. Kirk's conclusion could have come from the lips of Franklin Roosevelt:

> It is clear that if, instead of an armistice, there had been an unconditional surrender including, as implied, a speedy conclusion of a military settlement of the war, recovery might have been expedited, the peace conference would not have had hanging over it the fear of a renewal of hostilities by Germany, and German resentment over military aspects of the settlement might not have been so intense or prolonged.[15]

Kirk's paper was sent to the newly formed State Department Advisory Committee on Postwar Foreign Policy, a subcommittee of which was headed by Norman H. Davis, president of CFR and an intimate of President Roosevelt. This subcommittee rapidly endorsed the CFR's conclusions. On 20 May 1942, Davis told his group that he had discussed surrender with the president, who agreed with the committee's position.[16]

America's allies were fully aware of Roosevelt's intentions. The United Nations Declaration, signed 1 January 1942, did not use the unconditional surrender phrase, but said the same thing in other words: "The governments signatory hereto . . . Being convinced that complete victory over their enemies is essential . . . Declare . . . [etc.]"[17]

Shortly before the Casablanca Conference, Roosevelt discussed unconditional surrender with his Joint Chiefs of Staff (JCS). The minutes of the meeting of 7 January 1943 record: "The President said he was going to speak to Mr. Churchill about the advisability of informing Mr. Stalin that the United Nations were to continue on until they reach Berlin, and that their only terms would be unconditional surrender."[18]

At Casablanca, Roosevelt did speak with Churchill, who approved the idea and suggested that they issue a statement about it after the British cabinet was consulted. This was done, the Cabinet approved and suggested that Italy be included in the public statement.[19] Roosevelt was to make the statement at the end of the conference, and a script was prepared for him to read:

> The President and the Prime Minister, after a complete survey of the world war situation, are more than ever determined that peace can come to the world only by a total elimination of German and Japanese war power. This involves the simple formula of placing the objective of this war in terms of an unconditional surrender by Germany, Italy and Japan. Unconditional surrender by them means a reasonable assurance of world peace, for generations. Unconditional surrender means not the destruction of the German populace, nor of the Italian or Japanese populace, but does mean the destruction of a philosophy in Germany, Italy, and Japan which is based on the conquest and subjugation of other peoples.[20]

For some unknown reason, Roosevelt scuttled this script at the news conference and ad-libbed. What came out was a reference to "Unconditional Surrender Grant" plus a reasonably coherent statement about what the policy could mean, and *not* mean, for the Axis powers. He concluded, "This meeting is called the Unconditional Surrender meeting."[21]

Roosevelt did not say that the policy had been discussed in twenty-one meetings of a CFR study group, that it had been approved by a committee of the U.S. State Department, that it had been discussed with his Joint Chiefs of Staff, nor that Churchill had approved it and gained the approval of the British cabinet. No listening reporter knew that he and Churchill had written out a statement about it in advance. In truth, William M. Franklin's statement that "In 1943, unconditional surrender was a newly publicized slogan for an already well-known policy," is quite accurate.[22]

Roosevelt's casual handling of the announcement left the door open for all kinds of silliness. Churchill was the worst offender; his memory played tricks on him and he wrote to Robert Sherwood that "I heard the words 'unconditional surrender' for the first time from the President's lips at the [news] conference."[23]

Roosevelt's memory was hardly better; he told Sherwood: "We had so much trouble getting those two French generals together that I thought to myself that this was as difficult as arranging the meeting of Grant and Lee—and then suddenly the press conference was on, and Winston and I had had no time to prepare for it, and the thought popped into my mind that they had called Grant 'Old Unconditional Surrender' and the next thing I knew, I had said it."[24]

Elliott Roosevelt added to the confusion, Samuel Rosenman and E.L. Woodward gave misleading versions of the background, and anti-Roosevelt writers have perpetuated a mythical version ever since. The accurate version was published in Sherwood's *Roosevelt and Hopkins* in 1948: "What Roosevelt was saying was that there would be no negotiated peace, no compromise with Nazism and Fascism, no 'escape clauses' provided by another Fourteen Points which could lead to another Hitler. . . . He wanted to ensure that when the war was won it would stay won."[25] There were other reasons for using the phrase; it was intended as a morale booster for the Allies, and specifically for the Soviet Union. Stalin was outraged at continual postponement of a second front on the European continent. He feared the United States and Britain were unwilling to bear their share of the fighting and casualties, when the Soviet Union had already paid in torrents of blood on the eastern front. Roosevelt wanted some gesture of reassurance for Stalin, and unconditional surrender, which committed the Western powers not to compromise with the Nazis, seemed to be such a gesture.[26]

Partly because of Roosevelt's sloppy introduction of the phrase, much uncertainty existed as to exactly what it meant. One effort to clarify its application to Japan came at the Cairo Conference on 1 December 1943. The declaration of this Anglo-Sino-American gathering read "The three Great Allies are fighting this war to restrain and punish the aggression of Japan. They covet no gain for themselves and have no thought of territorial expansion." The declaration goes on to indicate that Japanese conquests (Manchuria, Formosa, and "all other territories which she has taken by violence and greed") should be taken away from it, and the independence of Korea granted.[27]

Both Roosevelt and Churchill provided definitions of a sort. They usually distinguished between the Axis leaders and the common people, as in this Roosevelt statement in 1943: "The people of the Axis-controlled areas may be assured that when they agree to unconditional surrender they will not be trading Axis despotism for ruin under the United Nations. The goal of the United Nations is to permit liberated peoples to create a free political life of their own choosing and to attain economic security."[28]

Similarly, Churchill told the House of Commons in February 1944:

> The term "unconditional surrender" does not mean that the German people will be enslaved or destroyed. It means however that the Allies will not be bound to them at the moment of surrender by any pact or obligation. There will be, for instance, no question of the Atlantic Charter applying to Germany as a matter of right and barring territorial transferences or adjustments in enemy countries. No such arguments will be admitted by us as were used by Germany after the last war, saying that they surrendered in consequence of President Wilson's Fourteen Points. Unconditional surrender means that the victors have a free hand. . . . If we are bound, we are bound by our own consciences to civilization. . . .[29]

Public opinion in both the United States and Britain was strongly behind the idea of being tough with the Axis powers. Michael Howard, in his essay, "The Challenge of Fascism 1935-1945," finds that British opinion changed radically after the outbreak of the war, and even people formerly sympathetic to Germany's placement of blame on Versailles were now ready for a war to the finish:

> It became accepted as much on the Left as on the Right that this was a war specifically against *Germany*, against a philosophy which appeared to be distinctively German and one which inspired a depressingly high proportion of the German people. In November 1941 even Aneurin Bevan wrote that "it was Prussian militarism, with

all its terrible philosophy, that had to be got rid of from Europe for all time": and the following September the President of TUC told his annual conference "that until the German people, not alone their gangster ruler, have meted out to them what they have meted out to millions of their fellow creatures . . . the German people will again, if not prevented, make another attempt to enslave Europe."[30]

In the United States, Japan was the object of more hostility than Germany. Every public opinion poll showed that large majorities wanted Japan thoroughly beaten and the emperor deposed or tried as a war criminal.[31] That the soft peace advocates ultimately won their main objective, the retention of the emperor, was due to Truman's sagacity in realizing that peace would not come without some flexibility on that topic. The slogan had to stay; the policy could give just a bit.

Hard peace advocates came in two flavors: left-wing New Dealers, who wanted Japan completely liberalized, with monarchy and industrial combines destroyed; and right-wing Japanophobes motivated primarily by racism.[32]

New Dealers such as Dean Acheson, Archibald MacLeish, Elmer Davis, and Owen Lattimore, all of whom worked either for the Department of State or the Office of War Information, believed the emperor, and the imperial system, were responsible for Japanese aggression, and believed the social system to be rigged against the common people. Unconditional surrender was necessary to reconstruct Japanese society. They accepted Roosevelt's geopolitical outlook: peace required complete destruction of Japan's war potential.[33] The American Communist Party also took this view. One of the last columns Louis Budenz wrote as editor of the *Daily Worker*, just before he renounced Communism and rejoined the Catholic Church, was a castigation of the "Anti-Soviet Gang" seeking a soft peace with Japan.[34] (Within a year, Budenz was attacking the same people for being pro-Soviet.)

Also supporting unconditional surrender was a conservative group that did not care what happened in Japan after the war; it was interested in punishing Japan for Pearl Harbor and other atrocities, and in destroying the country so thoroughly that it could never again challenge the West. Sen. Richard Russell, Rep. Roy O. Woodruff, and the *Chicago Tribune* were typical of these forces.[35]

Opposition to unconditional surrender in the United States came from two groups: Japanophiles, motivated by ideology; and the military, fearful of the huge casualties should Japan not capitulate before the scheduled invasion. Japanophiles, mostly conservative, felt that however mistaken Japan's rampage through the Pacific had been, Japan (not China) was the most plausible bulwark against the spread of Communism in Asia. If unconditional surrender was held to strictly, and the Japanese state was reduced to anarchy and impotence, the Soviet Union would assume hegemony in that area.

Foremost among the Japanophiles were Joseph Grew, the last pre-war American ambassador to Japan; Joseph Ballantine and Eugene Dooman of the State Department; Harry Kern of *Newsweek*; Hanson Baldwin of the *New York Times*; economist James Lee Kauffman; and a dozen others who later formed the American Council on Japan (ACJ).[36] These people wanted no mention of unconditional surrender, but rather a clear statement that the Japanese could choose their own form of government—which meant retention of the emperor system.

It was this Japan lobby, as much as the noisy but unwieldy China lobby, that first tagged New Deal reformers, who opposed the emperor, as Communists. The ACJ after the war worked quietly but effectively to overturn the liberal reforms of MacArthur's occupation forces, and then during the inquisition fingered their opponents to Joe McCarthy, Pat McCarran, the House UnAmerican Activities Committee, and the FBI.[37] During the war, the Japanophiles were unable to influence policy.

The most influential force for modifying unconditional surrender came from the military. During 1944, worried that the casualties likely to be caused by strict adherence to unconditional surrender would be unacceptable, Gen. George Strong, an army planner, drafted two sample surrender documents. Both implicitly allowed the emperor to continue to function under the control of American occupiers. These drafts were presented to Undersecretary of State Joseph Grew. In February 1945, the new State-War-Navy Coordinating Committee (SWNCC) considered and modified them, since they seemed to weaken unconditional surrender.[38]

SWNCC deliberations were overtaken by the Anglo-American discussions at Malta and Yalta, 30 January to 11 February 1945. Here the military leaders of the United States and Britain came to grips with problems of the Pacific War, including plans, logistics, and surrender policy. Churchill was then in favor of mitigating the harshness of unconditional surrender; he said this "would be worthwhile if it led to the saving of a year and a half of a war in which so much blood and treasure would be poured out."[39] After the defeat of

Germany, Churchill wanted the Allies to issue an ultimatum to Japan, retaining the unconditional surrender wording, but defining it to allow retention of the emperor. Brian Villa believes this proposal of Churchill's was the true origin of the Potsdam Declaration.[40]

From Yalta until the Potsdam Conference in July, the question of surrender terms was rarely off the agenda of SWNCC, the Joint Staff Planners, the Joint Intelligence Staff (JIS), the War Department Operations Division, the Department of State, or the desks of Grew, Stimson, Byrnes, and even President Truman. Military advice was strongly against a strict interpretation of unconditional surrender. On 7 April, for instance, the Joint Intelligence Staff distinguished between defeat and surrender, claiming that the literal meaning of unconditional surrender "is unknown to the Japanese." And even if a Japanese government surrendered unconditionally, the JIS thought, Japanese resistance would cease only if the people and army believed the emperor approved the surrender.[41]

Harry Truman, taking over the presidency 12 April, gave his first address to Congress 16 April. He had not been privy to Roosevelt's decision making, but he knew Roosevelt's rationale for unconditional surrender, and affirmed his own commitment in his speech to Congress. In his *Memoirs*, Truman notes that "There were many indications of approval of what I said. I was applauded frequently, and when I reaffirmed the policy of unconditional surrender the chamber rose to its feet."[42] Few events could have confirmed his support of the doctrine more indelibly.

Nonetheless, military efforts to modify the doctrine were felt in the White House. In his V-E Day press conference 8 May, Truman went further than Roosevelt had in explaining what unconditional surrender meant for Japan, and subtly modified the doctrine. Instead of assuming Japan to be monolithic, he separated the people from their leaders and especially from the military. He did not demand surrender of *Japan*, but only of the military and naval forces:

> Just what does the unconditional surrender of the armed forces of Japan mean for the Japanese people?
>
> It means the end of the war.
>
> It means the termination of the influence of the military leaders who brought Japan to the present brink of disaster.
>
> It means provision for the return of soldiers and sailors to their families, their farms and their jobs.

And it means not prolonging the present agony and suffering of the Japanese in the vain hope of victory.

Unconditional surrender does not mean the extermination or enslavement of the Japanese people.[43]

This change was noted in Japan. Advocates of peace saw a significant softening of the Casablanca attitude. The die-hard Japanese military ignored the change.

On 28 May, in a conference with the primary advocate of retaining the emperor system, Joseph Grew, Truman said he had been thinking of further modification of surrender terms, but he refused to include in his upcoming Memorial Day address the statement Grew suggested specifically allowing for continuance of the "present dynasty." Instead, Truman wanted the matter referred to the JCS and SWNCC.[44]

The military advised against any such statement. American forces were then being butchered by the fanatic defenders of Okinawa, and modifying the surrender terms at that time would be seen by the Japanese as a sign of weakness. Consequently, on 1 June, Truman issued a militant call for unconditional surrender. He was back on the same wavelength as his predecessor.[45]

But the controversy continued. Unconditional surrender dominated the meetings of the secretaries of war, state, and navy in June. On the 12th, Secretary Stimson mentioned a letter former President Herbert Hoover had written to Truman advocating flexibility on the surrender issue. Stimson said the unconditional part should be abandoned if the United States could secure its strategic objectives without it.[46] On 18 June, Truman met with the JCS and the secretaries; Stimson tried to get Truman to publicly define "surrender" to allow retention of the emperor. He was supported by Truman's chief of staff, Adm. William Leahy. They failed. The minutes of the meeting show Truman saying that "he had left the door open for Congress to take appropriate action with reference to unconditional surrender. However, he did not feel that he could take any action at this time to change public opinion on this matter."[47] Assistant Secretary of War John McCloy, who was present at this meeting, later told friends and journalists that Truman had approved a change in surrender terms, and had urged McCloy to take the matter up with James F. Byrnes, who was about to be appointed secretary of state, and who might have been persuasive with the general public.[48] But Byrnes was never to be an ally in this project; he was against retention of the Emperor.

On 19 June, the three secretaries (Artemus Gates sitting in for Navy Secretary James Forrestal) went over the same ground with the same results. Surrender simply had to be clarified before any invasion. Once American troops landed, it would be too late; they would face "cave-by-cave" battle to the bitter end.[49]

Truman agreed to appoint a high-level committee to word a public surrender demand. Drafting of the statement was in the hands of a group chaired by McCloy; at this stage, everybody in the War Department got into the argument. Brig. Gen. George Lincoln, Col. Charles Bonesteel, Col. Dean Rusk, and many others all had a say.[50] A Lt. Col. Fahey wrote a substantial memo saying, "It should be made perfectly clear that a Japanese 'Yes' or 'No' is the only type answer sought, and that no Allied-Jap negotiations will be tolerated."[51] Mark Howe, in Stimson's office, advised that "Although present plans being formulated . . . are based on the assumption that unconditional surrender will include the total capitulation of the Japanese Government and the Emperor (JCS 1275), the United States is neither committed to that assumption, nor to any particular definition of unconditional surrender. It is clear, however, that any modification of tacitly assumed policy would be unacceptable if it substantially jeopardized the objectives of the United States. It would be short-sighted in the extreme to save the lives of this generation only to lose those of the next."[52]

John McCloy, in charge of putting all this together, noted in a memo to Stimson on 29 June in regard to the emperor's retention, "This point seems to be the most controversial one and one on which there is a split in opinion in the State Department. The draft . . . may cause repercussions at home but without it those who seem to know most about Japan feel there would be very little likelihood of acceptance."[53]

Few historians of the long conflict over surrender policy realize that an event of 3 July tipped the balance against overt, explicit modification of unconditional surrender. James F. Byrnes was sworn in as secretary of state. Grew was now sidelined, efforts by Stimson, McCloy and Marshall failed, and Truman departed for the Potsdam Conference having turned over the issue to his new Secretary of State.

James Byrnes was nothing if not a politician. He followed the polls, and the polls showed 33 percent of Americans favored execution of the emperor, slightly more than that wanted him tried for war crimes, imprisoned for life, or exiled. Dean Acheson and Archibald MacLeish menacingly challenged the advocates of retaining the emperor: if such a departure from accepted policy were made, "the American people have a right to know it."[54] Former Secretary of State Cordell Hull told Byrnes that the Stimson statement "seemed too much like appeasement of Japan . . . it seemed to guarantee continuance not only of the Emperor but also of the feudal privileges of a ruling caste under the Emperor."[55] If Byrnes had been wavering, the "appeasement" warning from Cordell Hull would have stiffened his resolve. "Appeasement" in 1945 was as potent a charge as "Comsymp" in 1952. Moreover, Hull represented a link with Roosevelt, and Truman wanted to stick close to Roosevelt's policies. Both Truman and Byrnes would listen very carefully to Hull's opinions.

Byrnes, in his memoirs, has little to say about his handling of the reams of conflicting advice, or of the turmoil in Potsdam over wording of the surrender demand. In fact, he takes less responsibility for deleting the language about the emperor than most historians attribute to him. He writes,

> Secretary of War Stimson, on July 2, had submitted to the President a wise memorandum setting forth a proposed message to Japan. Using this memorandum as a basis, the president prepared a draft of a declaration to be issued jointly by the United States, the United Kingdom and China. The President and I spent some time on it. Then Prime Minister Churchill made some suggestions which were adopted. The declaration to which Mr. Churchill agreed followed the general lines of Secretary Stimson's proposal except that it did not contain a reference to the future of the Emperor.[56]

So the famous Potsdam Declaration (officially it was a proclamation, but that label did not stick) went out on 26 July 1945.[57] The first paragraphs warned the Japanese that unless they seized the opportunity to end the war, they would be devastated as was Germany. Paragraph five was also tough: "Following are our terms. We will not deviate from them. There are no alternatives. We shall brook no delay." Japan's experienced diplomats immediately saw that *if there were terms, this was not really an unconditional surrender*. Nor were the terms a surprise, coming on the heels of various Truman speeches and the Cairo Declaration: eliminate the power of the militarists, submit to occupation until a peaceful and responsible government is established, give up all conquered territories, and "proclaim now the unconditional surrender of all the Japanese armed forces."

All this was demanded *of* Japan. But there were also promises: the disarmed military would be permitted to return home and lead productive lives; freedom of speech, religion, and thought would be established; civilian industries would be permitted; international trade would be permitted eventually; and the Allied occupation would be ended when the new government was established.

The word "unconditional" was still there, but the rhetoric had softened. How much it had softened was revealed in an anonymous memo produced in McCloy's office on 4 September. The memo was headed "Rights and Powers over Japan." The first paragraph observed that although MacArthur had full power to "take such steps as he deems proper to effectuate the surrender terms," he was nevertheless bound by the Potsdam Declaration. Then:

> 2. In the sense in which "Unconditional Surrender" has been used in relation to Germany, the Japanese surrender is not an unconditional surrender. On the contrary it is based on the terms of the Potsdam Declaration, the exchange of notes resulting in the acceptance of those terms, and the surrender instrument, which itself constitutes an acceptance of those terms.
>
> 3. A moment's consideration of the effect of those documents will make this clear: Under the Potsdam Declaration we have bound ourselves to continue Japanese sovereignty in the home islands (par 8); to permit Japanese military forces "to return to their homes with the opportunity to lead peaceful and productive lives" (par 9); not to enslave the Japanese race, and to establish freedom of speech, of religion, and of thought. . . .

The rest of the Potsdam conditions were reviewed, and the memo concluded: "All of these are expressly 'terms' which were offered to Japan in order to induce her to surrender, and which were accepted by Japan. No such situation arises in our relations with Germany."[58]

Here is a conclusive answer to those who insist that unconditional surrender was a purely punitive stance, carried out by a malevolent president fanatically asserting American superiority over an inferior race. At the end, not even the rhetoric was that of a zealot. Potsdam can of course be interpreted different ways. Writers who wish to put Truman in the wrong see the declaration as just another instance of American and British vindictiveness. Martin

Sherwin, for instance, says, "The Potsdam Declaration of July 26 calling for the surrender of Japan was decidedly unhelpful to those Japanese who were searching for a means of bringing the war to a conclusion."[59] Leon Sigal, in *Fighting to a Finish*, is contemptuous of the Potsdam Declaration: "Adding little to the threats and promises that might alter Japan's calculations to continue the war, the declaration was also released in a way that denied time for rational choice. . . . Neither conciliation nor ultimatum, the Potsdam Declaration was no more than propaganda."[60]

Careful inspection of the attitudes of leaders of the Japanese peace party yields different conclusions. They saw in the Potsdam terms an acceptable alternative to the destruction Japan would otherwise sustain.

Foreign Minister Togo Shigenori was foremost among them. He felt that the phrase "Following are our terms" clearly indicated that there *were* terms, that surrender was not without conditions. Further,

> It appeared also that a measure of consideration had been given to Japan's economic position; at a time when such Draconian retribution upon Germany as the "Morgenthau Plan" for her reduction to a "pastoral state" was being proposed, I felt special relief upon seeing the economic provisions of the declaration—the gist of them being that the function of Japan as a processing nation, as contemplated by Secretary Hull during the Japanese-American negotiations [of 1941] would be recognized, and that to this end severe reparations would not be imposed.[61]

Baron Hiranuma Kiichiro, president of Privy Council, said "Following the Potsdam Declaration, I felt that we should accept it at once since it did state that the position of the Imperial House would be maintained."[62]

Kase Toshikazu, officer for American affairs in the Japanese Foreign Office in 1945, discusses the declaration in *Journey to the Missouri*:

> Instead of demanding unconditional surrender from our government the last item significantly called upon it to proclaim the unconditional surrender of all our armed forces. *This was a deft move*, as it spared the imposition of indignities upon His Majesty's government. . . . The Army at first opposed the publication of the proclamation, but it was

finally prevailed upon by the Foreign Office to agree to it. . . . Also, the newspapers were encouraged to denounce the proclamation as a device to intimidate our people into submission.

The popular reaction, however, was that the terms were far more lenient than had been generally expected. . . . I remember that quite a few people came to see the foreign minister in order to urge upon him the necessity of immediately accepting the offer. [italics added][63]

In his book *The Lost War,* reporter Kato Masuo offers similar interpretations of the declaration: "Foreign Office Officials quickly interpreted it as offering Japan considerable latitude, even though it called for 'unconditional surrender'. Actually, aside from purely military considerations, the Allied demand was far from 'unconditional'. It left Japan no sane alternative but acceptance."[64]

Shigemitsu Mamoru, an active member of the peace party and foreign minister before Togo, told Samuel Eliot Morison that despite the absence of an explicit statement about the emperor, the "reference in paragraph 7 to withdrawing occupation forces after 'a peacefully inclined and responsible government' had been set up indicated to the Japanese that they would be permitted to determine their own future government."[65]

Akira Iriye, one of the foremost contemporary students of Japanese foreign relations, also holds the Potsdam Declaration to have been just what the peace party was seeking, a "peace on the basis of something other than unconditional surrender."[66]

The Japanese officials in Switzerland, led by Minister Kase Shunichi and director of the Bank for International Settlements Kitamura Kojiro, after initial negative reaction to the Potsdam Declaration, decided that it was an "astute document which left a possible way out." According to an Office of Strategic Services (OSS) report sent to Truman through channels, the Kase-Kitamura group cabled Tokyo on 30 July stressing the favorable terms from Potsdam.[67]

At the Tokyo War Crimes Trial, counsel for Togo and Sato argued their innocence on the basis that "unlike Germany, Japan had surrendered not unconditionally, but conditionally, i.e. in the form of acceptance of the Potsdam Declaration."[68] Since crimes against peace and humanity were not mentioned in the declaration, Togo and Sato could not be charged with them.

In 1974, when the Japanese Northern Territories Issue Association published its brief for the return of Southern Sakhalin and the Kurile Islands to Japan (an issue that still poisons the relationship between

Japan and Russia), it depended on the *terms* of Potsdam and the preceding Cairo Conference to justify its claim against Russia.[69]

From the perspective of 1992, Japanese historian Iokibe Makoto emphasizes the importance of Potsdam:

> Between May and June 1945, the political leaders of the United States and Japan formulated the desire to avoid a continuation of the war. America showed itself prepared to step down from an insistence on unconditional surrender, if by doing so it could bring about an early end to war. The rational course for the Japanese government would have been to announce Japan's capitulation to the United States in the middle of June 1945. . . . However, at the time, the Japanese government did not have sufficient information to detect the crucial change that had taken place at the top levels of government in Washington. It had to wait until July 26 for the Potsdam Declaration. Although Minister of Foreign Affairs Togo Shigenori, Prime Minister Suzuki, and Emperor Hirohito recognized the declaration's significance as a step toward ending the war, the Japanese army exerted strong pressure on the prime minister to reject it. He was thus forced to make his famous mokusatsu statement to the press. . . .[70]

Unconditional surrender may have dampened the peace forces until Potsdam, but they were impotent anyway.[71] After reading the defiant statements of the Japanese generals to USSBS and MacArthur's staff, it becomes clear that they were not about to surrender with or without conditions. They were going to do exactly as they had done on Okinawa, but on a massive scale: punish the attackers so severely that the attackers would sue for peace. To carry out this policy, they defied the Japanese politicians, even the emperor, until the horror of the atom was brought against them. This, and only this, led them to bow to the imperial order to surrender. Even after the shocks of 6-9 August, military leaders were unwilling to surrender except on their totally unacceptable terms.[72]

The Japanese government finally decided on 10 August, after the atomic bombs and Russian entry into the war, to accept the Potsdam terms with the understanding that "the prerogatives of His Majesty as a sovereign ruler" would remain.[73] Thus, the Japanese did demand a condition that the Allies had not offered, but peace was too tantalizing to resist. President Truman and Secretary of State Byrnes found a way out by allowing the emperor to stay on as long as his rule was subject to MacArthur's directives.

So the policy changed, but the slogan remained the same. Truman handled it just right. He conceded what was necessary to concede indirectly, while maintaining the appearance of toughness.

Barton Bernstein's analysis of the way this was handled is perceptive. Stimson, Forrestal, and Leahy, who were less worried about public opinion than Byrnes,

> . . . may have believed that widespread American opposition to the Emperor and to modification of unconditional surrender would quickly pass in the glow of victory and the delights of peace. These military leaders may also have recognized that their government could manipulate public opinion by both retreating from unconditional surrender and denying it. In fact, such "double think" proved ultimately successful.[74]

Suppose Truman had scuttled unconditional surrender in June, when the revisionists claim he could have obtained surrender? Certainly relations with the Soviet Union would have been further embittered. Stalin would have been confirmed in his suspicion that the United States simply wanted to keep Russia out of postwar affairs in the Pacific by securing an early surrender. The domestic consequences in the United States could have been explosive. Dean Acheson, Cordell Hull, and Archibald MacLeish were right about this. Secretary Byrnes put it bluntly: he told Truman the American people would crucify their president if unconditional surrender were publicly renounced.[75] British historian A.E. Campbell emphasizes Roosevelt's sensitivity to Woodrow Wilson's failures at the end of World War I: Wilson "failed to carry either the Allied leaders or his own countrymen with him in his grand design."[76] Truman was well advised to also heed a strong public demand for unconditional surrender; it would have been unrealistic to reverse policy in the spring of 1945.[77] Only the atom, and the startling reversal of the *Japanese* position to acceptance of the Potsdam terms made it possible for Truman and Byrnes, on 11 August, to offer the Japanese "slight reassurance" that the emperor could remain.[78]

The Allies had conflicting objectives in the summer of 1945. They desperately wanted to end the war without a bloodbath on Kyushu. This objective required the cooperation and continued reign of Hirohito, hence tacit easing of unconditional surrender. But they also wanted to defeat Japanese forces so convincingly as to make a recrudescence of Japanese militarism unlikely.

Did they achieve both objectives? About the first there can be little doubt. Despite U.S. Army estimates at the conclusion of the Okinawa slaughter that Japan could not be brought down until late 1946, with the aid of the August shocks (the atom and Soviet entry) the war was over long before that.

About eradicating Japanese militarism, we cannot be so certain. Most early reports from the occupation were pessimistic. Richard Johnston's story in the *Washington Post* of 4 September 1945 said:

> Tokyo, September 4—The Japanese people do not know they lost the war. The Japanese Army is relatively intact and has no awareness of defeat. The Japanese Navy virtually ceased to exist, but its officers excuse the debacle on the basis of maladministration by the Army.
>
> Japanese intellectuals criticize the military—but not for taking Japan into war—only for failure to win it.
>
> The mass of the Japanese people believed the war was halted by the magnanimous gesture of the Emperor rather than as a result of Allied force. . . . "We are embarrassed at the failure of the Army and Navy to triumph for the Emperor—next time we will do better."[79]

Richard Russell quoted this dispatch in his long and bitter speech to the Senate 18 September 1945 to protest the coddling of the Japanese.[80]

On 5 September, Maj. Gen. Clayton Bissell, U.S. Army G-2, reported similar conclusions to his superiors:

> The Japanese government and Imperial Headquarters will insure complete compliance by the Japanese armed forces with the surrender terms and will keep the general public calm and under control. Japan's leaders hope to keep the present Japanese political and social structure essentially intact by avoidance of overt acts against the Allies and by well considered pressure for the mildest possible interpretation of the Potsdam terms. Fear of Communism will color their political outlook considerable [sic] in the immediate future. . . .
>
> Japan's present ruling groups will continue to try to create the impression that Japan is on the road toward democracy, with the purpose of hastening the evacuation of Allied occupation forces. Although many Japanese would welcome a truly democratic Japan, no fundamental change has occurred in Japanese psychology, aspirations to control the East or determination that Japan shall become a great world power. She is simply making the best of a bad situation

while she gains the power and knowledge for another try for a place
in the sun.[81]

The long story of Japan's development from a defeated military
empire to a triumphant economic empire under American tutelage
is well known. Less well known is the continuing campaign of suc-
cessive Japanese administrations to deny, explain away, justify, and
whitewash the events of its assault on the peoples of Asia and the
Pacific. Despite the peace clause in the Japanese constitution,
Yamato racism, the bushido spirit, belief in the right of Japan to rule
the Pacific area, contention that the only atrocity of World War II
was American bombing, denial of the rape of Nanking and the
Bataan Death March, and the prolonged pretense that there were no
Korean and other women conscripted into prostitution for Japanese
soldiers, and other distortions of history are still strongly supported
in Japan.[82]

These dogmas from the glory days linger, partly because the liberalization and democratization that Acheson, MacLeish, and
Lattimore wanted to impose on Japan was never completed. For the
first two years of the occupation, MacArthur and his New Deal
advisers sought to break the power of the great industrial combines,
to strengthen labor and liberal parties, and to reform agriculture and
education. The decision of the Truman administration to make
Japan into an anti-communist bulwark, which was intensified by the
Korean War, caused an about-face—"reverse course" is the term
most often applied to the 1948 change in occupation policy. The
elites came back into power, the textbooks were rewritten to glorify
the Greater East Asia Co-Prosperity Sphere, and government officials came once again to worship at the Yasukuni Shrine.[83]

Japan prospered. Most of what it failed to obtain by military force
it has gained with economic power.

These developments cast doubt on the viability of Roosevelt's
belief that a thorough trouncing of the enemy would make *this* war
stay won. Japan does not seem to be contrite (as the Germans seem to
be) for the horror and devastation it visited upon the rest of Asia.[84]
But one thing is positive; both Japan and Germany have learned that
prosperity and economic growth do not demand control of an
empire.

Thus on the big strategic question: Did substantially carrying out
Roosevelt's unconditional surrender doctrine in the Pacific War
teach Japan a lesson, eradicate militarism, promote "peace in our

time"? The answer is "perhaps." But had Truman officially abandoned the doctrine, the war party, not the peace party, would have benefitted. Anami, Umezu and Toyoda would have been better able to resist pressure from the emperor: "Look, now the Americans are backing down. If we just hold out long enough to severely punish their invasion forces we can get an armistice with no occupation, no war crimes trials, no American-conducted disarmament." As Brian Villa emphasizes in his discussion of the final tense moments, "There was present the eternal dilemma of truce making, the endless truism, 'If the enemy is weak, concessions are unnecessary, if he appears strong, concessions look like a confession of weakness.'"[85]

Thus, what Hiroshima cultists insist was a viable alternative for Truman to end the war early without using the bomb—retaining the emperor—was really no alternative at all. It would not have converted the Japanese military to surrender, but would instead have stiffened their resolve to fight the decisive battle of the homeland. Had the United States been willing to grant *all* of Anami's demands, the determination of the military to fight it out would have been even more intensified. Even if the emperor could have overpowered the military before Hiroshima and secured a cease fire on the basis of softening of the unconditional surrender demand, it would not have been wise. A Japanese conviction that they had not really been defeated would have taken firm hold.

There is also the tactical question: Did unconditional surrender help solidify the Allies, help convince the Soviets that America and Britain would not make a truce behind their backs? Probably it did. John L. Chase, in his perceptive 1955 study, says: "For the short run it prevented Russian recrimination in spite of the further postponement of the promised second front. At the same time it served notice on Germans, Russians and Americans [and Japanese] alike that there would be no compromise or deals with the Axis governments by any of the Allies. . . . On all counts, and contemporary criticisms of it notwithstanding, it was one of the most effective achievements of American statesmanship of the entire war period."[86]

When he wrote his memoirs, Truman was not so sure unconditional surrender could be as therapeutic as Roosevelt thought. He noted:

> This time unconditional surrender was decided on. The Allies wanted to be sure that there would be no room left for doubt in the German [and Japanese] mind as to the reason or the completeness of

their military defeat. I am not certain that things always work that way. . . . It seems to me that what happens is that national pride outlives military defeat. It is a delusion to think otherwise. I also think that it is a mistake to insist on unconditional surrender for moral or educational purposes. . . . If there were any reason for unconditional surrender, it is only the practical matter of taking over a defeated country and making its control easier.[87]

And on that rationale, Truman earned high marks for his handling of the end of the war.

4

Why No Warning or Demonstration?

Many critics of the bomb decision believe that it was the way in which the bombs were used as much as the devastation they created that was damning. If the Japanese had seen a demonstration of the bomb's power, and still refused to surrender, dropping another bomb on a Japanese city might have been warranted. Or if a specific warning had been given: "If you do not surrender by 5 August we will destroy Hiroshima with a new and terrible weapon"—then the Japanese could evacuate the city, saving many lives. Often associated with these approaches is the belief that if the United States had not been so secretive; had, perhaps, shared knowledge of the bomb and plans for its use with the Soviet Union, the postwar nuclear arms race might have been slowed or avoided. There is a moral component to these beliefs, but they rest primarily on a political basis: warning or demonstration would have brought speedy surrender; openness would have been advantageous to the postwar American position.

The stimulus for the Manhattan Project was defensive: fear that Germany would develop nuclear weapons, probably before the Allies did. German science was capable of major innovations; the V-weapons alone were evidence of German technological prowess. Once American authorities were convinced that atomic fission was possible, the race to beat Germany was on. But it was a tremendous task, and by the time the Manhattan engineers could set a timetable for producing useful bombs, the back of Germany's power had apparently been broken, and the end of that war was in sight. No Allied authority could be sure that Hitler would not at the last minute produce an atomic bomb, but by May 1943 the Manhattan Engineer District's Military Policy Committee (Vannevar Bush, Gen. William D. Styer, and Adm. William R. Purnell) realized that the first American bombs might not be ready before the European War was over, and would probably be used on Japan. The Japanese naval installation at Truk seemed the best target.[1]

This early concern with targeting seems not to have been followed up in the military. President Roosevelt, however, had it on his mind. When Winston Churchill visited Hyde Park after the Quebec Conference of September 1944, he and Roosevelt discussed how the first bomb should be used. The conclusion in an aide-memoir initialled by both: "It might perhaps, after mature consideration, be used against the Japanese, who should be warned that this bombardment will be repeated until they surrender."[2]

Use of the bomb came up again four days later when physicist Vannevar Bush conferred with Roosevelt. The president wondered if the bomb should actually be used against the Japanese, or merely held as a threat. Bush did not commit himself; there was no need to decide that yet.[3] But Roosevelt's inquiry stimulated Bush to discuss the matter with James B. Conant, and when a Bush-Conant memo went to Secretary of War Henry Stimson on 30 September 1944, their suggestion resembled the Churchill-Roosevelt position: "This demonstration might be over enemy territory, or in our own country, with subsequent notice to Japan that the materials would be used against the Japanese mainland unless surrender was forthcoming."[4]

One of Roosevelt's advisers, however, was pushing for a more specific plan. The first record of anything like a detailed proposal for use of the bombs came from Alexander Sachs, economist and Roosevelt confidant who had been instrumental (along with Albert Einstein, Leo Szilard, and others) in convincing Roosevelt to approve the atom project in the first place. Sachs saw the president irregularly, sometimes reading memos about the atomic project, the course of the war, or relations with U.S. Allies. In May 1944, Sachs first mentioned the need for target planning; in November 1944, he claims he handed the president a memo with some detail:

> Following a successful test, there should be arranged (a) a rehearsal demonstration before a body including internationally recognized scientists from all Allied countries and, in addition, neutral countries, supplemented by representatives of the major [religious] faiths: (b) that a report on the nature and the portent of the atomic weapon be prepared by the scientists and other representative figures; (c) that, thereafter, a warning be issued by the United States and its allies in the project to our major enemies in the war, Germany and

Japan, that atomic bombing would be applied to a selected area within a designated time limit for the evacuation of human and animal life, and, finally, (d) in the wake of such realization of the efficacy of atomic bombing, an ultimatum demand for mediated surrender by the enemies be issued, in the certainty that failure to comply would subject their countries and peoples to atomic annihilation.[5]

Sachs wrote that Roosevelt had accepted this plan, and that it was being set in motion in February 1945 when Sachs last talked with the president. Gen. Edwin (Pa) Watson, a Roosevelt aide, presumably knew of the plan, but FDR's administrative methods were so devious that no documentary proof remains.

There is much documentary proof of the endless discussions among Manhattan scientists about how the bomb was to be used and how atomic energy was to be managed after the war. The same discussions took place in the offices of Secretary of War Stimson and Army Chief of Staff George Marshall. On 1 May 1945, Stimson organized an "Interim Committee" to advise him on atomic matters; despite the innocuous name, the committee was to have great influence on the outcome of the Manhattan Project. It consisted of Assistant Secretary of War George Harrison, Vannevar Bush, Karl T. Compton of MIT, Under Secretary of the Navy Ralph Bard, Assistant Secretary of State William L. Clayton, and Secretary of State designate James Byrnes. Advising this group was a scientific panel: Arthur Compton, Ernest Lawrence, Robert Oppenheimer, and Enrico Fermi.

On 9 May, the Interim Committee met with Stimson. He told the committee its task was to develop proposals for controls on atomic information; texts of public announcements to be made after the bomb was used; and plans for postwar research, development, and control.[6] At this first meeting, use of the bomb against Japan was apparently not discussed, but since the members of the scientific advisory panel were under pressure from their colleagues at Chicago and Los Alamos to raise this matter in Washington, it soon appeared on the agenda.

Even without agitation from Szilard and colleagues, the issue of using of the bombs would have reached Stimson from an unknown engineer in a subcontractor shop in New York. On 24 May, O.C. Brewster, a specialist in uranium isotope separation, wrote a 3,000-word letter addressed to President Truman with copies to Stimson and Secretary of State Edward Stettinius. Brewster had willingly worked on the bomb when the United States seemed to be in a race with Germany. Now the bomb had become a monster, and the United States could not become the first to use it and thus set a precedent for a rogue regime to destroy the world. But if absolutely necessary in the Pacific War, it should be demonstrated to the Japanese before combat use. The United States should halt further production as evidence of good faith.[7]

Stimson was much impressed with Brewster's plea. He sent a copy to General Marshall with a covering letter, and said he would see that Truman got it too; that probably did not happen.[8]

In Chicago, Szilard was one of the most active agitators. He believed that the Soviet Union would get nuclear weapons in the near future; that American use of these weapons against Japan might alienate the Soviet Union and speed Soviet atomic research; and that in six years, the Russians would be able "to destroy all of our major cities in a single sudden attack."[9] In March 1945, Szilard wrote a long memo addressed to President Roosevelt covering this and many related matters. He did not, in this first memo, complain specifically about the inability of Manhattan Project scientists to influence government policy, nor did he emphasize the idea that if the bomb were used against Japan prematurely there would be adverse reactions. He left these two points to Einstein, who wrote a covering letter on 25 March. The Einstein letter and Szilard's memo were to be transmitted via Eleanor Roosevelt.[10] Franklin Roosevelt died on 12 April, before Szilard's letter reached him.

Undaunted, Szilard searched for an avenue to the new president. He found it in a Chicago lab employee from Kansas City, and via that channel, he got through to Truman's appointments secretary, Matt Connelly. Szilard and a Chicago friend, Walter Bartky, saw Connelly at the White House 25 May. Connelly read Szilard's materials, and then said, as Szilard reports, "The President thought that your concern would be about this matter, and he has asked me to make an appointment for you with James Byrnes, if you are willing to go down to see him in Spartanburg, South Carolina."[11]

Szilard was puzzled by this. He knew Byrnes had been a major player in Roosevelt's administration, but was then out of government service. Szilard guessed Truman intended to put Byrnes in charge of atomic matters, which was plausible but still short of the reality. Byrnes was to be secretary of state when the United Nations had been fully launched and Secretary Stettinius could be gracefully retired. Puzzled or not, Szilard, Bartky, and Harold Urey entrained for Spartanburg.

The confrontation of the three scientists and the canny politician was paradigmatic of the relations between scientists and power brokers during mid-century. The scientists were taking the long view, anxious to secure international control of atomic energy, concerned with avoiding an arms race in the future. The power brokers were straining to end a costly war, and to keep the Soviet Union from gobbling up all of Europe in the short run.[12] Alice K. Smith, in *A Peril and a Hope*, which is her version of the involvement of scientists in nuclear politics, also notes this phenomenon in these words: "What divided the seven scientists advising the War Department— three on the Interim Committee and the four panel members - from the [agitators at Chicago] far more than any difference in the realm of ideas was their degree of closeness to the nerve center of decision. Those who bore responsibility tended to deal first with the most palpable peril—the continuance of the war; those without this burden could take the longer view that the real impact of the bomb and its imminent peril lay in the future."[13]

The long view of the scientists was idealistic and commendable. To some extent, their position was conditioned by the experiences of the core of scientific refugees from Nazism. The very origin of the Manhattan Project was the result of fear of the triumph of Hitlerism if Germany were to develop nuclear weapons first. The Manhattan scientists as a group were Eurocentric, and since the European Fascists were near destruction the basic reason for the project disappeared. They had little knowledge of, or concern for, the equally malicious Japanese tyranny in the Pacific. Thus when they found out later how devastating their creation had been to Hiroshima and Nagasaki, and when they heard that some Japanese had been angling for a negotiated armistice through the Russians, many of them had guilty consciences.

So Szilard and friends visited James F. Byrnes on 28 May 1945, carrying with them a revision of Szilard's earlier memorandum designed for Franklin Roosevelt. It is possible that the many writers who castigate Byrnes for being so harsh with Szilard have not actually read this revised Szilard memo. It gives far less explanation of the various technical and political issues Szilard was concerned with than the original version designed for Roosevelt. Rhetorically, it was a much inferior product. In only two pages six complicated, almost arcane "points on which decisions appear to be most urgently needed" are set forth, staccato. Witness "point" number 3: "Can we materially improve our chances to obtain the cooperation of Russia in setting up such a system of controls by developing in the next two years modern methods of production which would give us an overwhelming superiority in this field at the time when Russian [sic] might be approached?"[14]

If the density and apocalypticism of Szilard's six points did not disturb Byrnes' equilibrium, the arrogance of Szilard's claim that only he and his colleagues could lead the Truman administration out of the wilderness would have sufficed:

> Thus the Government of the United States is at present faced with the necessity of arriving at decisions which will control the course that is to be followed from here on: These decisions ought to be based not on the *present* evidence relating to atomic bombs, but rather on the situation which can be expected to confront us in this respect a few years from now. This situation can be evaluated only by men who have first-hand knowledge of the facts involved, that is, by the small group of scientists who are actively engaged in this work. This group includes a number of eminent scientists who are willing to present their views; there is, however, no mechanism through which direct contact would be maintained between them and those men who are, by virtue of their position, responsible for formulating the policy which the United States might pursue.[15]

James F. Byrnes does not rank as a great world statesman; nonetheless it is easy to justify the acerbic statement he made about this event in his biography: "[Szilard's] general demeanor and his desire to participate in policy making made an unfavorable impression on me, but his associates were neither as aggressive nor apparently as dissatisfied."[16] Szilard too had a negative attitude toward the confrontation: "I was rarely as depressed as when we left Byrnes' house and walked toward the station. I thought to myself how much better off the world might be had I been born in America and become influential in American politics, and had Byrnes been born in Hungary and studied physics. In all probability there would have been no atomic bomb and no danger of an arms race between America and Russia."[17]

Szilard's assumption that had he not initiated action that led to the Manhattan Project, there would have been no atomic bomb, is certainly unwarranted. There might have been no crash program in the United States at that time; however *someone* would have produced a bomb.

Yet another player in the atomic drama was beginning to think about use of the bomb. On 29 May, General Marshall told Secretary Stimson and Assistant Secretary McCloy that the weapon should be used first on "straight military objectives such as a large naval installation." If that did not bring the Japanese to capitulate, bombs could be used against "large manufacturing areas from which people would be warned to leave—telling the Japanese that we intended to destroy such centers." The warning before bombing cities was particularly important: "Every effort should be made to keep our record of warning clear. We must offset by such warning methods the opprobrium which might follow from an ill-considered employment of such force."[18]

Two days after Marshall's conference with Stimson and McCloy, on 31 May, the Interim Committee held an all-day meeting; the scientific panel, plus Generals Marshall and Leslie Groves, Manhattan Project director, met with it. No council of war in American history was more fateful. Every major atomic development and prospect was discussed, and some urgent matters decided. Stimson explicitly stated that he and Marshall viewed the Manhattan Project in cosmic terms: atomic energy represented a new relation of man to the universe, and the conferees were to provide their best advice as to postwar organization, wartime controls, public announcements, legislation, and future research.[19] A proposal to bring the Soviet Union in on the project was discussed and rejected, largely on Byrnes's advice.

During the morning, Ernest Lawrence had suggested giving the Japanese a harmless demonstration before using the bomb for military advantage. This suggestion was taken up during the noon hour. General Marshall was not present; perhaps the outcome would have been different had he been able to argue for the moral position he had presented to Stimson. Without him, the demonstration idea was shot down. In hindsight it is easy to see why.

Where would such a demonstration be held? In neutral territory, as Alexander Sachs suggested, with many observers from other nations? Much time would be required to make arrangements, no one *knew* the bomb would work, and a dud would be disastrous. There was no warrant at all for believing that General Anami Korechika and his military colleagues would give up their determination to fight to the bitter end however spectacular the demonstration. Since the military firmly controlled what appeared in the Japanese press, the people would not be informed no matter what demonstration was staged.

If the demonstration were held very high over a Japanese city, where the fireball could be seen but would do little damage, the Japanese generals would treat it as so much pyrotechnics.[20] No one present at the luncheon believed that a bloodless demonstration would impress the Japanese military. If the time and place of a demonstration over a sparsely populated area of Japan were announced, the remnants of Japan's air force could still interfere with the planes.[21] American prisoners of war could be brought to the spot. Should the demonstration take place anyway, the generals could again deny that the weapon was lethal. And there was still the dud possibility. The Alamogordo test was of a stationary device, not a bomb.

Further, a demonstration, however impressive, would preempt the shock value of the weapon, and it would waste a bomb, very few of which would be available in 1945. The consensus on 31 May was "no demonstration."

The Chicago scientists were not immediately exposed to the full argument against a demonstration. In fact, their Eurocentrism and their isolation from the domestic pressures to keep down casualties and get the boys home caused them to ignore the administration rationale for using the bomb. When Arthur H. Compton returned to Chicago from the Interim Committee meeting, he reported to his staff what security allowed him to say about the committee's concerns. Most of this dealt with postwar control, organization, and legislation. He also noted that nothing was yet definite, and that the committee would meet again in two weeks at Los Alamos.

The Chicago scientists sensed that their worry about first use of the bomb was not being considered at the top. Therefore, with Compton's approval, they organized six committees to systematize their thoughts.[22] These committees dealt with future research, social and political implications of the bomb, educating the public about atomic energy, production, control, and organization. No committee was formed to study how to use the bomb to cause Japanese surrender. The scientists were distant-future minded. Military strategy and tactics in the Pacific War were minor matters to them.

The most significant committee at the Chicago lab, Social and Political Implications, was chaired by James Franck. Eugene Rabinowitch, Glenn Seaborg, and Leo Szilard were members, along with three others less well known. They quickly organized their thoughts; the first meeting was 4 June, and a final report was ready by 11 June. The Franck Report became the most prominent artifact of the Chicago scientists' beliefs and concerns, and a sacred text of the antinuclear movement. One needs to analyze this text carefully to understand where the scientists were coming from, and where they sought to guide their considerable following.

The report begins with the claim that "nuclear power is fraught with infinitely greater dangers than were all the inventions of the past."[23] These dangers, and the threat of nuclear weapons to the United States, can be avoided only by an international authority controlling all nuclear developments. The United States cannot depend on maintaining such a lead in nuclear arms that no one will dare attack us for fear of retaliation; too many other nations know the fundamental facts of nuclear power, and the United States cannot control the raw materials needed to make weapons.[24] Because of the great advantage in a future war of first use of such weapons, we cannot be safe from sudden attack even if we have a massive lead.

The only apparent defense is "dispersal of those industries which are essential to our war effort and dispersal of the populations of our major metropolitan cities."[25] This is of course a staggering task; we would be at a great disadvantage compared with nations more diffusely populated and more authoritarian.

What are the prospects for the essential international control? Even the Soviet Union would shudder at the thought of a sudden disintegration of Moscow and Leningrad: "Therefore, only lack of mutual *trust*, and not lack of *desire* for agreement, can stand in the path of an efficient agreement for the prevention of nuclear warfare" (italics in original).[26]

The report then shifts to the Pacific War. Some officials want "to use them [atomic bombs] without warning on an appropriately selected object in Japan. It is doubtful whether the first available bombs, of comparatively low efficiency and small size, will be sufficient to break the will or ability of Japan to resist, especially given the fact that the major cities like Tokyo, Nagoya, Osaka, and Kobe already will largely have been reduced to ashes by the slower process of ordinary aerial bombing."[27] What were they saying here? Were they saying, "This bomb is not so powerful after all"? Then how can its use be as provocative as the report claims: "Russia, and even allied countries which bear less mistrust of our ways and intentions, as well as neutral countries may be deeply shocked. It may be very difficult to persuade the world that a nation which was capable of secretly preparing and suddenly releasing a weapon as indiscriminate as the [German] rocket bomb and a million times more destructive, is to be trusted in its proclaimed desire of having such weapons abolished by international agreement."[28]

At this stage of the argument, two, and only two, alternative possibilities are presented: (1) it is possible to create international agreement on a total prevention of nuclear war, and (2) effective international control is impossible. Franck and his members obviously lean to the first. But somewhat obtusely, having already told us that dropping the bomb on Japan might not have much effect, they now shift to telling us that "the military advantages and the saving of American lives achieved by the sudden use of atomic bombs against Japan may be outweighed by the ensuing loss of confidence and by a wave of horror and repulsion sweeping over the rest of the world and perhaps even dividing public opinion at home."[29] Therefore, we should have a demonstration in the desert or on a barren island; then, when we obliterate a Japanese city (but will a low efficiency bomb really obliterate anything?) there will be no "wave of horror and repulsion."[30]

Yet more puzzling recommendations are to come. Atomic weapons have been compared to poison gas, which cannot be used because of public opinion.[31] Now we read that after a demonstration, and an "ultimatum to Japan to surrender or at least to evacuate certain regions as an alternative to their total destruction," we might just bomb them.[32] "This may sound fantastic," says the report, "but in nuclear weapons we have something entirely new in order of magnitude of destructive power. . . ."[33] No, not fantastic, just confusing; will military use on a Japanese city shock them into surrender or not?

Now the second alternative comes into focus. Perhaps effective international control is impossible. On this view, "early use of nuclear bombs against Japan becomes even more doubtful—quite independently of any humanitarian considerations. If an international agreement is not concluded immediately after the first demonstration, this will mean a flying start toward an unlimited arms race. If this race is inevitable, we have every reason to delay its beginning as long as possible *in order to increase our headstart still further*" [italics added].[34] What would be more likely to induce "a flying start toward an unlimited armaments race" than increasing our lead as fast as we can?

Of course all this argument takes place in an intelligence vacuum. The race was already on. Stalin ratcheted it up several notches the minute he knew the United States had a bomb, even though it had not yet been used.

There follows a technical discussion of "stages of production" of nuclear weapons. The United States had reached only the first stage, but was on the threshold of the second:

> This stage probably requires no elaborate plans and may provide us in about five or six years with a really substantial stockpile of atomic bombs. Thus it is to our interest to delay the beginning of the armaments race at least until the successful termination of this second stage. The benefit to the nation, and *the saving of American lives in the future*, achieved by renouncing an early demonstration of nuclear bombs and letting the other nations come into the race only reluctantly, on the basis of guesswork and without definite knowledge that "the thing does work," may far outweigh the advantages to be gained by the immediate use of the first and comparatively inefficient bombs in the war against Japan. [italics added][35]

Which nations did the Franck Committee think would "come into the race only reluctantly"?

The concluding sections of this document, about "Methods of International Control" were dead right about one thing: the decision on use of the first atomic bombs "should not be left to military tacticians alone."[36]

Alice K. Smith's discussion of the report contains a strange error: "The final report rested its argument against dropping the bomb on a target in Japan solely on the ground that announcing its existence to the world in this way would make agreement about international control virtually impossible."[37] This was not the sole argument against use. The committee clearly stated that the first "low efficiency bombs" might not achieve anything. This is quite a different argument.

Smith also says, "The accuracy with which the framers of the Franck Report forecast the course of the postwar armaments race has been often and truly remarked."[38] How could any observer of man's warlike history *fail* to predict that every nation capable of acquiring a new and potent weapon would rush to do so?

A more astute judgment from Robert S. Stone, director of the Chicago laboratory's health division, was found in committee files, and is printed without comment by Smith:

> The fact that we have developed this weapon without the knowledge of our allies other than the British convinces me that there will be a certain element of mistrust amongst the other allies no matter how

we introduce it. Moreover, it is inconceivable to me that the French and Russians are not already well aware of the possibilities even though they may not be as far along in the practical development as we are. Under these circumstances I feel that we would be losing nothing by using the weapon in our war against the Japanese. Any respect which the Russians have for us will not be increased if they later find that we had a valuable weapon which we did not use. . . . I feel quite strongly that we will be in a better position to secure international agreement on its suppression after its effectiveness has been demonstrated.[39]

Franck himself carried the committee's report to Washington, where on 12 June it was left with Secretary Stimson's assistant, George L. Harrison. Smith believes that Stimson never gave the report his "careful and personal attention."[40]

Peter Wyden's summation of where the major players stood in mid-June of 1945 is fair: "The scientists hoped to shock the entire world into disarmament. Stimson and his men wanted primarily to shock Tokyo into surrender. If coincidentally, they could also shock Moscow into international cooperation, that would be a welcome dividend."[41]

Not all the scientists agreed with the Franck Committee. Harold Urey was among the dissenters. He was not sure what the bomb would do if it were dropped, he didn't know if it would bring Japanese capitulation, and according to a story in the *New Yorker*, "if it were dropped as a demonstration, the world might not be sufficiently impressed with its frightful reality and the concomitant solve-or-perish problem of world peace. 'It was the difference between abstraction and reality,' he said."[42]

The Franck Report was classified and could not be circulated even in the Chicago lab; it dropped from sight until a sanitized version was declassified and published by the *Bulletin of the Atomic Scientists* 1 May 1946. It then began its life as the "I told you so" text of those who protested Hiroshima and the arms race.

Foremost among those who used the Franck Report to bolster a revisionist interpretation of Truman's Hiroshima decision was Patrick Maynard Stuart Blackett, Fellow of the Royal Society, prominent physicist at Manchester University, a member of Great Britain's Advisory Committee on Atomic Energy from 1945 to 1948, pioneer in the development of Allied anti-submarine measures during the war, the leader of the largest school of cosmic ray research in

Europe, and in the 1950s and 1960s one of the students of rock magnetism who challenged the mistaken (largely American) permanent view of continents and oceans for the current plate tectonic theory.[43]

In 1948, the same year he was awarded the Nobel Prize for physics, Blackett published *Military and Political Consequences of Atomic Energy* in Britain; a year later it was published in the United States as *Fear, War, and the Bomb*. Sensing, and deploring, the pathological American fear of the Soviet Union, Blackett (unwisely) accepted the unwarranted conclusions of the United States Strategic Bombing Survey about Japan's readiness to surrender in 1945 without the bomb, the Russians, or invasion. His lengthy analysis of the closing months of the war concludes "that the dropping of the atomic bombs was not so much the last military act of the Second World War, as the first major operation of the cold diplomatic war with Russia now in progress."[44]

Blackett's account is a reasonable formulation from the data available at the time. I believe it is wrong, but it is far superior to the convoluted and dishonest "atomic diplomacy" tracts of later writers. Blackett, like the authors of the Franck Report, does not give sufficient credit to the powerful and legitimate demands by the American electorate to forestall casualties, get the conscripts out of harm's way, and bring them home at the earliest moment consistent with destroying Japan's power to make war.

Blackett's book was a sensation in Britain. Lord Cherwell, Churchill's scientific adviser during the war, attacked it vigorously.[45] Soviet Foreign Minister Andrei Vyshinsky quoted it ten times in a speech at the United Nations. The American edition attracted less attention; the political climate was not yet hospitable for such a heretical work. The House Committee on UnAmerican Activities was riding high, and McCarthyism/McCarranism was about to dominate the domestic arena. The surge of anti-Truman sentiment was yet to come.

•   •   •

What James Franck and his colleagues hoped for in 1945 was a sympathetic hearing by the Scientists Advisory Committee at the mid-June meeting in Los Alamos. No minutes were kept of this meeting, and we have only later recollections to go on. Those of Arthur H. Compton are the most extensive:

Ten days later, at Oppenheimer's invitation, Lawrence, Fermi and I spent a long weekend at Los Alamos. . . . We were determined to find, if we could, some effective way of demonstrating the power of an atomic bomb without loss of life that would impress Japan's warlords. If only this could be done! Ernest Lawrence was the last one of our group to give up hope for finding such a solution. The difficulties of making a purely technical demonstration that would carry its impact effectively into Japan's controlling councils were indeed great. We had to count on every possible effort to distort even obvious facts. Experience with the determination of Japan's fighting men made it evident that the war would not be stopped unless these men themselves were convinced of its futility.

So again, they recommended military use, but Compton says their "hearts were heavy."[46]

There is some evidence that Enrico Fermi was the last to agree to military use.[47] Whatever the internal arguments, the committee presented a unanimous report. Its first point was that the bomb should be discussed with the Soviet Union, France, and China before it was used (Britain would necessarily be consulted). Its third point was that although the committee was consisted of scientists, it had "no special competence in solving the political, social, and military problems" of atomic power. This disclaimer tends to vitiate the most salient conclusion, which is number two in the report:

> (2) The opinions of our scientific colleagues . . . are not unanimous: they range from the proposal of a purely technical demonstration to that of the military application best designed to induce surrender. Those who advocate a purely technical demonstration would wish to outlaw the use of atomic weapons. . . . Others emphasize the opportunity of saving American lives by immediate military use. . . . We find ourselves closer to these latter views; we can propose no technical demonstration likely to bring an end to the war; we see no acceptable alternative to direct military use.[48]

Robert Oppenheimer later confessed that the disclaimer was based on the fact that the scientists "didn't know beans about the military situation in Japan," so they assumed invasion was inevitable because they had been told that.[49] But they did read newspapers, they did know about the escalating fanaticism of the Japanese defenders of Iwo Jima and Okinawa, and they did trust decisions of the Joint Chiefs of

Staff (JCS), who were planning the invasion. They had not yet been infected by the Strategic Bombing Survey hypothesis that Japan was ready to capitulate. And they did have special knowledge: they knew what had happened at Alamogordo. Oppenheimer referred to this insight in his testimony to the Atomic Energy Commission trial board during his loyalty hearing in 1954: "We did say that we did not think exploding one of these things as a firecracker over a desert was likely to be very impressive. . . . The destruction in the desert is zero, as I think Mr. Gray may be able to remember."[50]

However modest they were about their knowledge of the Pacific War, the advice of this committee was accepted by the Interim Committee, by the secretary of war, by the JCS, and by President Truman. The issues of demonstration, warning, and informing the Russians did not disappear, but the arguments and conclusions remained the same.

At Truman's crucial meeting 18 June 1945 with the JCS and the service secretaries, Assistant Secretary of War John J. McCloy raised the subject of the atom bomb; he thought the United States should use it after a warning to the Japanese. The suggestion was rejected; nobody present could *know* the bomb would go off as planned.[51] The Interim Committee met again in Washington 21 June; the opposition of Franck, Szilard and other Chicago scientists to use without warning was discussed, but the Oppenheimer committee's recommendation was retained.[52] The undersecretary of the navy, Ralph Bard, wrote a memo 27 June that he had had second thoughts, and that perhaps a warning should be reconsidered. This memo reached Stimson, but nothing came of it.[53]

Szilard was not willing to give up. On 19 July, he gave a petition signed by sixty-eight scientists to Arthur Compton for forwarding to the president. Compton sent it via the Manhattan Engineer District Office, not the most sympathetic courier.[54] It never reached the president; he was en route to Potsdam. Szilard's final effort was a more moderate and reasonable enterprise than the April memo he took down to Byrnes. All it called for was a warning to Japan before the bomb was dropped.[55]

•   •   •

When Szilard came to write his recollections, he acknowledged the futility of the demonstration proposal: "I think it is clear that you can't demonstrate a bomb over an uninhabited island. You have to demolish a city."[56]

In the interrogations of Japanese leaders conducted by the United States Strategic Bombing Survey, and by MacArthur's G-2, I have been unable to find any Japanese leaders who claim that the destruction of Hiroshima and Nagasaki could have been avoided, and Japan brought to surrender, by a nonlethal demonstration of the bomb. Instead, there is abundant testimony that the Japanese military even minimized the significance of the damage at Hiroshima. Fortunately the civilian elite, the peace party, knew that something disastrous had occurred; and the emperor used it to face down Anami.

Hiroshima cultists never come to grips with the very cogent reasons why the Interim Committee and its scientific advisers rejected the idea of a demonstration. Some writers, such as Peter Wyden, claim the idea never got "serious analysis," yet he devotes two chapters to the consideration it did get.[57] The pressure point of the argument is whether a nonlethal demonstration could have produced the triumph of the peace party and the acquiescence of the militarists. On this matter, the pro-demonstration argument is bankrupt. Its supporters do not even attempt to analyze the proposal from the Japanese viewpoint as of the summer of 1945; they assume a strictly Western point of view.

The only prominent scientist I have found who inquired into the probable reactions of Japanese to a nonlethal demonstration is Mitchell Wilson. As a young physicist he declined to work at Los Alamos on such a destructive weapon. In the late 1960s, the publisher Sir George Weidenfeld sent Wilson, as a senior physicist, around the world to investigate "the differences of national styles in doing science." Japan was one of his target countries. The Manhattan Project physicists he had come to know were still complaining that Truman had been wrong to reject a demonstration. From what Wilson heard,

> There are those who have become absolutely certain that the bombing of Hiroshima was a mistake. Not until I went to Japan did I realize that all the discussions I had heard had been among Western scientists only, thinking only in Western terms, and taking for granted that the Japanese High Command would necessarily have reasoned along similar lines. In Tokyo, I discussed the question at last with a number of Japanese scientists who were old enough to have lived

through the times. When I asked these men to describe for me what sort of demonstration of the atomic bomb by the United States in the summer of 1945 would have convinced the Japanese High Command of the inevitability of defeat and the need for immediate surrender, I drew a blank stare at the total unreality of the question in the light of the situation as it then existed.[58]

The situation, Wilson heard, was one of total fanatical devotion to the god/emperor, to Japan's imperial mission and the Greater East Asia Co-Prosperity Sphere; death for this cause was a blessing. Japanese did not quail before the first atom bomb; the government noted that people in shelters escaped unscathed, and in any case, said one admiral, "even America could not have enough radioactive material ready to make a sufficient number of bombs to carry on such attacks. Even when Nagasaki showed there was more than one bomb in the American arsenal, the cabinet debated for more than seven hours on what to do."[59]

Wilson concludes his reflections on this issue: "Whatever verdict history will pass on the need to destroy Hiroshima and Nagasaki . . . when the matter is put in terms of the Japanese values generally accepted during the war, Japanese scientists themselves can suggest no realistic alternative to what happened. That there might have been a premilitary demonstration of the atom bomb turns out to be another one of history's myths."[60]

One could expect that advocates of demonstration would have found powerful support for their position in the tens of thousands of pages of testimony from Japanese leaders. The Japanese bias was plain: atomic warfare was unfair. The government filed a formal protest with the Red Cross to this effect. Why, then, did not many of them tell USSBS, MacArthur's G-2, Butow, and other investigators, "You could have ended the war without totally destroying these two cities simply by a demonstration?" And why did not the outraged Western moralists produce significant testimony from *Japanese* that a demonstration would have been effective?

In its 1972 book, *The Day Man Lost*, the Pacific War Research Society naturally regards the atomic bombings as tragedies. But it does not tell us a demonstration would have made military use unnecessary. Nobody, in fact, offers any substantial case for a demonstration. Mitchell Wilson had it right. A demonstration would have wasted time, allowed the casualties in POW camps and naval encounters to continue, possibly have brought many Allied soldiers to the site of the demonstration, and still have been ineffective. William E. Juhnke, typical of the naive believers in a demonstration, says a "dramatic pyro-technical display over Tokyo Bay, at the window of the Japanese government as it were" might have ended the war.[61] His conception of the Japanese Government bears no resemblance to the reality of Anami and his bitter-end supporters. John J. McCloy, who as Stimson's assistant had recommended reconsideration of the "no demonstration" decision on 18 June, twenty years later was sure Stimson and the Interim Committee had been right:

> The decisions recommending the use of the bomb, made by the interim committee formed by President Truman, were reached after thorough exploration of every possible angle: Could you have a demonstration? What would be its effects? We had not at that time seen the explosion at Alamogordo, but I can just say that if I had been a Japanese observer and seen the bomb go off at Alamogordo, I would not have advised surrender. It's one thing to see something go off, causing no damage at all but creating a great ball of fire and obviously of tremendous power, but it's another thing to say: "Well, now, they set this off on a tower; maybe it weighs 50 tons. How do we know they can deliver it?" And I am sure that anyone who was a sound thinker would have said: "No, that doesn't convince us. In the first place, would they have another?" For example, the German scientists believed that it would be impossible for us to make an atomic bomb, and that if we did we could make only one. The Germans thought of an atomic bomb as something that would have to contain as much as 20 tons of uranium 235, a practically impossible quantity.[62]

The demonstration alternative was bankrupt.

•   •   •

But what about a warning?

Many scientists and philosophers felt a warning was called for; the very sober General Marshall felt the same way; even the Far Eastern Department of the British Foreign Office took that point of view.[63] Stimson and his advisers, and hence Truman, believed otherwise.

The only analyst to consider the "no warning" position in depth is Lawrence Freedman of the Royal Institute of International Affairs in London. In a 1978 article, "The Strategy of Hiroshima," he concludes: "As more thought was given to the most effective use of the bomb, the strategy evolved from a simple one based on maximizing the impact of the bomb's destructive power to one aimed at maximizing its shock value. To achieve this it became necessary to distinguish the use of this new weapon from conventional strategic bombing."[64]

Supporting this contention, he notes that in April 1945 Gen. Groves set the following as governing factors: (1) that the targets chosen should be places the bombing of which would adversely affect the will of the Japanese people to continue the war; (2) the targets should be military in nature, consisting either of important headquarters or troop concentrations, or centers of production of military equipment and supplies; and (3) to enable military planners to assess accurately the effects of the bomb, the targets should not have been previously damaged by air raids.[65]

The will of the people criterion was the most important, but let us examine the other two first. The second criterion was almost meaningless; there were few large, strictly military targets left in Japan. Ironically, Hiroshima came as close as any to meeting this criterion, since it was headquarters for the army charged with the defense of Kyushu.[66] The third criterion, designating targets not previously damaged, was important enough to become a bone of contention between Groves and Stimson. Groves thought Kyoto the best target; Stimson had visited there, regarded it as Japan's greatest cultural heritage, and refused to let Groves target it.[67] The four cities on the final target list met this third criterion reasonably well. But it was the first criterion that consciously or not predominated. The word "shock" was not used, but "affecting the will of the people" implies it. This had been the objective of Gen. Curtis LeMay's incendiary raids in the beginning, but his raids became routine, evolving into a strategy of cumulative pressure. In the Interim Committee meeting of 31 May, the minutes read:

VIII. *EFFECT OF THE BOMBING ON THE JAPANESE AND THEIR WILL TO FIGHT:*

   It was pointed out that one atomic bomb on an arsenal would not be much different from the effect caused by any Air Corps strike of present dimensions. However, Dr. Oppenheimer stated that the visual effect of an atomic bombing would be tremendous. It would be accompanied by a brilliant luminescence which would rise to a height of 10,000 to 20,000 feet.[68]

Robert Oppenheimer sensed the true potentialities of the new bomb. It was not just an extension of LeMay's conventional bombing campaign; it was something new under the sun. Lawrence Freedman observes, "It was on the basis of this spectacular quality that those considering the use of the bomb began to move away from the previous, implicit, strategy of cumulative pressure to one of maximum shock."[69] Maximum shock demanded maximum surprise; a specific warning would have eliminated this factor.[70]

It was precisely the shock of the bombs and the assumption that more were coming that brought about Japan's surrender *at that time*. The emperor, by mid-June, agreed with the peace party that the time to give up had arrived. He could not, however, despite his godlike stature, simply impose his will on a military machine determined to fight a decisive battle of the homeland, and capable of governing by assassination if thwarted. Kido, Suzuki, Togo could have been assassinated and the emperor taken into protective custody in order to keep fighting.

The shock of the atom gave the emperor the leverage he needed to compel compliance with his decision. William Manchester, whose experience in the Pacific gives him considerable insight, describes part of what transpired in Tokyo the sixth of August: Hiroshima just disappeared from the communication net. No one knew why. Then,

> At dawn the next day Lieutenant General T. Kawabe, deputy chief of the army general staff, received a single-sentence report that made no sense to him: "The whole city of Hiroshima was destroyed instantly by a single bomb." Subsequent details sounded to Kawabe like ravings. Later accounts to the contrary, Hiroshima had not been without military significance; the Japanese Second Army had been quartered there. At 9:15 August 6 the entire army had been doing calisthenics on a huge parade ground. The Thin Man had exploded almost directly overhead, wiping it out. That was one of the messages that reached Kawabe. It was as though the Pentagon had been informed that the United States Marine Corps had been annihilated in less than a second while turning somersaults.[71]

Anami and others made convincing arguments that the United States could not have more bombs. Nagasaki, when it came so soon after, was equally a shock. These shocks were fundamental to ending the stalemate in the cabinet and the Supreme Council for the Direction of the War, *and* needed to convince Anami, Toyoda, and

Umezu not to join Hatanaka, Ida, and the other insurgents who assassinated the commander of the Palace Guard and attempted to reverse the emperor's decision.

The centrality of the bomb in effecting capitulation is vigorously denied by Hiroshima cultists. For most of them Soviet entry was the key, but they do not engage the evidence on this matter.[72] Part of the relevant evidence consists of pre-surrender communications between Japanese commanders and staff as revealed in the ULTRA decrypts. Prior to September 1944, Japanese forces in Manchuria, known as the Kwantung Army, had operated under a plan for attack on the Soviet Union. As Japanese forces elsewhere were debilitated by Allied attack, and as Soviet capabilities for entering the Pacific War increased, these orders were changed to a defensive strategy. After discussing developments in Manchuria during 1944, Edward J. Drea summarizes Japanese expectations at the beginning of 1945:

> The Japanese, then, had no illusions about an eventual Soviet invasion of Manchuria. In late January 1945, then Vice-Chief of Staff of the Imperial Japanese Army, Lieutenant General Hata Hikosaburo, sent to Japanese military attaches in Europe a forecast of the world situation as it might appear in mid-1945. Concerning the U.S.S.R., the message acknowledged that the Soviets would probably abrogate the Japanese-Soviet Neutrality Pact (due for renewal in April 1945) but "for awhile" thereafter would remain neutral. Hata cautioned, though, that if a favorable opportunity presented itself, the Soviets would enter the war against Japan in the latter half of 1945.[73]

Drea then follows speculations about when the Soviets would attack. Japanese intelligence knew it was coming, but thought the Soviets would not have adequate forces until the spring of 1946.[74] The Kwantung Army was thus taken by surprise and overwhelmed. This constituted a "shock" of sorts, but nothing comparable to the atom bomb.

Not only did Japan expect Soviet entry, it expected the Russians to penetrate Manchuria. Tokyo's order to the Kwantung Army dated 30 May 1945 directed Japanese units to "conduct a delaying action designed to exhaust the Soviet invaders."[75] Japanese troops would slowly withdraw to the rugged terrain near the Korean border, where they could conduct a "protracted defense" for six months.[76] This delaying action would give the defenders of the homeland enough time to smash the first wave of the expected American invasion, at which time a cease fire favorable to Japan would be negotiated. *This military timetable was not upset on 8 August when the Soviets invaded*: only the illusory hopes of the diplomats for Soviet neutrality and mediation were upset.

Until the recent disintegration of the Soviet Union, the official line in that country was that its entry into the Pacific War was the deciding blow for Japan. Now that independent scholarship is again becoming possible in Russia, more candor is appearing. Oleg A. Rzheshevsky, in 1994 the head of the Department of the History of War in the Institute of World History of the Russian Academy of Sciences, wrote that "The atomic bombs dropped by U.S. bombers on Hiroshima and Nagasaki on 6 and 9 August were, of course, pivotal in the Japanese decision to surrender."[77]

Hiroshima cultists make much of a Combined Chiefs of Staff (CCS) "Estimate of the Enemy Situation as of 6 July 1945," prepared for the Potsdam Conference.[78] One section of this document reads:

> We believe that a considerable portion of the Japanese population now consider absolute military defeat to be probable. The increasing effects of sea blockade and cumulative devastation wrought by strategic bombing, which has already rendered millions homeless and has destroyed from 25% to 50% of the builtup area of Japan's most important cities, should make this realization increasingly general. An entry of the Soviet Union into the war would finally convince the Japanese of the inevitability of complete defeat.[79]

Note what this document does not say: that Soviet entry *would induce surrender*, which is the issue here.[80] The CCS believed that nothing would bring Japanese capitulation until the unconditional surrender doctrine was significantly modified. It was wrong about this, and for good reason the British and American leaders at Potsdam retained the unconditional surrender demand (see chapter three).

The really reprehensible failure of cultist argument on this point, however, is its total disregard of postwar interrogations of Japanese principals and of subsequent Japanese scholarship.

In the USSBS interrogations, many respondents commited themselves to the belief that the atom bombs alone brought surrender; a lesser number identified both Soviet entry and atom bombs as effective. Only one, Col. Hayashi Saburo, secretary to War Minister

Anami, implied that Soviet intervention, rather than the bomb, ended the war. Hayashi's interrogation includes this exchange:

Q. It is said that Minister of War Anami's attitude changed after the dropping of the atomic bomb and the entry of the SOVIET UNION into the war. Will you please elaborate on this point?

A. Although it is true that his desire for a quick termination of war suddenly became strong after the entry of the SOVIET UNION into the war, I nevertheless believe that he wanted somehow to ease the conditions even slightly [secure concessions from the Allies]. Up until that time, he spoke very little about the question of ending the war.[81]

This is not exactly a compelling statement.

One other military leader, Maj. Gen. Takashima Tatsuhiko (quoted in chapter two), denied that atom bombs had any effect on the army, though they did affect civilians.[82]

Thus the sum total of relevant Japanese testimony supporting the Hiroshima cultists is thin indeed.[83] Supporting the contention that the bomb ended the war is the judgment of a phalanx of Japanese authorities. It needs to be stressed again that with the official Japanese position holding atomic weapons to have been an atrocity, any acknowledgement by Japanese that the bombs served a useful purpose by ending the war has to be seen as reluctant and highly credible testimony. There is plenty of it.

At least seven principals in the Japanese surrender gave approximately equal weight to the atom and the Soviets: Prince Konoye, Toyoda Soemu, Funada Atsuyasu, Ikeda Sumihasa, Kawabe Torashiro, Abe Genki, and Arisue Seizo.[84] Those who believed the atom bombs deserved predominant credit for precipitating surrender were Hata Shunroku, Hiranuma Kiichiro, Nagano Osami, Sakomizu Hisatsume, Baron Suzuki Kantaro, Inaba Masao, Marquis Kido Koichi, and Prince Higashikuni.[85]

Many Japanese interrogated by USSBS and Far East Command refused to commit themselves; what caused the end of the war was even then an inflammatory subject.

The point at issue here is not what *defeated* Japan; naval, army, and air forces can all claim much credit. Nor is it *when* Japan realized it was defeated; this happened at various times, some admitting defeat after the loss of Saipan, others after MacArthur retook the Philippines, or after Iwo Jima or Okinawa. What is at issue is the trigger that motivated the emperor to surrender and emasculated military opposition. No revisionist historian even begins to come to grips with the best evidence here.[86]

Japanese historians, many of whom declare nuclear weapons immoral, nonetheless generally agree that the shock of the atom ended the war. Togo, writing his memoirs, states baldly that the Hiroshima bombing sent him to the emperor with advice that the war should be ended forthwith, and the emperor agreed.[87] The collective authorship of *Japan's Longest Day* endorses Togo's version of events.[88] Kase Toshikazu's *Eclipse of the Rising Sun* says, "both the bombs and the Russians facilitated our surrender."[89]

Ienaga Saburo, an anti-bomb pacifist, admits in his volume *The Pacific War* that "the twin shocks of the atomic bombings and the Soviet declaration of war broke the stalemate in Tokyo."[90]

Toyoda Toshiyuki, writing in 1986, is emphatic that the atom alone ended the war:

> The explosion of a uranium bomb over Hiroshima on August 6, 1945, and of a plutonium bomb over Nagasaki three days later gave a tremendous shock to Japan's wartime rulers. After studying the report of the Japanese scientists who surveyed the devastated cities, the leaders realized the extraordinary power of the atomic bomb: a single shot could instantly obliterate an entire city. They moved quickly to surrender in order to avoid a third use of this awesome and inhumane weapon on another Japanese city.[91]

Takemi Taro, a Japanese physician, has a slightly different scenario for activating the emperor; he says Count Makino convinced Hirohito to end the war in a conference lasting one hour and forty minutes. But his causal analysis is the same: "When I showed the data about the atomic bomb to Count Makino, he became gravely concerned and immediately asked for an audience with the Emperor to tell his majesty of the danger of the threat of bombing Tokyo. The Count was afraid that there would be no chance for peace talks if the atom bomb was indeed dropped on Tokyo."[92] Makino told Takemi, a relative, that the emperor then agreed to accept the Potsdam Declaration.

Other Japanese are equally emphatic. The widespread support of the Hiroshima cult has not extinguished candid historical analyses of what ended the war. Murakami Hyoe, Kato Masuo, Nakayama Takashi, and Nakamura Masanori are among other analysts who say the bomb was decisive; American revisionists ignore this compelling evidence that, terrible as it was, the atom brought peace.[93]

Henry Stimson and the Interim Committee did not perceive the true fulcrum of Japanese decision making in this crisis; the effect of bombs on the Japanese *people* was largely irrelevant. The people were kept in the dark about how destructive the atom had been. But the leaders knew, and they were shaken. Robert Butow captures the essence of the event:

> The revulsion with which these *samurai*-inspired men viewed defeat and surrender often made them blind to all other considerations. Their thinking processes were befuddled by the emphasis they placed upon the ability of the spirit to triumph miraculously over the power of material force. These men, who had once been the wardens of the prison in which they had confined the whole nation, had now joined the ranks of the inmates. The real significance of the explosions over Hiroshima and Nagasaki and the Soviet dash into Manchuria was that these events produced a shock great enough to crack the walls of the prison. Even this shock did not result in an escape but it did force everyone, the guards and guarded alike, to face the full and glaring light of day—to acknowledge a fact which could no longer be denied. It was not that the military men had suddenly become reasonable . . . it was rather that they, like the machinery of government with which they had been tinkering, had momentarily been caught off balance.[94]

In the furious controversy over surrender that shook the Japanese government in the first days of August 1945, the atomic bombing of Hiroshima and Nagasaki was the decisive event.

Assistant Secretary of War John J. McCloy in his 1965 retrospective says as much: "The reason that we did not have a demonstration of the bomb was, first, that it would have completely wiped out the element of surprise, which in my opinion was extremely important. As it turned out, that was one of the reasons why Japan surrendered so quickly. They weren't prepared for it. It was a bolt out of heaven. There has never been a surprise to equal it since the Trojan horse."[95]

Lawrence Freedman, in his analysis, is careful to note that the Japanese situation was unique, and that the shock effect of atomic bombs cannot be extrapolated to future wars.[96] So far, the desperate circumstances of the Pacific War have not been repeated, nor is it likely that they will be.

5

Was a Second Bomb Necessary to End the War?

To probe the warrant for the second bomb, one has to start with the Truman administration's objective. Lawrence Freedman believes, correctly, the objective was to shock a weakened Japan into early surrender.[1] *Mere quantitative destruction was not the objective; LeMay's B-29s were achieving that with conventional bombs,* but the Japanese military continued to hold out for a final decisive battle of the homeland that would yield lenient surrender terms.

The United States had no reason to think that *one* shock would be sufficient; the Japanese military could, and did, claim that there was only one bomb, and that it was not so terrible anyway.[2]

Hence a second bomb following close on the heels of the first one, keeping the Japanese off balance, was called for. Truman's order was that atomic bombs would be dropped as ready. Two were available in early August; a third was ready by mid-August but was canceled by Truman.[3]

Many commentators hold that the Japanese government did not have adequate time to settle on surrender in the three days between Hiroshima and Nagasaki, and if it had had more time, the war would have ended without dropping the second bomb.[4] Who would have used this time, and how, to overcome the rock-ribbed opposition of the military is never explained.

Despite Truman's euphoria at Potsdam about the Alamogordo test ("I am sure [the Japanese will fold up] when Manhattan appears over their homeland")[5] his military authorities were not counting on one bomb to cause surrender. Barton Bernstein notes, "Before Hiroshima, they did not believe that the nuclear attacks would produce a surrender within a few days or weeks, or even in August."[6] This pessimism was partly due to underestimating the bomb's power, hence its shock value, but mostly due to the increasingly bitter resistance of Japanese soldiers and to continued belligerent statements coming from Tokyo.

Consequently, when physicist Norman F. Ramsey was sent to Tinian as chief scientist to supervise preparation of the atomic bombs for loading on aircraft, he expected a long assignment. Peter Wyden's description of Ramsey's situation offers the best account:

> He had been instructed that fifty nuclear bombs might be required to force the surrender of the Japanese and end World War II. The dreaded alternative was an invasion of Japan against fanatical resistance. . . . Each bomb was equivalent to about one week of bombing raids with conventional explosives. . . . So when Oppie dispatched Ramsey, his most trusted senior physicist, to Tinian . . . Ramsey had expected routine duty. . . . Ramsey had told his crew of nuclear specialists that they would serve a six-month tour of duty on the island. . . . The Tinian contingent had planned their personal lives to fit this timetable. One engineer brought along hop seed in the belief that he would have ample leisure to brew his own beer.[7]

This preparation for a long run of atomic bombing represented excessive prudence, a worst case scenario. No one in the Manhattan Engineer District (MED) thought it would take so long. Adm. William Purnell, naval member of the MED Military Policy Committee, believed that two bombs would end the war.[8] But nobody could be sure.

Even on 12 August, after the atomic bombings, Soviet entry, and the first tentative Japanese offer to accept the Potsdam terms, Maj. Gen. Clayton Bissell, Army G-2, wrote a memo to General Marshall speculating on Japanese actions. "Atomic bombs," wrote Bissell, "will not have a decisive effect in the next 30 days."[9]

Fortunately Purnell was right, Bissell wrong.

The pressure point of the argument is this: "Would Japan have surrendered soon without the second bomb immediately following the first?" Of course no certain answer can be given. For rational analysis, this question must be translated into "Was the U.S. desire to keep the Japanese off balance, and to prove immediately that there was more than one bomb, sufficiently well-grounded to justify Nagasaki?" Certainly the demonstrated Japanese capacity to absorb punishment and still remain bellicose warranted the belief that just one superbomb might not cause them to give up. Since the Japanese militarists controlled information tightly and could easily minimize the significance of one superbomb and since every day that went by without another bomb would reinforce Anami's claim that, whatever it was, the United States only had one, the belief that two bombs in quick succession would be more potent than spreading them out seems reasonable.

Richard Rhodes interviewed naval Ens. Bernard J. O'Keefe, who was on the assembly team and recalled the "mood of urgency" as they got the Nagasaki bomb ready:

> With the success of the Hiroshima weapon, the pressure to be ready with the much more complex implosion device became excruciating. We sliced off another day, scheduling it for August 10. Everyone felt that the sooner we could get off another mission, the more likely it was that the Japanese would feel that we had large quantities of the devices and would surrender sooner. We were certain that one day saved would mean that the war would be over one day sooner. Living on that island, with planes going out every night and people dying not only in B-29s shot down, but in naval engagements all over the Pacific, we knew the importance of one day; the *Indianapolis* sinking also had a strong effect on us.[10]

On the other side of the Pacific, in the fevered councils of a reeling Japanese empire, the militarists were doing what they could to calm the fearful. Edwin Hoyt's narrative of events the morning of 9 August reconstructs what happened at the palace:

> At 11:00 in the morning, as the B-29 carrying the plutonium bomb approached Nagasaki, the generals, admirals, and civilian members of the Supreme War Council met at the Imperial Palace. . . . The military members began by arguing that if, as now seemed indicated, the bomb dropped on Hiroshima had been an atomic bomb, and if just one bomb was dropped when everyone knew the Americans had thousands of B-29s, then there must simply have been that one bomb. Therefore, said War Minister Anami, one need have no further fear of atomic attack. The destruction of Hiroshima was, quite to the reverse of the civilian way of thinking, really an asset to the government, because now it would be far easier to rally the people of Japan—who were admittedly growing restless in the shadow of constant defeat—to the last great struggle that should bring "victory."[11]

General Umezu took a slightly different approach. He argued that "even the United States could not possibly possess enough radioactive material to make a sufficient number of bombs to permit a continuation of such attacks."[12] Anami, Umezu, and Toyoda stood their ground. There was only one atomic bomb, Soviet entry had already been discounted, the decisive battle of the homeland must be fought.

Given these facts, Barton Bernstein's claim in the January-February 1995 *Foreign Affairs* is surprising: "Evidence now available about developments in the Japanese Government—most notably the emperor's then-secret decision shortly before the Nagasaki bombing to seek peace—makes it clear that the second bomb could undoubtedly have been avoided."[13] Evidence that the emperor made his firm decision to recommend peace after the Hiroshima bombing and before the Nagasaki bombing has been available for decades. The sticking point during this interim was not the will of the emperor; it was the refusal of Anami and the military to give up their hopes for a decisive battle of the homeland, at which they would finally convince the United States to back off and negotiate.[14]

No account of the deliberations in the Supreme Council for the Direction of the War, or in the Japanese cabinet, on 9 August warrants the belief that absent Nagasaki, the emperor would have been able to prevail when he finally declared himself. *Japan's Longest Day* is quite clear; the Hiroshima bomb, the Soviet entry into the war, and the Nagasaki bomb were *together* insufficient to move the military. Only the Emperor's opinion, stated twice, ended the war. How can one believe any lesser trauma could have been effective?[15]

So stubborn was the military resistance that Japanese waffling went on until 14 August. On that day, the British political affairs officer in Washington reported to the Foreign Office, "When I saw the President at midday on Tuesday morning (14 August) he was a very worried man, pinned down in his office at the White House by a mob of news-hungry journalists parked on a twenty-four-hour vigil in the anteroom. He had just received a report that the messages from Japan did not contain the expected reply and he sorrowfully remarked that another bomb now seemed the only way to hasten the end."[16] Then, of course, the Japanese acceptance arrived.

•   •   •

Everything we know about the death throes of the Japanese empire indicates that even with the modification of the unconditional surrender doctrine to allow continuation of the emperor, even with the devastation caused by conventional bombing and two atomic bombs, even with the feared entry of the Soviet Union, surrender hung by a thread. Twice the emperor had to direct his ministers to accept the Potsdam terms. When they finally gave in, obedience by the fanatical junior officers was not assured. The Pacific War Research Society emphasized in *Japan's Longest Day* that War Minister Anami stated bluntly, "Our men will simply not lay down their arms." Home Minister Abe "served notice that he could not promise civil obedience if the Cabinet decided to attempt to end the war through capitulation."[17]

Of all the histories of the emperor's triumph over the militarists, *Japan's Longest Day* is the one that shows most clearly how narrow was his victory, and how dangerous to the surrender process were the several insurrections.[18] None of the "bomb wasn't necessary" theorists acknowledge the fact that the Japanese Foreign Office was so alarmed at the rumor that a third bomb was to be dropped on Tokyo on 12 August that Domei News Agency was ordered to broadcast the text of Japan's conditional acceptance of the Potsdam Declaration even before the status of the emperor had been settled, to convince the United States not to drop another.[19]

Samuel Eliot Morison's oft-quoted metaphor, that "the atomic bomb was the keystone of a very fragile arch" that brought Japan's surrender,[20] needs to be modified; there were two bombs, two keystones.

Although the known bias of Japanese participants in the surrender decision was to deplore atomic bombs as atrocities, there is a glaring absence of "Nagasaki was unnecessary and cruel" statements in their interrogations. Fuchida Matsuo offers the only strong comment. According to Gordon Prange, "he didn't blame the United States, but he did resent the timing of the second bomb. An interval of only three days between the Hiroshima and Nagasaki bombings was unrealistic."[21] Fuchida, however, does not factor into this opinion Anami's stubborn insistence that the Hiroshima event was not an atomic bomb, or that if it was, it was the only one. Fuchida himself claims to have felt as soon as he learned of Hiroshima that the bomb was atomic, and that "The war is over."[22] And he admitted that "If Japan had had the atomic bomb we would have dropped it on the United States."[23]

The most probative testimony comes from Marquis Kido. The affidavit he introduced at the Tokyo War Crimes Trials shows the following entry:

304. On August 10, 1945 [9 August U.S. time] atomic bombs were dropped at Nagasaki City causing a large number of victims. This gave a great shock to the nation, together with the Soviet Union's participation in the Pacific War on the Allied side, imparting a sudden and powerful stimulus to controversies as well as moves and countermoves between the peace and war parties in this country. Surveying the situation, I foresaw various difficulties ahead, to overcome which I thought that there would be no course left but to broadcast an Imperial rescript to the nation on the part of the Emperor terminating the war.[24]

There is no countervailing testimony. Kido was assuredly prime mover in the emperor's decisions to end the war; he was also on the assassination list of the army insurgent groups.

Hayashi Saburo, military secretary to the minister of war (Anami) from April to August 1945, also credits the Nagasaki bomb with a significant effect. He explains in *Kogun: The Japanese Army in the Pacific War* how the army denied that the Hiroshima bomb was formidable, and claimed that countermeasures were available. Truman's broadcast claiming that the bomb had been atomic was rejected by the Japanese military as

. . . strategic propaganda directed against Japan. On-the-spot investigations failed to make satisfactory progress. It was only later that it was tacitly understood that the Truman statement was not a lie; i.e., after a second bomb had been dropped upon Nagasaki. City dwellers were gripped with great fear that their own communities might become the next target. In Tokyo, when air raid warnings were sounded, not a soul was to be seen out of doors. In particular, the psychological effect upon the authorities conducting the war was tremendous. It could not be denied that sentiment for accepting the Potsdam Declaration was growing stronger.[25]

One of the most perplexing treatments of the importance of the Nagasaki bomb is in Martin Sherwin's *A World Destroyed*. Sherwin approaches the bomb by asserting: "The rationale that had loosed the first atomic attack was about to unleash the second one too—

unconditional surrender had to be accepted immediately or, as Truman announced, the Japanese 'may expect a rain of ruin from the air, the like of which has never been seen on this earth.'"[26] By then, however, as chapter three shows, unconditional surrender rhetoric had already been modified by the Potsdam terms, and the Japanese knew it.

Sherwin goes on to quote Robert Butow: the atomic bomb and Soviet entry were a "supreme opportunity" for the peace party; Sherwin implies that the Nagasaki bomb contributed nothing to this "opportunity."[27] Butow says of the morning of 9 August that "By the time Marquis Kido arrived at the palace in midmorning, the city of Nagasaki was on the verge of becoming a graveyard with not a tombstone standing, and the forces of the Soviet Union were well into Manchuria. Without wasting either time or words, His Majesty requested the Privy Seal to get in touch with Premier Suzuki and to urge upon him the need for action."[28] But, contrary to Sherwin, Butow factors the Nagasaki bombing into his analysis.

In discussing the deadlock in the Supreme Council for the Direction of the War that morning over whether Japan should demand more concessions than just the retention of the emperor, Butow very clearly asserts what Sherwin is so anxious to deny:

> The council was deadlocked, with Suzuki, Togo, and Yonai on the one side, and Anami, Umezu, and Toyoda on the other. Although the atomic attack upon Hiroshima had made it impossible for anyone present to continue to deny the urgency of Japan's situation, it apparently had not made a deep enough impression upon the chiefs of staff and the War Minister to make them willing to cast their lot outright for a termination of the war.
>
> While the two sides were still debating the issue, however, the news that Nagasaki had suffered the fate of Hiroshima was carried into the council chamber. There had been an interval of only two days between the two attacks. This seemed to suggest that in two more days, or three, the map of Japan might grimly sport another black-faced X drawn through the name of a third or even a fourth Japanese city. Certainly the fact that a second A-bomb had been dropped did not offer much consolation to those who were wistfully speculating about the total number the United States might have on hand.[29]

Having conveniently overlooked the awkward passages in Butow, Sherwin confronts the Nagasaki issue directly: "What effect did this second holocaust delivered only three days after the first have on the decision of the Japanese to surrender? The fact that Nagasaki was destroyed before Japan's leaders had absorbed the shock of Hiroshima, or the shock and implications of the Soviet declaration of war, precludes an accurate assessment. The rapid succession of crises blurred the significance of each."[30]

Of course it did. The rapid succession of crises was intended to destabilize Japan. It was one more disruption of the military dominance that had existed in the Japanese polity. It threw the Supreme Council for the Direction of the War off balance. This turbulence benefited the peace party, which was seeking change. Then the controversial assumptions of Yamato racial superiority, of Japanese military invincibility, of inevitable triumph were shaken to their foundations.[31] Turmoil strengthened the people who knew what they wanted, and weakened the people who then had to contemplate, in addition to all their other troubles, atomic bombs and Russians.

Sherwin quotes Joseph L. Marx, who writes that the bombing of Nagasaki "did give the Emperor a means by which to convince the military that the Potsdam terms had to be accepted," which is a misstatement of the situation.[32] The emperor didn't convince the military; he simply overpowered them. But Marx's misstatement does not justify Sherwin's next claim: "[This argument] assumes that until the emperor was informed about Nagasaki he was not inclined either to accept or to advocate surrender."[33] No such assumption is legitimate, nor does Marx say that the Nagasaki bomb *by itself* enabled the Emperor to win out. It was simply another argument in his brief. The balance of argument is clearly supportive of the validity of the U.S. dual shocks strategy.

There is another attack on the use of a bomb against Nagasaki, based on the claim that since it was a different kind of bomb than that dropped on Hiroshima, the U.S. military wanted to drop it to see how it worked—as an experiment.

The pacifist A.J. Muste was one of the most vociferous critics. To him, since he could see no military justification at all for the second bomb, the basic evil was the scientist's "urge for experimentation running wild."[34] *Christian Century* cited with approval a *Human Events* commentary that "The bombing of Nagasaki, on the other hand, was a 'purely experimental matter'; scientists wanted more data on atom bomb results."[35] Even crusty old Adm. William Halsey, no lover of the air force, said the Nagasaki bomb was dropped because the scientists "had this toy and they wanted to try it out. . . ."[36]

Certainly the Manhattan scientists had a paternal interest in the product of their labors. To assert that the Nagasaki bomb was dropped *primarily* because of this interest, however, flies in the face of *all* the artifacts of the scientists' strenuous activity. They, no less than other Americans, wanted desperately to bring the war to a close. Had they been interested primarily in experimentation, they could have exploded their progeny under less stressful and dangerous conditions far away from the war zone—as they did in the following years of Cold War excesses.

Could the necessary convulsion in the Japanese government have been produced if the second bomb had been held off for, say, a week? We will never know. What we do know is that every day without a follow-up to Hiroshima played into Anami's hands.

6

Was Dropping These Bombs Morally Justified?

The fundamental moral dilemma remains for me unsolved. The infliction of suffering is in itself an evil, corrupting the agent as well as harming the patient. The conduct of war consists of deploying armed force so as to inflict, or threaten the infliction of suffering on an adversary—which may mean, under contemporary political and economic conditions, on all members of his society. War, thus, is in itself inescapably an evil. But those who renounce the use of force find themselves at the mercy of those who do not; and the value-system which enables us to see the infliction of suffering as an evil is in itself the product of a certain kind of society which is as liable as any other social system in history to destruction from without, as it is to corruption and disruption from within. On one horn of the dilemma lies suicide, on the other a moral degradation which may be a more subtle form of self-destruction. There are no easy answers: we have no right to expect them.

Michael Howard[1]

There *are* easy answers to the question of this chapter from a host of commentators. No dilemma or moral ambiguity exists for them: Truman's decision was clearly and unquestionably immoral.

John Haynes Holmes of the Community Church of New York called Hiroshima "the supreme atrocity of the ages."[2] Lewis Mumford wrote in a prominent essay that "our moral nihilism has brought us down to the level of Genghis Khan, or, if that is possible, somewhat lower."[3]

A commission of the Federal Council of Churches concluded, "the surprise bombings of Hiroshima and Nagasaki are morally indefensible."[4] Dwight MacDonald, writing in his magazine, *Politics*, placed the United States on a moral level with the Nazis and their extermination camps.[5] Father Edgar R. Smothers in the Jesuit journal

115

America acknowledged that the bombs might have shortened the war, but their use violates "a primary principle of sound morality: no end—however good, however necessary—can justify the use of an evil means."[6] *The Christian Century*, in an editorial entitled, "America's Atomic Atrocity," said, "What the use of poison gas did to the reputation of Germany in World War I, the use of atomic bombs has done for the reputation of the United States in World War II."[7]

It is not always easy to tease out a clear basis for these moral judgments. One basis for condemnation rests on the belief that nuclear weapons are intrinsically evil, like poison gas; they are qualitatively different from other weapons in their horrible effects, both immediate and latent. In this respect, as with poison gas, mankind should regard them as beyond the pale and forbid their production and deployment.

A second ground on which some condemn the use of atomic bombs against the Japanese is that it violated the principle of noncombatant immunity. Such bombs cannot be targeted or restricted to fighting forces. Truman and his advisors knew that thousands of women and children, most of whom were not engaged in prosecuting the war, would be killed. This argument also applies to any bombing that will kill noncombatants, as well as to conventional blockades and sieges designed to starve or otherwise incapacitate enemy populations.

Many moralists acknowledge this principle, but some qualify it. They hold that noncombatants may be killed incidentally to a legitimate military action (the current term is collateral casualties) if the prospective benefit of that action outweighs the evil of noncombatant injury. This is a utilitarian calculation; the ends achieved must be in proportion to the means used. This proportionality principle allows the commentator to generally approve area bombing of Germany when that was the only way in which Britain could engage the Nazis, while condemning area bombing (especially atomic bombs) in Japan, which did not appear to pose the same threat to the Allies as did Germany.

Third, many critics claim that the bombs were used on the basis of invalid motives: retribution, revenge, reprisal. We were, in using them, lowering ourselves to the level of our opponents; or we used the bombs against Japan where we would not use them against Germany because of racism; or we were merely experimenting or justifying a $2 billion expenditure.

Fourth, some attack the morality of the Hiroshima and Nagasaki bombings because no specific warning was given. The force of this argument is diminished by the certainty that despite any conceivable warning thousands of Japanese would have been killed anyway. The use of poison gas, for instance, would not be excused by warning the enemy.

•   •   •

The "intrinsically evil" argument is made by those opponents of nuclear weapons who are most outraged. It is preemptive. If one accepts it, all other arguments are irrelevant. The judgment that the bombs used at Hiroshima and Nagasaki are inherently cruel, barbaric, unconscionable is a private and personal judgment: the ends to which such weapons are directed do not matter. No conceivable benefit of atomic bombing, such as shortening the war, or diminishing total casualties, cancels out its cruelty.

One explicit statement of this point of view comes from Thomas Nagel:

> . . . one can justify prohibitions against particularly cruel weapons: starvation, poisoning, infectious diseases . . . weapons designed to maim or disfigure or torture the opponent rather than merely to stop him. . . . The effect of dum-dum bullets, for example, is much more extended than necessary to cope with the combat situation in which they are used.[8]

Nagel is here concerned with American conduct of the Vietnam War, but the strictures apply equally to nuclear weapons.

Robert Jay Lifton is among those who emphasize the inherently evil nature of nuclear weapons. He titles the book he wrote with Richard Falk *Indefensible Weapons*. To him, when we discuss the use of atomic bombs, "we are no longer talking about war or weaponry but about a technology of destruction so extreme, of such a quantum jump from anything we have known, as to border on the absolute." His visceral rejection of these weapons was reinforced in 1962 by six months he spent in Hiroshima. What he found was "not just death; it was grotesque and absurd death, which had no relationship to the life cycle as such. There was a sudden and absolute shift from normal existence to the overwhelming immersion in death."[9] Lifton's descriptions of the pathologies left in the wake of this first use of atomic weapons are chilling.

Norman Cousins took the "inherently evil" position after reading John Hersey's *Hiroshima*: "Do we know . . . that many thousands of human beings will die of cancer during the next few years because of radioactivity released by the bomb? Do we know that the atomic bomb is in reality a death ray, and that the damage by blast and fire may be secondary to the damage caused by radiological assault upon human tissue? Have we as a people any sense of responsibility for the crimes of Hiroshima and Nagasaki?"[10]

Dwight MacDonald emphasizes "that the real horror of the Bomb is not blast but radioactivity." He attacks not only Truman but the scientists who "whelped this monstrosity . . . the white coat of the scientist is as blood-chilling a sight as Dracula's black cape."[11] Hanford, Los Alamos, and Oak Ridge were equal to Frankenstein's laboratory.

Despite such colorful rhetoric, the preemptive argument on intrinsic evil is far from compelling. Hanson Baldwin deplored Hiroshima, but on pragmatic grounds; he thought "the atomic bomb is no worse qualitatively than other lethal weapons; it is merely quantitatively more powerful; other weapons cause death in fearful ways; the atomic bomb caused more death."[12]

Ralph McGill, prominent editor of the *Atlanta Constitution*, also belittled the qualitative argument: atomic weapons were "fully as moral as the shotgun, the spear, the ax . . . the tommy gun . . . the slingshot of David . . . or any other weapon of death."[13] Even Thomas Nagel, whose list of immoral weapons is as long as any, acknowledges in a footnote that the matter may not be certain: "Ordinary bullets, after all, can cause death, and nothing is more permanent than that."[14]

McGill is right; there *are* ways of killing, commonplace in every war, that are as grotesque and repulsive as the bombs used on Hiroshima and Nagasaki. Consider the intolerable incidence of mass slaughter, maiming, debilitating, incinerating, from the trenches of World War I; the destruction of Guernica by the Luftwaffe in the Spanish Civil War; the rape of Nanking by Japanese soldiers; Mussolini's target practice on Ethiopians; the atrocities of the Gestapo throughout Europe; the Bataan Death March; the Japanese "construction" camps throughout Southeast Asia; the flamethrowers American soldiers used on Pacific islands; the firestorming of Hamburg, Dresden, Tokyo—these terrible events were as traumatic for their victims as the horrors of Hiroshima and Nagasaki. They *all* involve degradation and cruelty. Perhaps the aftereffects of radiation are worse than the aftereffects of flamethrowers, or high explosive amputations, or fragmentation grenades; in 1945, this was unknown. The two atomic bombs loosed on Japan were not worse than many other events in mankind's sordid history. They were simply more spectacular, with a fireball and a mushroom cloud, concentrated in time and space, affecting thousands of people all at once, appearing mythically as the vengeance of God.

However one evaluates the "intrinsic evil" argument, it has little purchase on Harry Truman's decision in this case. Until late in 1946, neither Truman nor his top advisers knew the range of damages caused by atomic weapons, hence they could not be aware of the extent to which this weapon might be viewed as different from conventional explosives. They knew from Robert Oppenheimer that there would be danger from radiation, but not how much nor how long it would last; and Oppenheimer predicted 20,000 casualties from one bomb, far short of the reality.

Plans for tactical use of atomic bombs in proximity to American troops show complete disregard for radioactive effects of early bombs. Barton Bernstein and Marc Gallicchio have reconstructed General Marshall's plans for battlefield use of bombs that were to be ready in November for the invasion of Kyushu. One bomb would be exploded at a height of 1,800 feet. It could "wipe out resistance over an area 2000 feet in diameter . . . paralyze it seriously over an area five miles in diameter. . . ." Damaging effects of residual radiation? None: ". . . we think we could move troops through the area immediately, preferably by motor but on foot if desired."[15]

There was consideration of tactical use of atomic bombs right up to the Japanese surrender. General Marshall recalled in 1957 that he had planned to use nine atomic bombs, three for each of the three army corps scheduled to land on Kyushu. One bomb was to be dropped in each corps area right in the path of the American invaders, shortly before they went ashore.[16] These were the plans of a military commander to whom the atomic bomb was merely a powerful explosive. Given the 1945 state of knowledge of atomic explosions, one could hardly call them more immoral than the strategic bombing carried out by all the major participants (except China).

Full knowledge of the destructiveness of nuclear weapons came later. Jack Schubert and Ralph E. Lapp, in their study, *Radiation*, observe, "Alamogordo, then, provided only a mild foretaste of things to come. Nor did the two bombs exploded over Hiroshima and Nagasaki reveal the true dimensions of fallout as a biological hazard. . . . Our first real taste of what residual radioactivity from a bomb would be like came from the Operation Crossroads (Bikini) bomb tests in the summer of 1946." After these tests, the U.S. Navy built a laboratory at Hunter's Point, San Francisco, to explore the nature of fallout.[17] Today, we know our nuclear arsenals to be lethal far beyond the two bombs loosed in 1945. The case for immorality of today's overkill arsenals and war-fighting doctrines is strong. To apply the same case retrospectively to 1945, however, is senseless.

●　　　●　　　●

The legitimacy of wars, and of the means by which they are fought, have long been concerns of Christian moralists. In this, they depart from their Judaic predecessors. As Michael Howard notes, "The Old Testament describes with bloodthirsty relish a succession of massacres, deceptions, trickeries, and assassinations which were considered not only innocuous but positively praiseworthy since they forwarded God's purpose for the Children of Israel."[18] Christ, however, preached a different gospel. "Love thine enemy" was to replace "an eye for an eye." Beginning at least with Augustine, the tortuous process of reconciling an ethic of love and forgiveness with the political practices of militaristic nations has occupied a great number of moralists.

Augustine began the process of rationalizing Christian participation in war, and Robert L. Holmes is right in claiming that Augustine "turned Christ's teaching on its head."[19] Certainly no subsequent Western moralist who deals with war can afford to neglect Augustinian doctrine. This is not to hold that Augustine was right in his convoluted doctrine of Just War. As with all problems of moral philosophy, arguments still rage, and will continue to rage, about the morality of initiating war, and equally of fighting it. Nuclear weapons have only intensified controversy over what is moral in war.

The prime pressure point of controversy in contemporary argument about the morality of fighting wars arises from the inevitability of massive civilian casualties from strategic bombing. There are three positions here. "Realists" hold that war is by its very nature immoral, that both sides in a war must do whatever is necessary to win, and that only the law of the jungle prevails. This point of view I will disregard.

Other observers agree that some means of fighting are not to be tolerated, and that killing innocent civilians (the wording Holmes uses) or noncombatants (the more common term) is presumptively wrong. "Absolutists" (Richard A. Wasserstrom's term) insist that to knowingly kill noncombatants is always and absolutely wrong; "utilitarians" or "consequentialists" believe that if the end achieved is crucial, killing of noncombatants is justified.[20] This is the ancient means/ends controversy.

Ironically, the first major theorist of strategic bombing advocated a kind of war that would kill many civilians in order to avoid the horrible bloodbath of World War I trench warfare. Italian general Giulio Douhet was the most influential of the military theorists; after observing the carnage of that war, where hundreds of thousands of young men died needlessly seizing or defending inconsequential pieces of territory, he thought that air power could put an end to such madness in the next war. Ronald Schaffer's summary of the kind of war Douhet envisaged puts the matter succinctly: it would be

> a conflict of whole peoples, employing the entire human and material resources of society, a struggle in which the distinctions between combatant and noncombatant vanished. In modern war everyone took part, "the soldier carrying his gun, the woman loading shells in a factory, the farmer growing wheat, the scientist experimenting in his laboratory." In this total war the primary object of military action would no longer be the enemy's armed forces, as in Clausewitz's time, but the vitals of the nation itself, the source of enemy military power, now exposed by technology to attack from the air.[21]

Douhetian-style, total war clearly rejects the noncombatant principle.

The statesmen who gathered periodically to draw up conventions for the conduct of war, however, refused to condone a concept of total war. The Fourth Hague Convention (1907), which was adopted by most Western nations, forbids any bombardment of undefended towns, but allows bombardment of defended towns, or towns that are under attack on the ground.[22] This prohibition was disregarded in World War I. Balloons and zeppelins were used by both sides to deliver bombs behind the combat areas, but these unwieldy delivery vehicles did little damage. By 1917, German Gotha and R-bombers were able to carry 2,000 pounds of explosives, and the world's first "serious strategic bombing campaign" attacked London; 1,400 people were killed.[23] Few subsequent wars have been without some strategic bombing.

The advent of aircraft carrying bombs made existing rules of acceptable conduct obsolete, and in 1923 another meeting convened at the Hague to consider rules of aerial warfare. Its work was never ratified, though some countries indicated they would comply. Paragraph 3 of Article XXIV of the 1923 Hague Draft Rules of Aerial Warfare reads: "The bombardment of cities, towns, villages, dwellings or buildings not in the immediate neighborhood of the operations of land forces is prohibited."

This rule worked to the advantage of the Fascist powers. Thus, when the German Condor Legion obliterated Durango and Guernica in March and April of 1937, the Fascist bombers were able to claim that these acts were permitted by the "rules" of warfare, since Franco's army was about to attack those towns.[24] Similarly, when the Germans bombed Warsaw and Rotterdam, Hitler claimed that their destruction was justified by the nearby operation of land forces. Later, when the Germans blitzed London, razed Coventry, and launched their Baedeker Raids, there was no longer any pretense of following the Hague rules.

At the beginning of World War II, both Churchill and Roosevelt endorsed the principle of noncombatant immunity, and for a while Allied bombers attempted precision bombing of military and industrial targets. But the power of the German Wehrmacht, the rout of British and French armies, and the losses to British air crews in daylight precision bombing made it seem as if the only way in which the lone defenders of Western civilization could injure the Nazis was by strategic or area bombing. By early 1942, the British were attacking German cities as such.

The history of bombing escalation in World War II is long and complicated. Here it is only pertinent to note that Harry Truman was in no way involved.

Those who spoke out against strategic bombing in the 1940s were the absolutists, for whom no conceivable objective could justify killing civilian populations. Vera Brittain, a popular English essayist, was the most outspoken of the protesters. Her book, *Seed of Chaos*, was bitterly assailed in England; it roundly condemned the Bomber Command's targeting. In 1944, extracts from Brittain's book were published in the United States by the Fellowship of Reconciliation under the title "Massacre by Bombing"; the reception there too was frosty. But strong Catholic voices came to her defense, among them John C. Ford, S.J., who in "The Morality of Obliteration Bombing" acknowledged Brittain's pioneering work, and agreed that "the majority of civilians in a modern nation at war enjoy a natural law right of immunity from violent repression."[25]

Hiroshima and Nagasaki expanded the influence of the anti-bombing position. One surprising convert was Norman Cousins. In 1944, he was a gung ho bomber, specifically disagreeing with Brittain. His ground was retribution: "But once the enemy *starts* it, it becomes no longer a moral but a military question, no longer a matter of argument but a matter of action. . . . And the only question remaining is whether we can beat the enemy at a type of warfare which he has made inevitable because he himself had initiated it."[26]

By 14 September 1946, Cousins had reversed himself. As noted earlier, his editorial in the *Saturday Review* of that date called the atom bomb a death ray, and castigated American leadership for using it. Cousins had been turned around by John Hersey's *Hiroshima.*[27] Prior to this, the residents of Hiroshima were faceless, nameless enemies who had done great damage to the United States. Hersey made them seem innocent and human; the ethics of obliteration bombing suddenly concerned not just philosophers and moralists, but a broad attentive public. As the Cold War developed, criticism of bombing merged with fear of nuclear proliferation to activate a lasting antinuclear constituency. Leading this constituency were Catholic theologians. We need not go into the fine points of their doctrine; it was basically simple: the primary principle of sound morality is to "uniformly insist on the innocence and consequent immunity of civil populations."[28]

There are two influential full-scale attacks on the morality of Truman's bomb decision. One comes from a rigid absolutist (Catholic), the other from a secular consequentialist.

The first is the 1957 pamphlet by Elizabeth Anscombe, entitled *Mr. Truman's Degree.*[29] In the spring of 1956, G.E.M. Anscombe was a research fellow in Philosophy at Somerville College, Oxford. When she heard of the proposal to award Truman an honorary degree, she decided to oppose the move in Oxford's deliberative body, Congregation. Normally, Congregation is about as exciting, and well-attended, as the average American faculty meeting. When word got out that Anscombe would oppose the motion to honor

Truman, the dons bestirred themselves, and more than 100 turned out on 1 May 1956. As Anscombe describes the event,

> I informed the Senior Proctor of my intention to oppose Mr. Truman's degree. He consulted the Registrar to get me informed on procedure. The Vice-Chancellor was informed; I was cautiously asked if I had got up a party. I had not; but a fine house was whipped up to vote for the honour. The dons at St. John's were simply told "The women are up to something in Convocation; we have got to go and vote them down." In Worcester, in All Souls, in New College, however, consciences were greatly exercised, as I have heard. A reason was found to satisfy them: *It would be wrong to try to PUNISH Mr. Truman!* I must say I rather like St. John's.
>
> The Censor of St. Catherine's had an odious task. He must make a speech which should pretend to show that a couple of massacres to a man's credit are not exactly a reason for not showing him honour. [italics in original][30]

The head of St. Catherine's, Alan Bullock (now Lord Bullock), who proposed the degree, hardly defended Truman on the merits. He "admitted that the dropping of the atomic bombs was probably a mistake, as we could now see. At the time, however, the decision to use them appeared unavoidable, and was pressed on Mr. Truman by all his senior advisors." Further, Mr. Truman had "substantial claims on England's gratitude" for securing the continued U.S. presence in Europe, and for defending South Korea.[31] This argument was enough for Congregation; the motion was carried by acclamation. Anscombe did not press for a recorded vote.

But she got back at Truman in her pamphlet. It was widely circulated, and along with her 1961 article, "War and Murder," it is still cited by philosophers. It is a curious bit of argument, strong on emotion and lamentably weak on its historical claims. Her first paragraph reminds us that in 1939, Franklin Roosevelt asked the European belligerents not to attack civilian populations. Her second paragraph says, "In 1945, when the Japanese enemy was known by him to have made two attempts towards a negotiated peace, the President of the United States gave the order for dropping an atomic bomb on a Japanese city; three days later a second bomb, of a different type, was dropped on another city. No ultimatum was delivered before the second bomb was dropped."[32]

Two things stand out. (1) Truman was in no way responsible for failure of the Allies to continue observing the prohibition against bombing cities. All the belligerents conducted obliteration bombing before Truman came on the scene. (2) The Japanese enemy had not made two serious attempts toward a negotiated peace. Some members of the peace party had made unauthorized peace feelers through Switzerland, the Vatican, and Sweden. The first authorized peace feelers, made through Japan's ambassador to Moscow, were so vague and insubstantial that Ambassador Sato, who was to explore them, cabled Tokyo, in effect, to get serious.[33]

Even had the peace feelers through Moscow been clear and firm, they would have been of no consequence. War Minister Anami, who had absolute veto over such things, and his two like-minded colleagues on the Supreme Council for the Direction of the War, wanted to stage another Okinawa when the Americans landed, and only then negotiate an armistice. Their terms? As stated in chapter one, they were totally unacceptable: no change in government structure, retention of Hirohito, the Japanese military to disarm itself, no occupation of the home islands, and any war crimes trials to be conducted by the Japanese.[34] U.S. Strategic Bombing Survey interrogations, as well as extensive intelligence gathered by others, show that the Japanese military firmly intended to kill so many Americans when Kyushu was invaded that the United States would offer lenient peace terms.[35]

No doubt Professor Anscombe read somewhere (probably in P.M.S. Blackett) that the Strategic Bombing Survey said Japan was ready to surrender; she definitely had heard of the peace feelers through the Russians.[36] But before committing herself to such draconian rhetoric, she should have probed a bit deeper. The facts were available when she wrote. Robert Butow's 1954 book, *Japan's Decision to Surrender*, could have suggested to her that she modify her charge that Truman acted in defiance of a clear Japanese intent to surrender.[37] Any one of a dozen accounts of the Pacific War could have helped her see that Truman had reason to believe that the bombs might eliminate a bloodletting on the invasion beaches.

The fourth paragraph of Anscombe's pamphlet begins, "The only condition for ending the war was announced to be unconditional surrender."[38] For Germany, this was true. But Japan is the focus of Anscombe's attack, and Allied conditions for the surrender of Japan were spelled out, most specifically, at Potsdam. Anscombe belittles the Potsdam Declaration; the terms set forth, she writes, "were mostly of so vague and sweeping a nature as to be rather a declaration of what unconditional surrender would be like than to constitute conditions."[39] Anscombe seems not to have read the Potsdam Declaration. The Potsdam terms were not vague; they were sweeping; and they were conditions. They told Japan what would happen when it surrendered.

Surprisingly, Anscombe appears to credit the argument that the bomb, by hastening the end of the war, had a good result:

> "It pretty certainly saved a huge number of lives." Given the conditions, I agree.
>
> That is to say, if those bombs had not been dropped the Allies would have had to invade Japan to achieve their aim, and they would have done so. Very many soldiers on both sides would have been killed; the Japanese, it is said—and it may well be true—would have massacred the prisoners of war; and large numbers of their civilian population would have been killed by "ordinary" bombing. I do not dispute it. Given the conditions, that was probably what was averted by that action. But what were the conditions? The unlimited objective, the fixation on unconditional surrender. The disregard of the fact that the Japanese were desirous of negotiating peace.[40]

But these were not the conditions. The Allies did not have an unlimited objective, as the Potsdam Declaration showed and Japanese peace leaders acknowledged. Nor did they have a fixation on unconditional surrender. When the right time came to enunciate the conditions the Allies would impose, they did so.

Yet another surprise in this censorious pamphlet is Anscombe's attack on pacifism. It is a false doctrine, she says: "The state actually has the authority to order deliberate killing in order to protect its people or to put frightful injustices right." This authority warrants going to war to ameliorate the plight of the Jews under Hitler, she adds. But we must not commit murder in such a war, and killing noncombatants is murder. Harry Truman is the prime murderer.[41]

The fundamental objection to Anscombe's attack is that it rests on an absolutist doctrine. There *are* ends that justify bombing of cities, even, in 1945, with atomic bombs. (There is no conceivable justification for using hydrogen bombs.) R.M. Hare is right: the consequences of an act are always morally relevant. George Mavrodes is also right: choosing the greater evil by letting this war go on would have been wrong.[42]

Beyond that, Anscombe compromises her position by applying it selectively, ignoring the most glaring instance of destruction— Dresden—that was disproportionate to whatever end was achieved. She weakens her case by implying that a warning would have mitigated Truman's guilt, by asserting that Truman was fixated on unconditional surrender when he was not, and by accepting uncritically a claim that Japan was ready to surrender without the shock of atomic bombs. She asserts that Allied strategic bombing policies were "taken largely out of a villainous hatred."[43]

Sheldon Cohen comments on Anscombe's position:

> The generation that fought WWII was well aware that Germany started the war only 21 years after WWI ended. I imagine their first priority after defeating the enemy was to ensure that Germany and Japan wouldn't rise up again in 20 years to start the cycle once more, and this was a legitimate goal, and one they achieved with stunning success: it is 50 years later, and we are all still famous friends. The benign and even magnanimous nature of the post-war occupation, given the ferocity of the war, was part of what made this possible, and this must give pause to anyone who thinks that two weeks earlier we were acting out of blind hatred, as Anscombe thought.[44]

Hers was an intensely felt campaign. Her last paragraph reveals how intense: "It is possible still to withdraw from this shameful business in some slight degree; it is possible not to go to [the awards ceremony]; if it should be embarrassing to someone who would normally go to plead other business, he could take to his bed. I, indeed, should fear to go, in case God's patience suddenly ends."[45] It is difficult to understand how God could wait until 1956 to evince His wrath if the matter were really so heinous as she claims. Anscombe's absolutist position as well as her application of it to Truman's decision must be rejected.

The second influential document relevant here is Michael Walzer's book *Just and Unjust Wars*.[46] First published in 1977, reprinted with a new preface in 1992, it has been widely hailed in the United States. Walzer subtitles his book *A Moral Argument with Historical Illustrations*. It is hard to quarrel with his theoretical position, that strategic bombing of cities, and nuclear bombs, are horrible and *presumptively* wrong, but may be moral in some cases. He errs, howerver, in talking about the war with Japan, about which he seems to have read very little. He attempts to deal with historical events reaching from the Peloponnesian Wars to the Persian Gulf War of 1991; unfortunately this breadth of coverage assured superficiality in dealing with the Pacific War.

Walzer supports the principle of noncombatant immunity in general, but unlike Anscombe, waives the principle in the case of the war against Germany, at least in the early years when Britain appeared lost. Thus British obliteration bombing was justified as a response to a "supreme emergency"; the very existence of the British polity was at stake, Allied forces had been swept from Western Europe, and "the decision to bomb cities was made at a time when . . . the specter of defeat was ever present. And it was made when no other decision seemed possible if there was to be any sort of military offensive against Nazi Germany."[47] German victory appeared imminent, and a Nazi-controlled Europe was very frightening: these two factors justified talking of a supreme emergency. By February 1945, when Dresden was obliterated, the emergency was past and Allied triumph was assured; hence the destruction of Dresden, according to Walzer, was wanton and evil.

In the case of bombing Japan, however, Walzer does not acknowledge even a minor emergency. We had already "won" the war when General LeMay started his incendiary campaign against Japanese cities; what was at stake, according to Walzer, was "only the speed or the scope of victory."[48] To Walzer, Japanese militarism was nothing like the threat of German Nazism: "Japan's rulers were engaged in a more ordinary sort of military expansion, and all that was morally required was that they be defeated, not that they be conquered and totally overthrown."[49]

Here Walzer reveals his ignorance of the Pacific War and of Japan's depredations throughout Southeast Asia. It is monstrous to contend that in early 1945, U.S. forces should have withdrawn from combat (since Japan was then "defeated"), leaving the crew of Japanese torturers in charge of so much of Asia and the Pacific. Nor was it tolerable that U.S. forces should simply "tighten the noose" of blockade, hoping to achieve surrender by imposing mass starvation on Japan—eventually. Millions of subject peoples would then have perished with the Japanese. Our forces would have continued to be subject to kamikaze and submarine attack (the *Indianapolis* was sunk by the Japanese on 29 July 1945 with a loss of 883 American sailors). No administration that ever occupied the White House could have ridden out the storm that would have erupted had the United States at that stage repudiated clear-cut victory and simply waited for Japan to collapse. Millions of overseas GIs would have demanded discharge, and the Japanese militarists, claiming they were right that the United States did not have the fortitude for a long war, would have dug in and made life even more horrendous for the conquered peoples.

The millions of subjects of the Greater East Asia Co-Prosperity Sphere would not have tolerated cessation of the drive to bring Japanese militarism down. There may not have been a "supreme emergency" for the United States, as Walzer thinks necessary to justify bombing, but there certainly was for Japan's Asian subjects, especially the Chinese, on whose behalf we had originally restricted exports of war materiel to Japan and hence triggered the attack on Pearl Harbor.

Walzer wants us to believe that the United States should not have pressed the war further: "In the summer of 1945, the victorious Americans owed the Japanese people an experiment in negotiation. To use the atomic bomb, to kill and terrorize civilians, without even attempting such an experiment, was a double crime."[50] In the summer of 1945, Americans owed the Japanese people exactly nothing. Nevertheless, the United States gave them deliverance from their military masters, and an enlightened occupation that started them on the road to such prosperity as their previous rulers could not even envisage.

Walzer also sees unconditional surrender as crucial in the bombing of Japan: "If killing millions (or many thousands) of men and women was militarily necessary for their conquest and overthrow, then it was morally necessary—in order not to kill these people—to settle for something less."[51] Like continuation of the Japanese empire? Like a recrudescence of Japanese expansionism later? Sheldon Cohen answers this argument summarily:

> Our first priority was to end the war by compelling an Axis surrender that would allow us to restructure their political process. Walzer spends a great deal of ink arguing, rightly, that nations have a right to live in peace, and that aggression is a very serious crime. . . . We were ready to invade Japan to end the war on lasting terms. It would have been cheaper to walk away, at least in the short term, but we didn't want to have to come back a decade or two or three later. . . . The U.S. was willing to take 100-200,000 casualties to end the war on terms that

would prevent another such war in the 50's, 60's, or 70's, and these terms were legitimate and right.

They did so with amazing success . . . the peace has lasted for 50 years, and it is hard to imagine France and Britain at war with Germany in the foreseeable future, or Japan at war with the U.S.[52]

We did not completely restructure the Japanese political process, but no one would contend that the present Japanese polity is no better than the one operated by Tojo Hidecki.

Hiroshima was no Dresden. The Japanese, even more than the Germans, threatened to fight to the last death and take tens of thousands of Allied soldiers with them. Churchill was right on this matter, and the quotation Walzer uses from Churchill to show the latter's insensitivity instead goes precisely to the heart of the reason for using the atomic bombs: "To avert a vast, indefinite butchery . . . at the cost of a few explosions seemed, after all our toils and perils, a miracle of deliverance."[53]

Averting a vast indefinite butchery even at the cost of several hundred thousand noncombatant casualties was worth it. The doctrine of noncombatant immunity needs contemporary rethinking. In previous times when soldiers were volunteers, in the business of soldiering for money, a distinction between them and ordinary folk had some moral force. In times when soldiers are mostly conscripts, when noncombatants are often as implicated in the war-fighting policies and economies of the state as those in uniform, it is not self-evident why the lives of conscripts should be valued less than their fellow-citizens. In the case at issue here, Japanese citizens were not abject (and hence innocent) victims of a militaristic regime. As Bamba Nobuya describes his fellow countrymen:

> According to the Marxist interpretation of imperialistic war, the "people" should have been innocent, but they were not. The Japanese populace did not [just] passively support the nation's military expansion, nor did they back the government simply because they feared the police. On the contrary, most people competed to get front seats on the fascist bandwagon, as the then common saying "Basu ni noriokureruna" (Don't miss the bus) vividly suggests. It was rather the people that agitated for tough diplomacy.[54]

Hiroshima cultists do not come to grips with analyses like this.

•   •   •

Truman's detractors view his use of atomic bombs through lenses with a significant moral blind spot. They resolutely ignore the facts that Japan also had an atomic bomb project, that this project was regarded as of potentially supreme importance, and that the Japanese had every intention of using atom bombs on American targets had they succeeded in producing them. The atomic bomb project never got off the ground, unlike the Japanese Unit 731 that experimented with lethal biological weapons successfully enough to use such weapons against the Chinese.[55] But the intention to make and use atomic weapons cuts the moral ground out from under hypocritical Japanese claims that American production and use of such weapons was illegitimate and an atrocity. If it was legitimate for them, they cannot claim it was illegitimate for the United States.

The point is not that the Japanese intention to make and use atomic weapons settles the moral argument. What is at issue is *moral standing*; in the atomic weapons case, Japan has no moral standing to criticize the United States. Japanese condemnation of Harry Truman is therefore hypocritical.[56]

Nor is it true that the Japanese tried to conceal, and then deny the existence of, their nuclear project. John Dower makes clear the falsity of charges published in *Science*, the *New York Times*, and the *Bulletin of The Atomic Scientists*—that the Japanese conspired to keep their atomic project secret, and are therefore culpable.[57] Naturally the Japanese did not publicize their atomic intentions extensively. They could hardly do this and maintain the posture of victimization that underwrites the Hiroshima cult. Nor was the United States in an atomic "race" with the Japanese; neither Gen. Leslie Groves nor the Manhattan Project scientists worried about a Japanese bomb as they did about a German one.[58] But the pressure point of moral controversy here is not whether there was a "race"—it is instead Japanese intentions.

A relatively full account of Japan's efforts to produce its own bomb is in *The Day Man Lost*, written by the Pacific War Research Society (PWRS) in Tokyo and published by Kodansha. PWRS, writing of the year 1941, observes "Japan, recently so determinedly isolationist, was now, like some of the 'advanced' countries of Europe, preparing for armed world conquest; and, though a late starter in the Western science sweepstakes, she was also keenly aware that the ability to make destructive use of atomic fission was a virtual guarantee of total victory in the fast approaching conflict."[59]

Originally, both army and navy (whose cooperation was sometimes nil and at best minimal) had a hand in atomic research; the army program was at Japan's Physical and Chemical Research Institute under Nishina Yoshio, who had studied with Niels Bohr in Copenhagen. He had working under him "a total of 110 researchers, including many of Japan's brightest young scientists. Nishina's laboratory was, at that time, not only the nerve center for Japanese physical research, it was a magnet that attracted all the most brilliant minds in the field."[60]

Despite this enthusiastic beginning for the army program, PWRS tells us that in spring 1942 the navy also started an atomic program to be housed in its Technological Research Institute. The navy was manic at having completed the battleships *Yamato* and *Musashi* ahead of schedule; at the second meeting of the navy committee for the study of atomic research, Capt. Ito Yoji chided some pessimistic scientists enlisted for the navy program: "You college professors are apt to be too conservative. You tell us that the problem is so difficult that success within a reasonable time is impossible to hope for. But listen to me. People who make warships have a different way of approaching problems. . . . I ask you, then, not to tell us that you are unable to produce the bomb within the necessary time but rather to exert every effort to do so. I want you to continue your research."[61] At the end of 1942, PWRS believed that "Japan, however belatedly, was at last a serious contender in the atomic sweepstakes."[62]

In 1943, things seemed to be progressing. Nishina's laboratory announced on 5 May that the staff felt production of an atomic bomb was technically possible. Prof. Tanakadate Aikitsu, an aerodynamics engineer, tried to persuade the Diet to appropriate more money for the project by telling it, "You gentlemen who are gathered here today are probably unaware of the fact that the progress of nuclear physics has made it possible to utilize atomic energy. It is now possible to produce a bomb the size of a matchbox which has the explosive power to sink a battleship."[63] PWRS says the legislators yawned; but the newspapers picked up the story. Good news was needed by then. Despite the handicap of material shortages, the researchers worked at the problem assigned to them "with almost demonic fury."[64]

The rest of the story must be skipped over, but it merits note that not just shortages of uranium plagued the Japanese effort. On 13 April

1945, a B-29 raid on Tokyo hit the Research Institute, and "Japan's last forlorn hope of developing an atomic bomb" went up in flames.[65]

But the scene shifts to Kyoto, and in July 1945, PWRS tells us "Japan was making a frantic, last-minute effort to produce an atomic bomb. This was taking place in one of Kyoto Imperial University's two physics research laboratories."[66] Here the navy was in charge, and pessimistic professors were still giving impatient naval officers fits. Says PWRS,

> . . . in the research laboratory headed by Professor Arakatsu Bunsaku, work was going on, both by day and by night, in an attempt to separate U-235 through the centrifugal method. . . . The Arakatsu project in Kyoto was proceeding under the orders of the navy, which, having lost most of its ships, was now trying to reestablish itself through a new and decisive weapon. When it had first approached Arakatsu, he had replied that producing the bomb would be impossible in time for it to be used during the war. The navy countered blandly that in that case it could be used in the next war; Arakatsu and the scientists who worked with him were ordered to carry out research around the clock.[67]

PWRS was clearly supportive of Japanese efforts to produce nuclear weapons. Only when the United States succeeded at the same task did such weapons become reprehensible.

It does not solve Michael Howard's dilemma to observe that we did to Japan what it would have eagerly done to us. This truth does, however, invalidate the moral warrant for the cult of Hiroshima.

•   •   •

Racism was a major factor in the Pacific War. It was virulent on both sides. John Dower's *War Without Mercy* has been cited many times in this book. Was racism behind the use of atomic bombs on Japan?

Allied soldiers were arguably less racist than the Japanese; atrocities committed by the Allies were not supported by official policy, such as Japan's claim of Yamato right to rule Asia. Nor were racist incidents by American troops as ubiquitous as were those by Japanese. Nor was Allied treatment, of the few Japanese who surrendered, characterized by racism.[68] Japanese in Australian and New Zealand POW camps were dumbfounded by the amenities available to them; they explained it on the assumption that the Australians and New Zealanders were storing up credits for themselves, knowing that Japan would win the war.[69]

Nor was the American occupation of Japan after the war significantly racist. The Japanese were astonished how few incidents attributable to American feelings of racial superiority took place. Nevertheless, the claim of racism as the major explanation for the use of atomic weapons has fallen on fertile soil, as chapter seven will show. Most Japanese accept the claim with an invincible ignorance that no argumentative discourse can puncture. Even some Western observers, such as Robert Guillain, accept the racism explanation.[70]

The most careful student of the Hiroshima decision, however, does not. Barton Bernstein's 1975 statement is: "Probably policymakers found it easier to use the bomb against yellow people (the Japanese) than against whites (the Germans), but racism did not dictate the decision to drop the bombs on Japan. U.S. leaders would undoubtedly have used the bombs against Germany if they had been developed in time to speed a surrender in Europe."[71]

The 1944 orders to Col. Paul Tibbets to prepare atomic attacks on *both* Germans and Japanese cannot be explained away, nor can the timing of the bomb's availability, nor the destruction of Dresden with atomic-like ferocity. Perhaps the most persuasive argument of all is a counterfactual one. Imagine the Normandy invasion being repulsed; or the German attack in the Battle of the Bulge cutting British forces off from American, creating another Dunkirk; or, earlier, Soviet loss of Leningrad, Moscow, or Stalingrad, with consequent Soviet demoralization and successful German occupation of European Russia. *With any one of those events*, who can seriously maintain that the United States would not have used any atomic bomb it possessed against Hitler's hated regime?

Alistair Horne, in his biography *Monty*, speculating on what would have happened had the Normandy invasion failed in 1944, is certain that American atomic bombs would have been used on what remained of Germany in 1945.[72]

•   •   •

The question of revenge (reprisal, retaliation, retribution) also merits discussion. Statesmen, soldiers, intellectuals, even divines have justified bombing of all kinds because "they" did it first, and "they" deserve to have it meted out to them.

Those who seek guidance from Holy Writ are confronted with the vast divergence between the Old Testament and the New. The *lex talionis* simply cannot be reconciled with Rom. 12:19: "vengeance is mine; I will repay, saith the Lord."

Many pundits follow the Old Testament ethic. Norman Cousins invoking revenge as a reason for bombing before Hiroshima has already been noted.[73] A.L. Goodhart, Professor of Jurisprudence at Oxford, asserted in 1940 that what he calls reprisals are morally justified: "It has occasionally been said that no acts of reprisal are ever justifiable because two wrongs cannot make a right. The answer is that one wrongful act can make the other act rightful. International Law is therefore correct when it speaks of the *right* to reprisal. This right has been exercised by nearly all belligerents in nearly all wars, so that, whether we like it or not, we cannot close our eyes to its existence."[74]

Many Americans talked as if revenge were their prime motive for bombing the Japanese. Opinion polls showed a healthy minority (23 percent) favored dropping even more atomic bombs on Japan, largely in retaliation for Pearl Harbor. Churchill, Roosevelt, and Truman frequently sought to stimulate enthusiasm for the war by what seem to be calls for revenge. One of FDR's purple passages: "Yes, the Nazis and Fascists have asked for it—and they are going to get it."[75] But this is not necessarily a call for revenge; it is simply a promise to give "them" a hard fight.

The coolly practical men in the American War Department, and the politicians of Truman's White House, were not significantly vengeful. Truman recoiled from the possibility of a third atomic bomb on Japan, and ordered that it not be scheduled without his express directive. And try as one might, it is impossible to paint the promises of the Potsdam Declaration as vengeful; disarmed soldiers were to be able to return home and resume productive lives, in contrast to Japan's enslavement of conquered Europeans and Asians; freedom of speech, religion, and thought were offered; civilian industries would be permitted, and trade would be allowed on an equitable basis when a responsible civilian government was established. These are not the terms of a conqueror bent on vengeance.

Despite the "eye-for-an-eye" precept of the Old Testament, revenge does not seem to be a legitimate motive for dropping the bombs. The evidence that the bombs were necessary to force an early end to the war simply made revenge, whether legitimate or not, moot.

But this is not the end of the matter; a more sympathetic view of the desire for retaliation expressed by so many Americans in the 1940s comes from reading about Japanese atrocities on Allied prisoners of war and to Asian peoples whom the Japanese conquered. One must also consider this analysis from Sheldon Cohen:

> I agree with you in being unhappy with [revenge as a motive for dropping the bombs], but that's not the same thing as being against revenge tout court. In some cases I am not sure how justice and revenge differ. Julius Streicher's execution was just; it may also have been an act of revenge—certainly we weren't trying to reform him. If so, taking revenge can sometimes be morally justified, or even obligatory. Not to punish the miscreant might be, as St. Anselm said in *Cur Deus Homo*, to make light of his crime, and therefore, a moral affront.
>
> I also believe that adult German and Japanese civilians in the 30's and 40's bore some responsibility for the acts agents of their government were performing or soon would be performing. It seems inconsistent to hold a right of national self-determination, and to grant that these were the legitimate governments of Germany and Japan, while denying that the population shares *any* responsibility for the deeds of their governments.[76]

How *do* justice and revenge differ? Is it not true that the people and factories of Hiroshima and Nagasaki, as well as the rest of Japan, armed Tojo's butchers and sent them forth on their campaigns of pillage, rape, and murder?

Despite the official effort to rehabilitate Japan's wartime record, the passage of time has loosened lips of Japanese who regretted participating in that war—who, in fact, had guilty consciences. One poignant instance is in Haruko Taya Cook and Theodore Cook's volume of interviews with Japanese who lived through the war. The Cooks were talking to Hayashi Shigeo, who had been an engineer in Manchuria, and was sent in late 1945 on a team to Hiroshima and Nagasaki to determine what actually happened there. Hayashi was in Nagasaki:

> One day I went to the Mitsubishi arsenal and was photographing the torpedo plant. I was being escorted around by a Mitsubishi man. At some point he said to me, "This is where we made the first torpedoes,

the ones dropped on Pearl Harbor at the onset of the Pacific War." The wrenches and tools used by the workers were lying there, all around me, as if they'd been set down a minute ago. I could have reached out myself and picked them up. Finally he said quietly, "Mr. Hayashi, the very first torpedo was launched from here in Nagasaki, and in the end here's where we were stabbed to death. We fought a stupid war, didn't we?" The two of us just stood there in silence.[77]

It is not the relatively rare Japanese mea culpas that are important here, but the overwhelming anguish of the millions of victims of the Japanese empire. Reading these accounts, sympathy for the 200,000 or so victims of the atom begins to fade. The books describing what the Japanese did to other human beings are never ending. These people had no John Hersey. Their stories are not often in his gripping prose. But they are heartrending accounts nonetheless. Had John Hersey visited Nanking or Manila and written about those catastrophes; had there been no competing and overshadowing spectacle in Japan fueled by supernatural science; had Hiroshima not become a shrine to the peaceminded, the anguish of Japan's victims might be more on our consciences.

And it is not just their anguish; it is their sheer numbers. Only after several years of study did I realize that, for some reason, I could find no one who had put together comprehensive figures showing the extent of Japanese-caused *deaths*. Statistics of the numbers who died at Hitler's hands are in every account of his crimes. The same for victims of Stalin. Deaths during World War II's battles in the European-African theaters are readily available. Why is there no similar compilation for deaths caused by the Japanese? Perhaps that would be more difficult to compile than Hitler's statistics. Japan did conquer more different and far-flung territories and put Allied captives in 424 prison camps scattered over one-quarter of the globe.[78]

Nevertheless, it is possible to put together an estimate of how many people perished at Japanese hands. John Dower gives death figures for nine countries in his book; a United Nations (UN) document covers four other countries.[79] Problem cases are China, where estimates of deaths from 1931 to 1945 range from two to thirty million; the Burma-Siam railway, where Murakami Hyoe gives a low estimate of 32,000, the Associated Press lists 116,000; and the Dutch East Indies, where the UN lists three million for Java, one million for the other islands; but the probable error must be high. I use the lowest figure in all cases except China, where ten million is a consensus figure, and the Burma-Siam railway, where I use the figure of the Allied War Graves Registration Unit:[80]

Deaths Attributable to the Japanese Empire, 1931-1945

China	10,000,000
Java (Dutch Indies)	3,000,000
Outer Islands	1,000,000
Philippines	120,000
India	180,000
Bengal famine	1,500,000
Korea	70,000
Burma-Siam railway	82,500
Indonesia, Europeans	30,000
Malaya	100,000
Vietnam	1,000,000
Australia	30,000
New Zealand	10,000
United States	100,000
Total	17,222,500

These were not painless deaths. They served no legitimate purpose. Many of them were nonbattle atrocities.

Gavan Daws, in his *Prisoners of the Japanese*, summarizes the incredible record:

> Asia under the Japanese was a charnel house of atrocities. As soon as the war ended, evidence of war crimes began piling up, in mountains. POWs, civilian internees, and Asian natives starved, beaten, tortured, shot, beheaded. The water cure. Electric shock. Cannibalism. Men strung up over open flames or coiled in barbed wire and rolled along the ground, nails torn out, balls burned with cigarettes, dicks cut off and stuffed in mouths. Women dragged naked behind motorcycles, raped and ripped open, babies skewered on bayonets. Cities in China and provinces in the Philippines laid waste, mass murders in the Indies, towns and villages wiped out, all the way to the remotest of small places in the Pacific, the island of Nauru, where the thirty-four sufferers in the leprosy hospital were taken out to sea and

drowned, and Ocean Island, where days after the war ended all the native laborers were pushed over a cliff.[81]

The summary cannot do justice to the details. From the viewpoint of seeking justice, Pearl Harbor is no big deal; a mere 2,400 casualties. This pales before seventeen million. At least ten million of these occurred between 7 December 1941 and 30 August 1945. During these forty-five months, 200,000 to 300,000 persons died each month at Japanese hands. The last months were in many ways the worst; starvation and disease aggravated the usual beatings, beheadings, and battle deaths. It is plausible to hold that upwards of 250,000 people, mostly Asian but some Westerners, *would have died each month the Japanese Empire struggled in its death throes beyond July 1945.*

Battlefield deaths, in the time after Okinawa, were slackening, but the carnage at sea and in Marshal Terauchi Hisaichi's domain, where several hundred thousand Westerners were imprisoned, went on apace. Laurens van der Post, in one of Terauchi's prisons, watched conditions of prisoners worsen as the Japanese cause became more hopeless, and Japanese morale plummeted. He feared that unless the war ended in a way that left the Japanese some shred of honor (as the atomic bombs did), the Japanese would try to "pull down their own sprawling military temple, Samson-like, and to destroy the European Philistine along with themselves rather than endure defeat with ignominy."[82] It is an apt analogy, but even with the excuse of the bomb and the emperor's firm order to cease fighting, there were hundreds of subsequent deaths at the hands of sadistic POW camp guards.

There is no way to represent adequately the "mountains of evidence" from the Tokyo War Crimes Trials, or from survivors of Japanese conquest and rule. The most graphic and repulsive events are recorded in the stories of Western POWs; occasional apologists for Japan attempt to impeach these accounts, but such attempts fail utterly. Former POWs usually bear physical scars of their mistreatment. Many photos exist of their emaciation when rescued. Some kept clandestine diaries, the authenticity of which can be established. With the passing of time and Hirohito, in whose name Japanese tyrannized so many nations, some of them have even begun to describe atrocities committed fifty years earlier. The Cooks, in *Japan at War*, give one of the chilling accounts, from Tominaga Shozo, who was sent to China in 1941 as a green second lieutenant.

His first week there was an orientation with the twenty other new officers reporting for duty; at the end of the week, to prove themselves fit for command, they had to demonstrate the ancient samurai art of chopping off heads.

> In the final day, we were taken out to the site of our trial. Twenty-four prisoners were squatting there with their hands tied behind their backs. They were blindfolded. A big hole had been dug—ten meters long, two meters wide, and more than three meters deep. The regimental commander, the battalion commanders, and the company commanders all took the seats arranged for them. Second Lieutenant Tanaka bowed to the regimental commander and reported, "We shall now begin." He ordered a soldier on fatigue duty to haul one of the prisoners to the edge of the pit; the prisoner was kicked when he resisted. The soldier finally dragged him over and forced him to his knees. Tanaka turned toward us and looked into each of our faces in turn. "Heads should be cut off like this," he said, unsheathing his army sword. He scooped water from a bucket with a dipper, then poured it over both sides of the blade. Swishing off the water, he raised his sword in a long arc. Standing behind the prisoner, Tanaka steadied himself, legs spread apart, and cut off the man's head with a shout, "Yo!" The head flew more than a meter away. Blood spurted up in two fountains from the body and sprayed into the hole. The scene was so appalling that I felt I couldn't breathe.

But Tominaga did breathe, and he did cut off a prisoner's head, and "At that moment, I felt something change inside me. I don't know how to put it, but I gained strength somewhere in my gut." Other candidates were not so accurate, and slashed the prisoner's head rather than his neck: "One prisoner ran around crazily, his blindfold hanging down, his head gashed. 'Stab Him,' Tanaka ordered. The candidate officer swung and missed again. 'You fool!' Tanaka scolded. This time Tanaka swung his sword. All of us did. Everyone got covered with blood as we butchered him."[83]

Hiroshima cultists, both Japanese and American, set forth vivid descriptions of the horrors inflicted on residents of that devastated city. These can be matched in intensity, and buried in quantity, by the horror stories of those who suffered Japanese captivity. Where is the goddess of justice, when the travail of 300,000 victims generates a cult following, but the deaths of seventeen million, *equally as horrible*, go unremembered?

Gavan Daws felt the Japanese bayonet but vicariously. His search for the truth about prisoners of the Japanese was awesome, his conclusion terrifying:

The Japanese were not directly genocidal in their POW camps. They did not herd their white prisoners into gas chambers and burn their corpses in ovens. But they drove them toward mass death just the same. They beat them until they fell, then beat them for falling, beat them until they bled, then beat them for bleeding. They denied them medical treatment. They starved them. When the International Red Cross sent food and medicine, the Japanese looted the shipments. They sacrificed prisoners in medical experiments. They watched them die by the tens of thousands from diseases of malnutrition like beriberi, pellagra, and scurvy, and from epidemic tropical diseases: malaria, dysentery, tropical ulcers, cholera. Those who survived could only look ahead to being worked to death. If the war had lasted another year, there would not have been a POW left alive.[84]

There were a mere 100,997 deaths of Americans at the hands of the Japanese.[85] This number by itself is not startling. Comparison of death rates of Allied POWs in the two major arenas of conflict is. Few authors discuss this, for obvious reasons. Gavan Daws is not inhibited: "In German prison camps, the death rate was only four percent. In Japanese prison camps, it was 27 percent. The Japanese camps were between seven and eight times more lethal. To be a prisoner of the Japanese was like being caught in a twentieth-century version of the Black Plague."[86]

By far the greatest carnage was of other Asians, especially Chinese. In an effort to get Japan to finally acknowledge its wartime destruction, secure reparations, and convince American readers that unrepentant Japan did not warrant a permanent seat on the United Nations Security Council, the Chinese Alliance for Memorial and Justice placed a full-page ad in the *New York Times* of 17 June 1994. Grant some possible exaggeration; basically the Chinese case holds up:

Japan has a problem remembering history. Its officials even try to distort and erase history.

On the occasion of Japanese Emperor Akihito's state visit to the United States, we are obliged to present a record of atrocities committed by the Japanese Imperial Army during World War II, for which

Japan has never acknowledged or compensated. Japanese troops, acting in the name of the late Emperor Hirohito, carried out an orgy of killing, raping, and looting in the Chinese city of Nanking. These savage crimes lasted from the day Nanking fell, on December 13, 1937, to as late as March 1938. 340,000 civilians and unarmed prisoners of war were massacred. At least 80,000 women were raped. (Tokyo war crime trials held in 1946 recorded that in the first six weeks alone, an estimated 20,000 women were sexually mutilated and murdered.) The three month pillage reduced a third of Nanking to dust.

From 1937 on, more than 1,300 occasions of germ warfare were inflicted over 14 provinces throughout China, costing hundreds of thousands of lives. 26 secret military laboratories in occupied China engaged in human experimentation, vivisection and mass production of germs of various diseases, including the bubonic plague and cholera. One of these biological warfare death camps, the notorious Unit 731, whose use of human guinea pigs caused the deaths of over 3,000 captured Chinese, Korean, Russian, and American civilians and POWs, was under direct Imperial jurisdiction in Tokyo and visited by Hirohito's brother, Prince Mikasa, then Lt. Col. of the Imperial Army.

Throughout the war, under the euphemism "comfort women," the Japanese Imperial Army coerced more than 200,000 Korean, Chinese and other Asian, as well as European young girls into sexual slavery. 90% percent of these girls died from abuse, diseases, and desertion by retreating Imperial units.[87]

Perhaps emboldened by Chinese efforts to embarrass the Japanese into action, Filipinos are now organizing to press their claims. The leader is Vicky Quirino, daughter of one of Manila's prominent families, who has been unwilling for fifty years to discuss the terrible events of 1944. She was prompted by the celebration of the American recapture of Manila: "It's only now that the remaining survivors are telling each other what really happened," she said. Her own story is typical. She was running for cover from American shelling when Japanese machine guns opened fire, killing her mother and elder sister. Her two-year-old sister lay on the street, still alive; "A Japanese soldier walked over, tossed the girl in the air and speared her with his bayonet."[88] U.S. Army records show an estimated 100,000 civilians killed when Japanese troops put the city to the torch.

Not only the Chinese and Filipinos; in August 1945, according to a Japanese Foreign Office report obtained by General MacArthur,

6,516,959 servants of the emperor were stationed abroad, tyranniz-
ing the people of China, Korea, the Bonins, Formosa, Indochina,
Thailand, Burma, Malaya, Sumatra, Java, the Lesser Sundas and
Timor, Borneo, Celebes, Moluccas, New Guinea, Bismarcks, and
Solomons.[89] Even if only 10 percent of Japanese occupiers committed one atrocity per week, the sum total of the trauma inflicted far
outweighs the pain and suffering of Hiroshima and Nagasaki. The
Greater East Asia Co-Prosperity Sphere was no "ordinary military
expansion," as per Michael Walzer.

Part of the uniqueness of the Japanese empire was its development and battle use of biological warfare (BW). The Japanese did not
deliberately exterminate millions of people as did the Nazis, though
had they been better organized and informed when the Soviet
armies crashed into Manchuria in 1945, perhaps their BW victims
would have numbered in the millions rather than the tens of thousands.

Knowledge of this Japanese BW activity was concealed from the
West for many years. The managers of the enterprise plea-bargained
with their American captors: no war crimes prosecution, you get our
BW data. This devil's compact was covered up in the West until the
1980s, but it was sufficiently well known in Japan to compromise the
reputation of the International Military Tribunal for the Far East
(IMTFE). Lt. Gen. Ishii Shiro, the major promoter of BW usage,
escaped prosecution; thousands of Japanese knew that he was far
more culpable than Hirota Koki or Kido Koichi.[90]

The Japanese BW program was originally designed, according to
Sheldon Harris' 1994 book, *Factories of Death*, for use against the
Russians. Harris writes of General Ishii, "His plans for BW research
met with an enthusiastic response from almost every key player in
Manchuria, since the principals were convinced that war with the
Soviet Union was inevitable, and BW theoretically could play an
important role in defeating enemy armies. . . . Bolsheviks greatly
outnumbered the Japanese. . . ."[91]

The story of Japanese BW use is too long to present here in anything but bare outline. For this purpose, the treatment in
Calvocoressi, Wint, and Pritchard is adequate:

> Briefly, the story of Japanese biological warfare implicates more than
> half the persons tried by the International Military Tribunal for the Far
> East, and more than 5,000 others who worked on the BW programme in
> some capacity. It involved a genuine conspiracy of silence that began

soon after the Japanese occupation of Manchuria and spread its tentacles throughout all Japanese occupied territories. . . . Thousands of people were butchered in the name of science and for the sake of war technology. . . . Field trials of Army biological munitions were conducted, first in Manchuria and then in China proper. Attacks were made at Ningpo in 1940, at Changteh in 1941 . . . and elsewhere. Later the mad Japanese medical scientists operated in Burma, Malaya, French Indo-China, Thailand. . . . They applied their skills at Nomonhan against the Russians and sent saboteurs across the Soviet Union itself in a succession of secret missions. . . . A ship carrying a biological warfare assault team was dispatched to Saipan to slow down the American advance: it was sunk *en route* by an American submarine.[92]

American BW researchers were only too eager to learn from the Japanese. Six chapters of Harris' *Factories of Death* relate how the transfer of the Japanese information to U.S. BW centers at Fort Detrick and elsewhere took place under tight secrecy. The Japanese information was mostly crude and many of their experiments had been ineffective; they had never developed a reliable distribution package for plague, typhoid, cholera, anthrax, or any of the virile toxins. Yet the U.S. scientists exerted themselves to pick the Japanese scientists' brains.

Harris writes that "One hypothesis that appears to be credible is that American scientists hungered after forbidden fruit. They were prohibited by law and a code of ethics that denied researchers access to involuntary human experimentation."[93] Much about this subject is still unavailable, but Harris is clear that "The cost to the United States in terms of honor and integrity appears to be high in comparison to the worth of the material it purchased from Ishii and the remaining BW specialists."[94]

Harris's opinion of Truman is as low as his opinion of the BW scientists and soldiers. Had the invasion of Japan actually produced an Okinawa from one end to the other, Harris has no doubt Truman would have authorized the use of BW or gas.[95] This is doubtful. Atomic bombs were just a step up in power from explosives that had come into common use by all belligerents; clearly, BW would have been qualitatively different from anything practiced in the West. The later Communist charge that the United States used BW in Korea is not warranted.

The Japanese were so uneasy about their experiments on human beings and their field usage of BW that they destroyed every installation as they retreated before the Russians. Animals used in their experiments were turned loose, and according to Harris, "the area surrounding the ruins was a veritable Noah's Ark."[96] All human subjects still alive were killed.[97] The Chinese Alliance for Memorial and Justice claims in its ad that "From 1937 on, more than 1,300 occasions of germ warfare were inflicted over 14 provinces throughout China, costing hundreds of thousands of lives."[98] Grant some exaggeration, the charge is not unreasonable given what we know about Japanese behavior throughout its empire. Calvocoressi, Wint, and Pritchard, writing in 1989, say that BW research "has become a matter of great public concern in Japan today."[99] As it should.

For all its horrors, Japanese bestiality does not justify terror bombing as revenge. Only shocking the Japanese into surrender warrants the use of 20,000 kiloton atom bombs. The appropriate revenge would have been to put Lt. Gen. Ishii Shiro and all his accomplices in the dock at IMTFE. The Allied failure to do this is inexcusable.

•   •   •

One of the more indefensible moral judgments was made by the writers of the original script for the Smithsonian Air and Space Museum's *Enola Gay* exhibit, scheduled for May 1995, then cancelled. They included this statement: "For most Americans, this . . . was a war of vengeance. For most Japanese, it was a war to defend their unique culture against Western imperialism."[100] This whitewashing of Japanese motives miscarried.

There were two main forces driving the Japanese into Manchuria in 1931, then into China proper, and on to the Pacific War. The first of them, as described by Hilary Conroy in 1970:

It will no doubt come as a shock to many Americans to learn that Japan's war in China, which later became merged into the Pacific War, was to the Japanese government and the majority of the Japanese people in many ways like today's war in Vietnam. To them it was not at all a war of aggression, not a war against China, not a war to seize Chinese territory. It was not a war at all, but a defense action against Communists and their allies in China.[101]

Unfortunately, the Japanese action in China got out of hand. Conroy points out that there is no real historical parallelism with U.S. fighting in Vietnam: "The United States is a functioning democracy; Japan was not. The United States has civilian control of the military; Japan apparently did not. The United States has a deep tradition of freedom of speech and press; Japan did not. However, lest we become too sanguine. . . . There was no national referendum, no declaration of war in either case."[102]

Another landmark study of Japan's descent of the slippery slope, Robert J.C. Butow's *Tojo and the Coming of the War*, also emphasizes the anti-Communist theme. Tojo was not a Hitler, but a Japanese chauvinist determined to hang on to Manchuria and defend it against anticipated Soviet aggression.[103]

More than fear of Communism was involved, however; Japanese appetite for empire grew with the growth of its armies. Maruyama Masao, who reconstructed Japanese actions from the testimony offered at the Tokyo War Crimes Trial, gives a non-pejorative analysis of the process:

> The men in the dock at the Tokyo trials had unquestionably been motivated by a common aspiration: the desire to establish a Greater East Asia Co-Prosperity Sphere, to build up a new order with "Eight Corners of the World under One Roof," to proclaim the Imperial Way throughout the world. Not one of the defendants ever indicated that he regarded this as a mere quixotic dream. Some of them, it is true, were inhibited by intellectual scruples from openly voicing their dream, while others . . . placed the happy date rather farther in the future; and even the most fanatic among them, as they gradually drew near to the windmill, were momentarily daunted by its size when compared with the puny lances in their hands. Yet all of them were driven ahead, as if by some invisible force.[104]

None was defending unique Japanese culture against Western imperialism. Countries that initially welcomed Japanese as liberators from European colonialism soon turned against them; Japanese oppression was worse than European.

Ienaga Saburo, no admirer of the United States, is as authoritative and blunt as any writer about the depths to which Japanese soldiers descended: "World War II brought atrocities on an unprecedented scale, and they were an infamous hallmark of the Japanese military. . . . Here I wish to elaborate on this theme, and show by concrete examples that the Greater East Asian War, which has been glorified as a moral cause, was a dirty war of sadistic cruelty."[105]

It was also a war of imperialistic expansion beyond East Asia. Hawaii was one of the targets. Most documents about Japan's extensive plans for conquest and incorporation of the Hawaiian Islands were destroyed out of fear of postwar trials, hence many writers did not know about them, and assumed Japan carried out a simple hit-and-run attack. In 1984, John J. Stephan published the results of a long investigation: "On 9 December 1941, less than 48 hours after the attack on Pearl Harbor that launched the Pacific War, Admiral Isoroku Yamamoto, commander in chief of the Combined Fleet and at that moment the most celebrated officer in the Imperial Japanese Navy, ordered his staff to prepare plans for an invasion of Hawaii. This order set in motion what was to be the most ambitious and far-reaching Japanese operation of the Second World War."[106]

Japan did not have similarly elaborate plans for all its actual and hoped-for conquests; but its appetite grew with each victory. Indochina fell so easily that the rest of Southeast Asia seemed ripe for plucking. At the manic height of its 1942 successes, India and even Australia went on the Japanese wish list. Had American aircraft carriers been in port at Pearl Harbor when Yamamoto struck, American forces could not have stopped Japan's advances at Midway. It would have been a wholly different war. For Japan, however, it was *never* a war to "defend their unique culture" against Western imperialism or anything else.

Former Ambassador to Japan Joseph C. Grew, universally known as a Japanophile, was never taken in by rationalizations for Japan's aggression:

> We know what that euphemistic slogan "Co-Prosperity" means: it denotes absolute hegemony—economic, financial, political—for Japan's own purely selfish interests, and the virtual enslavement of the peoples of those territories to do the bidding of their Japanese masters. This statement is not a figment of the imagination; it is based on practical knowledge of what happened in other regions already subjected to Japan's domination. . . .
>
> During all my ten years in Japan I have read the books, the speeches, the newspaper and magazine articles of highly placed Japanese, of Generals and Admirals, of statesmen and diplomats and politicians. Sometimes thinly veiled, sometimes not even veiled, has emerged their

overweening ambition eventually to invade and conquer these United States.[107]

Defenders of Japanese aggression in the twentieth century have excused it as being no worse than the imperialistic policies carried out in previous centuries by the Western powers. Japan was merely following their example, but then the Western powers wanted to change the rules. Western leaders did indeed want to change the rules, Woodrow Wilson foremost among them. Had the League of Nations established after World War I been universally supported, and had it functioned as Wilson intended, self-determination would have become the norm and imperialism would have been phased out. It was the attempt by Germany, Italy, and Japan to reverse Wilsonian principles that brought on World War II.[108]

This picture of Japan as innocent victim of a rule change by the Western powers cannot be completely sustained. Not only the intent of their aggression but its scope and tactics put Japan at odds with the international community. The 1933 League of Nations vote condemning Japan's attack on China was all but unanimous, and Japan withdrew from the league. Many Japanese were aware of their country's reversion to unacceptable practices, but the bushido mentality and Japanese racism blunted all protest. Kinoshita Junji, prominent Japanese critic speaking at a 1983 symposium on the Tokyo War Crimes Trial, refers to what he calls "the three original sins of Japanese modernization . . . the plunder of Okinawa, the colonization of Korea, and the aggression in China." These sins had been identified by a historian named Fujushima, and Kinoshita does not think they cover everything:

> There are still other "original sins" in Japan's modern history besides the three identified by Mr. Fujushima. Japanese aggression against China was the origin of the Fifteen Year War, which was the object of judgment at the Tokyo trial. But what made that aggression possible, the very source from which it sprang, was the contempt with which the Japanese Empire, and the people of that empire, viewed other Asian peoples. This, I think, was the greatest original sin of all. Even after Japan was defeated and forced to relinquish its colonial empire, this contempt remained deeply rooted. How deeply rooted can be appreciated, I think, if one considers that even today an extremely large number of Japanese fail completely to grasp the meaning of the loss of Japan's former colonies. Despite what may appear on the

surface, they have inherited this ideology of contempt for other Asian peoples without the slightest fundamental change.[109]

The same symposium at which Kinoshita spoke was addressed by B.V.A. Roling, the remarkable Dutch jurist who sat on the IMTFE bench as The Netherlands representative, and who had written the most penetrating critique of that tribunal. Roling was asked, in 1983, to comment on the opinions of the one IMTFE justice, Rodhabinod Pal of India, who accepted completely the Japan-as-victim position, hence voted to acquit all defendants.

> Dr. Roling: Justice Pal's attitude, from the very beginning, was that the war fought by Japan was a war for the liberation of Asia and that therefore it should not be regarded as an aggressive war. It was a more or less belated reaction against the (Western) aggressive wars by which the (Western) colonial system was established centuries ago. That was his opinion in respect to crimes against peace. In regard to conventional war crimes, Pal's opinion was that every party in war will commit war crimes, and that it was unfair in principle to punish only the war crimes committed by defeated nations. His attitude can be easily understood, and I have respect for the opinions of my friend Pal.
>
> But I regretted very much that his attitude prevented him from seeing the Tokyo trial as an expression of the belief that redressing the injustices of the world by war is now a thing of the past. In former times, such wars were fought and they were tolerated. But that time is over, for our history of wars has left behind weapons of destruction that no longer permit war for any cause.
>
> Therefore, I think Pal's judgment is understandable if we look at the past, but not when we look at the future. It takes away from the Tokyo trial the important aspect that the judgment contributes to the opinion, which is an essential condition for survival, that wars are no longer possible, and that we should learn other ways of conducting international relations and maintaining peace.[110]

Roling's wisdom is hard to fault. Had he been in charge of IMTFE, the world would have had more justice and less polemic from both the conquering Allies and the unrepentant Japanese.

●   ●   ●

Much anger still lingers from the Pacific War. Many of Japan's victims harbored vengeful thoughts for decades. Lord Mountbatten told his biographer that he "knew just how horrible [the Japanese] were after seeing such terrible things in Singapore and in the camps. It was the one thing during the war that seared my mind. There were no extenuating circumstances, and I could find no compassion for them at all."[111]

On the other side, Japanese have turned Hiroshima and Nagasaki into a victimization cult, which allows them to flush their responsibility for wartime atrocities down the drain. As William Lanouette says of this phenomenon, "In a flash, the villains of the Pacific War became its greatest victims."[112]

Neither of these positions is sound. The most cogent treatment of the emotional aftermath of the war is the tale of suffering in captivity, and eventual one-minute-to-doomsday release, by Laurens van der Post, published in the United States as *The Prisoner and the Bomb*, in Britain as *The Night of the New Moon*. By August 1945, van der Post had been in Japanese captivity, unbelievably traumatic, for more than three years. His prison, in Java, was under the command of Field Marshal Terauchi, the conqueror of Malaya, the builder of the Thai-Burma Railway. Van der Post and his fellow prisoners were informed that Terauchi had issued orders for all prisoners to be executed when the Allied attack on Southeast Asia began.[113] This attack was set for 6 September.

To van der Post, who knew a great deal about Japanese ways of thinking and feeling, the atomic bomb alone enabled the emperor to gather sufficient support to beat down the militarists:

> if the bomb had not been dropped and the Emperor had not been able to intervene, Field Marshal Terauchi would have fought on and the prisoners in his power would have been killed. . . . I had heard enough from prisoners-of-war in other areas of Field Marshal Terauchi's command to estimate that anywhere between 200,000 and 400,000 people would have been massacred. Even had we not been deliberately massacred, we were near our physical end through lack of food. The war had only to drag on some months for most of us to have perished.[114]

Despite his suffering and narrow escape, van der Post was unwilling to join in the cry for vengeance. He writes, "There seemed to me something unreal, if not utterly false, about . . . war crimes investigators from Europe, who had not suffered under the Japanese, more bitter and vengeful about our suffering than we were ourselves. . . . I came out of prison longing passionately . . . that the past would be recognized as the past and instantly buried before it spread another form of putrefaction in the spirit of our time."[115]

Not until 1970 did van der Post write about his imprisonment and release. By then, Japanese atrocities had faded from the Western mind, Japanese education was ignoring the wartime transgressions of its empire, the Yasukuni shrine was again drawing chauvinistic politicians to its war relics, and Hiroshima had become a cult, useful for bashing Americans, especially because of the shame of Vietnam.[116] Van der Post saw something that was out of perspective:

> I would have been silent even now if it had not been for the fact that I see another kind of one-sidedness being introduced into the thinking of our time, as dangerous as the other one-sidedness that I feared in ourselves at the end of the war. This one-sidedness results from the fact that more and more people see the horror of Hiroshima and Nagasaki out of context. They tend to see it increasingly as an act of history in which we alone were the villains. I have been amazed to observe how in some extraordinary kind of way my own Japanese friends do not seem to feel that they had done anything themselves to provoke us into inflicting Hiroshima and Nagasaki on them and how strangely uncurious they are about their own part in the war. I felt that it was extremely important for them as well as for us to maintain a view of this cataclysmic event as steady as it was whole.[117]

My judgment is that van der Post does see the war, and its denouement, steady and whole. He welcomed the war's coup de grace to European colonialism. He forgave Japanese cruelties to himself and millions of Asians. He deplored the Allied urge for revenge, and wanted to start with a clean slate. But he also knew that the bomb had served a purpose—a purpose that needed only one historical fulfillment. The *Prisoner and the Bomb* was about a miracle of deliverance for him, and for 200,000 plus Allied prisoners of one fearsome Japanese general, but it was also a compelling plea for a moral code willing to erase the past and create a future in which nuclear weapons would not exist.

We have not done that. Perhaps we never shall, but in chapter eight, we will see how World War II might have turned out differently, and worse.

There are no final answers to moral questions, as Michael Howard says; but Albert Einstein comes the closest:

> It should not be forgotten that the atomic bomb was made in this country as a preventive measure; it was to head off its use by the Germans, if they discovered it. The bombing of civilian centers was initiated by the Germans and adopted by the Japanese. To it the Allies responded in kind—as it turned out, with greater effectiveness—and they were morally justified in doing so.[118]

7

Why Has the "Japan-as-Victim" Myth Been So Attractive?

By the last years of World War II, the Japanese were perceived as villains almost everywhere. The Asian and Pacific powers, some of whom (Thais, Burmese, Indonesians) had originally bought into the Greater East Asia Co-Prosperity Sphere, were by 1945 largely alienated by Japanese cruelty and racist arrogance. The Chinese and Koreans, with long experience of Japanese brutality and clear memories of atrocities such as the Rape of Nanking, had never entertained illusions about Nippon.

In the United States, endemic Caucasian racism directed at the Japanese, coupled with outrage over the sneak attack on Pearl Harbor, was intensified in January 1944 when President Roosevelt authorized release of the horror stories from American servicemen who escaped from Japanese POW camps in 1943. These stories about the victims of the Bataan Death March and similar incidents brought the emotional pitch of what was already a War Without Mercy (the title of John Dower's book) to a high level of outrage.[1] From the first stories about Bataan until at least the end of 1945, no week went by without a new account of Japanese atrocities. The end of the war did not shut off the flow; it was several months before all the inmates of Japanese prisons were recovered; those who were not psychically numbed told unimaginable stories of systematic mistreatment by their captors. There is no argument here; at the beginning of 1946, the whole world viewed Japan as villainous.

In Japan, of course, images were reversed during the war. Yamato chauvinism and military control of public information led Japanese citizens to regard Caucasians, especially Americans, as evil incarnate. American incendiary bombing strengthened this hatred. William Chapman, in his account of postwar Japan, notes:

For the average Japanese, Japanese atrocities were the rumors of war. The facts of the war, those that they knew to be true, were all on the other side. The atomic bombings of Hiroshima and Nagasaki, the incendiary raids on Tokyo and other cities—these were indisputable. When looked at from the perspective of these terrible events alone, the war made sense only if Japan were a victim, and that is how a great many people remembered it.[2]

Even many of those who had been in the West were learning to hate Caucasians. Some few Japanese servicemen had surrendered to Americans despite the cultural taboo against such disloyalty, and they knew their captors had treated them fairly; but they were out of communication with their home towns. The average Japanese viewed occupation by an American army with great trepidation.

Very little of this trepidation was due to the atom bombings. Asada Sadao has written the best analysis of Japanese perceptions of the atomic bomb events. He notes that the U.S. Strategic Bombing Survey poll of 5,000 Japanese in late 1945 showed only 19 percent of the respondents resented Americans for the atom bombs. The figure probably "underestimated the actual extent of hostility toward the United States,"[3] but it is nonetheless surprising.

Asada notes several reasons why Japanese might not blame Americans for the bombing:

. . . the fatalistic attitude best summarized in the expression "c'est la guerre"; the respondents' unwillingness to express their true feelings out of fear or "politeness"; the total discredit into which Japanese war leaders had fallen and the all-time high prestige of the Americans in Japan under the great "Shogun" General Douglas MacArthur.

These and other biases seem to have been borne out thirty years after the Strategic Bombing Survey, when a monthly magazine *Ushio* searched out and reinterviewed as many as possible of the same persons who had been interviewed in 1945. They were asked what their feelings toward the United States had been then and what they were now. Many stressed the fears they initially had about the American troops, then their great relief at seeing the friendly behavior of the ordinary GIs, and their emerging sense of gratitude for the non-retributive occupation policies.[4]

Emperor Hirohito never stated what Westerners would regard as an adequate apology for Japan's conduct of the war, but he did refuse publicly to blame the United States for atomic bombs. In response to a journalist's question about war responsibility, Hirohito said "I feel it is very regrettable that nuclear bombs were dropped, and I feel sorry for the citizens of Hiroshima. But it couldn't be helped because it happened in wartime."[5] A similar posture is taken by Imai Ryukichi, writing in 1971 of Japanese perceptions twenty-five years earlier: "The great shock which descended on them in that unusually hot and tragic summer of 1945 was almost an 'act of God' before which humans were powerless."[6]

Japanese were not only remarkably favorable toward their conquerors during the early occupation years, they were not basically disillusioned about their own polity. The emperor (as distinct from Premier Tojo and the militarists) was still held in esteem, and ordinary citizens had no knowledge at first about Japan's role in beginning the Pacific War. Pearl Harbor was not wrong. Japan was only doing in the twentieth century what Europeans had done earlier. The attempt to establish a Japanese empire was not wrong; only the inept conduct of the war was wrong. There was little guilt in postwar Japan.

Nor, except for a tiny minority, was there guilt among the Allies. They had fought against tyranny, for democracy, had been outrageously provoked by Japan's sneak attack, and wanted only to achieve a lasting peace, not to deny prosperity to their enemies. The atom bomb? Just another weapon. Given Japan's transgressions, it was not only a legitimate weapon, it provided warranted retribution. Even many religious leaders endorsed use of the bomb, *by God's people*, that is, against an evil foe.[7]

At war's end, most of the world agreed; the Allies were the good guys, the Axis—including Japan—the bad guys.

By and large, the Germans admitted they had been in the wrong. Why did they, both as a nation-state (West Germany) and a people acknowledge their guilt for waging aggressive warfare (and for genocide), whereas the Japanese state and its people refused with minor exceptions to admit any guilt? Answers to this question will throw light on the propagation of the "Japanese as victims" myth.

The only book-length treatment of the factors producing candor from Germany, evasion and suppression from Japan, is *The Wages of Guilt* by Ian Buruma.[8] Buruma explains well why there was no Dresden cult. I borrow from that work, as well as other sources, for this comparison:

Factors in German Acknowledgement of Atrocities	Factors in Japanese Denial of Atrocities
Many Germans resisted Hitler, especially toward the end.	Few Japanese resisted Tojo.
German atrocities were high visibility; reporters saw the death camps, which were in Central Europe.	Japanese atrocities were (mostly) low visibility, carried out in distant lands, with few contemporary observers.
An influential international activist constituency (Jewish) pressed the case against Germany.	No influential international constituency pursued the case against Japan; the Korean comfort women, Indonesian slaves, etc. were not organized.
German atrocities left spectacular artifacts: Buchenwald, Auschwitz, etc.	Japanese atrocities left few artifacts: nothing to match the German death camps.
Germany had an indigenous religious minority hostile to aggressive war (Christians).	No indigenous minority hostile to aggressive war; Shinto and Nichiren Buddhism supported the military.
Germany was not furnished with any spectacular event to *distract* attention from German atrocities—Dresden was not as spectacular as Hiroshima.	Japan was given a promethean novelty in atom bombing that took attention away from their own atrocities.
The Nuremberg results were generally accepted by Germans.	After their conclusion, Tokyo War Crime trials were not generally accepted by Japanese.
The man in whose name German atrocities were committed was execrated as a devil.	The man in whose name Japanese atrocities were committed was exonerated by MacArthur and continued to rule.
None of the shrines of German fascism continued to function.	Japanese patriotic shrines (particularly Yasukuni) continued to function.
German government was totally abolished; the successor government had no loyalty to its predecessor.	Japanese government continued to function with slight modification.
Germany had to face a powerful literary work, the *Diary of Anne Frank*, that highlighted German guilt.	Japan had no similar challenge; instead it had a powerful literary work, Hersey's *Hiroshima*, that evoked great sympathy.

Given such a powerful set of factors conducive to Japanese denial of guilt for the Pacific War, it is not surprising that some Japanese began to focus on Hiroshima as an American atrocity of sufficient importance to overshadow, cancel out, or neutralize their own wartime conduct. Eventually this Hiroshima cult became dominant.

Murakami Hyoe explains the slowness of the Hiroshima campaign to catch on as due in part to "the Buddhist idea that one should forget what is past and done with; it was peculiarly characteristic of the Japanese people, moreover, that most of them should have viewed the atomic bomb as a kind of natural disaster akin to an earthquake or a typhoon."[9] Ienaga Saburo adds another reason: MacArthur's staff required the textbooks put out by the Ministry of Education in the first years after the war to contain phrases such as, "Military leaders suppressed the people, launched a stupid war, and caused this disaster"; "Japan and Germany must accept the greatest responsibility for World War II, which caused vast suffering, distress, and dislocation in the world." Ienaga adds that "These publications were not perfect, but at least as far as the war was concerned, they were unequivocal on its 'recklessness' and Japan's 'responsibility.'"[10]

Would-be anti-bomb activists were largely shut down by occupation censorship. During the late 1940s, very little about the continuing health problems in the two atom towns made it into the press. Items that might "invite mistrust or resentment" of the United States were forbidden. This censorship, coupled with the general liberality of occupation economic and political policies, and the friendliness of the GIs, created a strong barrier to the flourishing of the Hiroshima myth.

Later, when censorship was lifted and the anti-bomb activists could saturate the publishing and entertainment channels, things began to change. But even then as Ian Buruma notes:

> . . . despite these diatribes, the myth of Hiroshima and its pacifist cult is based less on American wickedness than on the image of martyred innocence and visions of the Apocalypse. One moment there was normal life—laughing children, young girls singing, housewives cleaning, good men working—then, in an instant all was turned to ash. The comparison between Hiroshima and Auschwitz is based on this notion: the idea, namely, that Hiroshima, like the Holocaust, was not part of the war, nor even connected with it, but "something that occurs at the end of the world . . . we had been flattened by a force—arbitrary and violent—that wasn't war."[11]

The significant foundation of *c'est la guerre* attitude in Japan was strongly supported beginning on 3 May 1946 when the International Military Tribunal for the Far East (IMTFE) opened for business in Tokyo. Tales of Japanese atrocities had reached the Japanese public before from trials in the Philippines and Indonesia; now a veritable torrent of their countrymen's misdeeds assaulted them. The trials were later to backfire, primarily because many culpable militarists were not tried, and several people (Hirota Koki, for one) were convicted on flimsy evidence.[12] But enough credible evidence was produced about wartime leaders to impress the Japanese.

Today most of what one reads about IMTFE is negative, but there is powerful witness to its effectiveness in counteracting bitterness about the atom bomb and helping at least some Japanese to a realization of what their agents abroad had done. Ienaga says, "Despite the IMTFE's imperfections, the majority of the Japanese people were certainly not opposed to the tribunal. . . . A genuine shift of opinion occurred even among those who had patriotically supported the conflict because it was national policy."[13] Murakami agrees: "The war-crime trials were particularly effective in breaking the pride of the Japanese and casting a pall over the nation."[14] The high point of acceptance of American use of atom bombs was probably 1948. After that, the "Japan-as-victim" myth began to snowball.

Powerful novelistic treatments of the Hiroshima experience were written in the years of the occupation. Most of them were suppressed by the MacArthur censorship, but some anti-bomb writings were more successful at outwitting the U.S. authorities, as Lawrence Wittner puts it.[15] There were mimeograph machines in Japan, and copies of anti-bomb writings were distributed as samizdat documents were in the Soviet Union. Religious groups held memorial services for the dead. Intellectuals held poetry readings. In 1947, peace groups in Hiroshima held a memorial day festival, and MacArthur was constrained to send a message to the 10,000 people who attended; he said the bomb had changed war, which must be abolished.[16] But there was still no possibility of overt criticism of the American decision to use the bomb; peace groups merely supported disarmament and world government in the future.

In 1948, American leaders began building up Japan as an ally against the Soviet Union, and the aims of the occupation shifted from democratization and liberalization to economic reconstruction and support of Communist containment. Japanese intellectuals began to sense that the "no armed forces" clause MacArthur had demanded in the Japanese constitution was phony. The constitution had originally been popular with all but bitter-end militarists; then, as Buruma observes:

> . . . when the Cold War prompted the Americans to make the Japanese subvert their constitution by creating an army which was not supposed to exist, the worst of all worlds appeared: sovereignty was not restored, distrust remained, and resentment mounted. Kamei's hawks are angry with the Americans for emasculating Japan; Oda's doves hate the Americans for emasculating the "peace constitution." Both sides dislike being forced accomplices, and both feel victimized, which is one reason Japanese have a harder time than Germans in coming to terms with their wartime past.[17]

Nineteen forty-nine was a watershed year. John Hersey's *Hiroshima*, which had been prohibited in Japan by MacArthur but about which many Japanese had heard, was published in Japanese in April. Asada Sadao believes it to have been the most notable American document about the bomb to reach Japanese readers.[18] In August, the Soviet Union exploded an atomic bomb; Japan was then ringed by atomic powers who were at each other's throats. And on 31 January 1950, Truman added to the anxiety by announcing a program to build the H-bomb.

From then on, almost every international development, and a host of American domestic developments, strengthened Japan's belief that it had been victimized, and would be a cosmic casualty should war between the two nuclear superpowers break out.

It did break out, in Korea. The Japanese knew who controlled the North Koreans and who supplied their armaments and training, and who alone could cause them to settle the war. The United States was fighting a Soviet surrogate. American pressure on Japan to rearm and to supply American forces in Korea fixed the Japanese even more firmly into the superpower rivalry, and made them ground zero for a looming nuclear Armageddon.

By 1951, occupation censorship was slackening, and a book that probably did more to alter the opinions of younger Japanese than any other was published by Hosei University Press: P.M.S. Blackett's *Fear, War, and the Bomb*. Asada Sadao believes: "This book had a seminal influence in shaping Japanese views of the A-bomb decision, because the Japanese public tends to hold Nobel prize scientists in such high esteem that their words are taken almost as an oracle even when they venture into the unfamiliar area of international politics and history. One index of Blackett's influence on our students is the fact that his translated book is recommended and excerpts from it included in high school teachers' manuals."[19]

With the end of the occupation in 1952, there was a "flood of publications on the 'A-bomb problem'" in Japan.[20] This increased criticism of the IMTFE and other war crimes trials. These were now seen as simply "victor's justice."[21] They had not indicted many of the main criminals, but had tried and convicted Yamashita Tomoyuki, Hirota Koki, Kido Koichi, and others against whom many observers believe there was no case. Fifteen million Japanese signed a petition to release all those still in prison. The relatively candid textbooks that had introduced students into at least some comprehension of the enormity of Japan's aggression were replaced by books with little or no criticism of Japanese militarists, and considerable sympathy for the glorious aims of the Greater East Asia Co-Prosperity Sphere.

And in 1954, in one of the first publicly exposed imbecilities carried out by the U.S. Atomic Energy Commission (AEC), the Japanese experienced their third taste of atomic destruction. The BRAVO test of a very powerful H-bomb was scheduled for 1 March 1954 in the Bikini Atoll.[22] Wind patterns, expected fallout, and other danger factors were calculated—or miscalculated—and several islands in the area were evacuated. Ships were warned not to be within an area of 50,000 square miles around Eniwetok.

There was, however, a Japanese tuna trawler, the *Lucky Dragon*, eighty-five miles east-northeast of Bikini. This was well outside the proscribed area. It was not outside the area where capricious nature sent an upper-level wind that day. And the force of the explosion far exceeded anything the scientists had predicted. Radioactive debris (Bikini Ash, as it came to be known in Japan) fell on the *Lucky Dragon* and its twenty-three crewmen. One of the crew members saw a dazzling light in the west, and seven minutes afterward they felt the shock wave from BRAVO. Suspecting they had been near an atomic test, they shortly thereafter pulled up their nets and headed for their homeport, Yaizu.

One might, perhaps, forgive the scientists who miscalculated the risks involved in BRAVO. Perhaps one can forgive Truman, who first decided the United States should build H-bombs; and Eisenhower, for testing the creature in the sensitive Pacific areas, where two A-bombs had already been dropped on Asian cities. What cannot be forgiven is the lying and stonewalling that followed. Unfortunately, the chairman of the Atomic Energy Commission at the time was Lewis Strauss, whose talents included the ability to make money selling shoes, selling stocks, and selling himself first to James Forrestal, then to Harry Truman, and finally to Dwight Eisenhower. Robert Divine compares Strauss to John Adams: "pompous, shrewd, patriotic but often mean, petty, and unpredictable."[23] He was also a certifiable paranoid; he told James Hagerty, Eisenhower's press secretary, that "the *Lucky Dragon* was not a fishing boat at all—it was a 'Red spy outfit' snooping on the American nuclear tests."[24] Strauss was instrumental in cancelling Robert Oppenheimer's security clearance. Altogether, Strauss was the worst conceivable person to handle American relations with the Japanese whom all Asia then perceived as victims of a third nuclear detonation.

All the *Lucky Dragon* crew were sickened and hospitalized. The radioman, who had tasted the Bikini Ash out of curiosity, died 23 September 1954. The rest lived, but recovery was long and painful.

The fish brought in by the *Lucky Dragon* were radioactive and had to be condemned. All fish brought in to Japanese harbors from suspect areas were checked for radioactivity for several months; 683 tuna boats were found to have contaminated fish. The Japanese fishing industry was well-organized and politically powerful, employing one million workers. One of its most popular products was now suspect. Thousands of pounds were condemned, and the bottom dropped out of the market. Tokyo's Tsukiji Central Fish Market was closed for the first time since a cholera scare in 1935. For the Japanese media, the tuna panic was more important than the sick fishermen.

Japanese citizens had clearly been victims of an atomic *test*; this reinforced the 1945 charge that the bombs dropped on Hiroshima and Nagasaki had also been mere experiments. The *Lucky Dragon* fishermen had become surrogate guinea pigs for the whole Japanese people. Even if most of the crew lived, it was clear that many of them would not be able to work for a long time, and in Japan, this was a living death. The five most important Japanese newspapers took a common position: this was the third atomic bombing.[25]

Japanese doctors could not know the best treatment for their patients, since they did not know the chemical composition of Bikini Ash, and the AEC would not tell them. It had to be kept secret from the Russians. Not only were the fishermen's blood counts dangerously low, their hair fallen out, and their gums bleeding, many of them were sterile. (Some recovered, and fathered children.) To demonstrate his contempt for the alarmist Japanese, Merrill Eisenbud, director (without a doctorate or any scientific distinction) of AEC's Health and Safety Laboratory, flew to Japan and visited the *Lucky Dragon* with an armful of instruments. As Ralph Lapp describes it, "The jaunty AEC expert refused to put on gloves, mask or protective clothing and rather horrified some of the Japanese scientists by his nonchalance."[26] They were also put off by his lack of credentials. Meanwhile, in the United States Sen. Joseph McCarthy of Wisconsin was tearing the American government apart with charges that the army was infiltrated by communists. A.M. Halpern in a RAND monograph dated 1 September 1954 noted that all this gave final confirmation to Japanese newspapermen of "their conviction that freedom was dead and hysteria reigned in the United States."[27]

On 31 March 1954, Eisenhower directed AEC chairman Strauss to appear at the end of a presidential press conference to read a statement about the BRAVO test and the *Lucky Dragon* mishap. After explaining why search planes had not seen the ship before the test, and how the wind changes were unexpected, Strauss misrepresented what had happened: he claimed none of the Marshall Islanders had been injured, there was no significant contamination of fish, the skin lesions of the fishermen were not due to radioactivity, and the fault for the whole thing lay with the tuna captain—he had entered the proscribed zone. All these things were false.[28] One cannot claim that the chairman of the U.S. Atomic Energy Commission lied. His paranoia was intense enough, and the self-protectiveness of the super-secret agency was powerful enough, that he could have believed what he was saying.[29]

No Japanese did. And if the head of America's atomic energy agency could so misrepresent American motives and actions in 1954, *so could America's president have misrepresented the reasons for obliterating Hiroshima and Nagasaki nine years earlier.*

Worse: Chairman W. Sterling Cole of the Joint Committee on Atomic Energy of the U.S. Congress suggested publicly that the *Lucky Dragon* might have been a spy ship.[30]

Eisenhower, who was more composed than Strauss, moved to mend relations with Japan, and eventually the United States gave $2 million to the *Lucky Dragon* and other claimants. But Japan's honeymoon with its conquerors was over.

Asada notes that "the Bikini incident of 1954 . . . suddenly galvanized the Japanese peace sentiment into a mass movement against nuclear weapons."[31] Tanaka Yasumasu, in his 1970 study of

"Japanese Attitudes Toward Nuclear Arms," says *Lucky Dragon* "literally ignited the fiery resentment and protests against nuclear weapons."[32] Roger Dingman's careful study of the incident shows that the fishermen who did not die recovered reasonable health, most married and had children, and all but three were still living thirty years later: "But the Lucky Dragon incident generated fallout that influenced relations between the United States and Japan for decades to come. The 'ashes of death' that rained down on March 1, 1954, formed part of the antinuclear mantle in which Japan wrapped itself."[33]

The Japanese *were* victims of this third atomic incident, and there was no supreme emergency to justify it, no horrible war to bring to an end, no stubborn militarists whose determination to fight to the end had to be overcome. There was only the atomic-military complex riding on the growing American paranoia about the Soviets.

There was much tension in the United States-Japan relationship which strengthened the Japanese peace and antinuclear forces, and contributed to Japan's feeling of victimization. Contributing to the tension were two treaties: the mutual defense treaty signed at San Francisco 5 September 1951, and the peace treaty between Japan and the Western Allies (no Communist nations signed).[34] The mutual defense arrangements gave the United States extensive basing rights on Japanese territory. Japan's conservative governments supported these bases strongly; the antinuclear activists did not, partially due to fear that nuclear arms would be stationed on Japanese soil or brought into Japanese ports.

Tension over the mutual defense treaty came to a boil when the treaty was up for renewal in 1960. Historian Nishi Toshio, then a college student, viewed the situation this way:

Popular sentiment in Japan was overwhelmingly against renewal. Massive street demonstrations, one after another, day after day, kept Japan on the edge of open revolt. University students . . . staged many violent confrontations with the special riot police force. My friends and I joined in massive street demonstrations for we felt that Japan did not need this defense treaty and that the United States was making a convenience of us for the sake of its own hegemony in Asia. We felt that if war started between the United States and the Soviet Union, the Soviets would attack us first, and worse yet, the war would be fought upon our soil. "Yankee, Go Home!" was a slogan spontaneously inspired by Japanese nationalism.[35]

Prime Minister Kishi Nobosuke was determined to renew the treaty. He went to Washington to sign it on 16 January 1960. Left wing students occupied the Tokyo airport lobby in protest, but failed to prevent Kishi's departure. Kishi was well received in Washington, and invited Eisenhower to Tokyo in June for a ratification exchange ceremony. In May, when the treaty was before the Diet, 330,000 people surrounded the building in protest.[36] Kishi pushed it through with opposition members absent, and the country exploded. Eisenhower's visit was cancelled, Kishi resigned 23 June, an assassin attempted to kill him 14 July, and on 12 October, the most vocal leader of the anti-treaty forces was assassinated by a right wing student.

Growing out of the mutual defense treaty was another major contretemps: Japanese involvement, as staging area and important supplier, for the American war in Vietnam. Japanese opposition to this was visceral. Thomas R.H. Havens calls the 1965 escalation of that war a "shuddering jolt" to Japan, the "most powerful shock" to the previously favorable opinion of the United States.[37] Despite Hiroshima and Nagasaki, John Hersey, P.M.S. Blackett, *Lucky Dragon*, and the other irritants in the U.S.-Japan relationship, in 1964 public opinion polls showed 49 percent of the public listed the United States as their favorite foreign country. Anguish over Vietnam was probably the most important factor in the decline of this popularity to 18 percent by 1973.[38]

The main target of Japanese displeasure was the bombing. Many more tons of bombs were dropped on Vietnam than on Japan in World War II. The many antiwar demonstrations in Japan were triggered by the bombing escalations. Havens' thorough study, *Fire Across the Sea: The Vietnam War and Japan, 1965-1975*, explains the intricate relationship of the antiwar movement to the antinuclear movement.[39] They were not identical. Antinuclear forces had become politicized, and were spearheaded by leftist groups. Opposition to the Vietnam War was more broadly based; photos of B-52 raids reminded Japanese of the B-29s twenty years earlier. Opinion polls in 1965 showed 74 percent of Japanese opposed the bombing.

The conservative government of Sato Eisaku calculated correctly that it could ride out domestic opposition if it supported the United States in Vietnam, but the price was high. When Sato visited South Vietnam on 8 October 1967, protesters staged a bloody clash with police at the Tokyo airport; this was "The first violent moment in a vast chain of rallies and demonstrations over foreign policy that drew 18,730,000 participants during the next two-and-a-half years."[40]

One high point of protest was the visit of the nuclear powered aircraft carrier *Enterprise* to Sasebo on 19 January 1968. Havens writes:

> Conventionally powered aircraft carriers capable of carrying nuclear weapons visited Sasebo regularly during the Vietnam War without major opposition. What was different about the *Enterprise* was the synergy of its gigantic size, its nuclear fuel, its pivotal function in the war, and the timing of its arrival in port. . . . The *Enterprise* affair was a moment of high theater in the antiwar movement, a week-long drama that is remembered more vividly in Japan two decades later than any other Vietnam protest. . . . The *Enterprise* offended the sensibilities of many Japanese who did not like having the United States and Japanese governments deliberately irritate their innate nuclear allergy. Few of them enjoyed being forcibly awakened from the non-nuclear idyll they had created for themselves since Hiroshima and Nagasaki.[41]

The *Enterprise* visit sparked a week of riotous demonstrations, with police clubbing students in front of the television cameras, and all Japan watching. At this stage, the protesters were generally non-violent, and won much sympathy. Their failure to influence government policy led them to more vigorous measures later. No nuclear carrier came to Japan again until 1983, but the dreaded atom sparked headline stories for nearly a month, when in May 1968 high levels of radioactivity were found in the waters of Sasebo harbor close to the nuclear-powered submarine *Swordfish*.[42]

The siege of Khe Sanh, February to April 1968, brought another crisis. B-52s based on Okinawa dropped 10,000 tons of high explosives a week on Vietnamese attacking the U.S. Marine post.

Stories about the My Lai massacre began to appear in Japanese papers in November 1969; they coincided with Prime Minister Sato's departure for Washington to renegotiate the mutual security treaty and to secure an American promise to return Okinawa to Japanese control. This time the five days of demonstrations drew fewer people than before, but led to more arrests.[43] Turmoil continued to the end of the war. By the time President Nixon actually got out of Vietnam, many Japanese were convinced that the U.S. effort in that tortured nation was inspired not just by anti-Communism, but by racism.

Not all the factors promoting the Japan-as-victim myth were due to American stupidities and blunders. One powerful cause was the determination of the Ministry of Education to indoctrinate Japanese students with a sanitized picture of Japan's 1931 to 1945 rampage throughout East Asia and the Pacific.

As soon as the occupation ended in 1952, the ministry began to eliminate from history texts all accounts that showed Japanese aggression in its true light. The horrors brought out by the IMTFE were by then fading from memory, and beginning in the mid 1950s, the only story known to younger Japanese was one of glorious achievements in freeing Asia from Caucasian imperialism, establishing a wholly altruistic Greater East Asia Co-Prosperity Sphere, and defending the holy Japanese homeland from the aggressive racism of the Americans.

In February 1953, Minister of Education Okano Seigo told the Diet, "I do not wish to pass judgment on the rightness or wrongness of the Greater East Asian War, but the fact that Japan took on so many opponents and fought them for four years . . . proves our superiority."[44] Hattori Takashiro's *History of the Greater East Asian War*, published in 1953, described the bravery of Japanese forces as "so gallant that the gods would be moved to tears."[45] Ienaga Saburo, an iconoclast who has no kind word for any World War II combatant, was one of the few scholars who tried to keep a picture of Japan's depredations before students. A high school history text he wrote in 1963 was rejected by the Education Ministry. Ienaga sued:

> During the trial a government brief elaborated on the shortcomings of my manuscript. Certain phrases such as "The war was glorified as a 'holy cause,'" "atrocities by Japanese troops," and "reckless war" were objectionable because "These are excessively critical of Japan's position and actions in World War II and do not give students a proper understanding of this country's position and actions in the war."
>
> . . . Whereas the great majority of students and children used to have a negative attitude toward the war, recently approval of Japan's actions has been increasing.[46]

The court battle went on for decades. The ministry was determined to allow only a whitewashed version of the Pacific War to be presented. Ienaga kept coming back with new challenges to his opponents. In 1993, twenty-eight years after he filed his first suit, the Japanese Supreme Court ruled "that the Government was well within its rights when it forced Mr. Ienaga to delete uncomfortable particulars about how Japan invaded Korea and Manchuria, and to skip by the rape and killings that accompanied the occupation of Southeast Asia."[47]

A year later, in 1994, the Court reversed itself, condemning Education Ministry censors and upholding Ienaga.[48] It remains to be seen whether the history taught in Japanese schools will now change significantly.

Japan's textbook controversy was never a hot news item in the United States. In China it was one of the greatest irritants in Sino-Japanese relations. Allen Whiting, in his book *China Eyes Japan*, devotes a chapter to the intense Chinese reaction in 1982 and 1986 when the Japanese Education Ministry authorized textbook changes to further prettify Japan's wartime record. Whiting quotes a 15 August 1982 editorial in the official Chinese youth newspaper warning that the Japanese "attempt to deceive the younger generation through education" was part of a dream of reviving militarism, but it would fail; "how could historical facts written in blood be concealed by lies written in ink?" There follows a brief but graphic list of Japanese atrocities and the contention that "even the German fascists labeled Japanese soldiers as a 'group of beasts.'"[49] China was not buying any "Japan as victim" scenario. China's killed and wounded at Japanese hands may not have been as high as the Chinese now claim (21.8 million), but Japan was certainly in the category of perpetrator rather than victim.

Whiting is correct on the significance of Chinese bitterness about this matter:

> The repeated references in the Chinese media to the Nanjing death tolls as greater than the combined casualties from the atomic bombs dropped on Hiroshima and Nagasaki convey multiple messages. First, these references imply that there is a double standard at work: world attention focuses on the victims of the atomic bombs and ignores China's greater loss. Second, these references also seek to point out that Japan wins sympathy as the victim and the United States is cast as the nuclear villain even though Japan started the war. This allows Japan to avoid any feelings of guilt for the invasion of China and the Nanjing atrocities. Third, these references make the point that the Nanjing Massacre was worse than Hiroshima and

Nagasaki because it occurred piecemeal through the personal actions of individuals whereas the atomic holocausts occurred instantaneously from high-altitude bombing.[50]

The third implication should perhaps be amended. The atomic bombings were justified not because they came from great altitude, but because they had a legitimate purpose: to end the war. The Nanking massacre was sheer bestiality.

Filipinos are close behind the Chinese in rejecting Japanese attempts to conceal their wartime atrocities and portray themselves as victims. F. Sionil Jose, a Filipino who has studied extensively in Japan, laid out the folly of Japanese pretenses in 1988. We must hope atom bombs will never be used again, he said, but the ones in 1945 were necessary. Truman was right in promptly going to sleep after issuing the orders. Not only was the war shortened, "Japan did not have to contend with Soviet occupation. . . . We must also continually remind the Japanese of what they did during the war and should not be deluded about their weeping over Hiroshima."[51]

But in Japan the victimization myth holds full sway. Asada Sadao, one of the most accomplished Japanese historians, has written more candidly about this than anyone. He begins with the "steady diet of popular histories, journalistic writings, and tendentious treatises that harp on the two themes of 'atomic blackmail' against the Soviet Union and American racism." This was "reinforced by analogy with what happened in Vietnam—the My Lai case, incidents in Cambodia, and other reported expressions of the contempt in which Asian lives were held by the American military. Suddenly revived was the old image of white men against yellow men, which became superimposed on Japanese views of the A-bomb decision."[52]

But this is not all. The early *c'est la guerre* attitude, the view that the atom bombs were a natural catastrophe such as a typhoon or an earthquake, has changed to attribution of personal responsibility:

> Regarding the "responsibility" for the A-bomb disasters, the polls indicate an increasing tendency among the Japanese, especially among the atomic survivors, to focus their resentment on one individual, former President Truman, rather than direct it toward the American people in general . . . what has baffled, irritated, and offended the Japanese was Truman's repeated disavowal of any sense of "guilt" or "regret."[53]

As Asada goes on to show, Truman did indeed have regrets. He expressed these to Henry Wallace when he reflected on his decision to cancel the third bomb even though the Japanese had not surrendered.[54] But that the first two bombs were necessary he had no doubts.

Thus, the deep-seated Japanese belief in their own righteousness, their delusion that the Greater East Asia Co-Prosperity Sphere was for the benefit of Asian colonies oppressed by Europeans, and their belief in the need for aggressive action to prevent economic strangulation by America and Britain, all predisposed them to see themselves as victims of American atrocities. By 1989, Hatana Sumio could describe majority opinion even among Japanese scholars as accepting the Blackett thesis and racism as explanations for Hiroshima and Nagasaki.[55]

• • •

Acceptance of the Japanese-as-victims belief in the United States is harder to explain. The tiny pacifist constituency was without influence. With the exception of the Vera Brittain pamphlet mentioned in chapter six, there was no significant attack on terror bombing. Polls in 1945 showed that a substantial number of citizens thought the air forces should have dropped more atomic bombs on Japan. Belief that Japan got what it deserved was almost universal.

William B. Breuer has one of the clearest descriptions of how things changed. "Hardly had the ink dried on the surrender document signed aboard the battleship *Missouri* in Tokyo Bay on 2 September 1945, than the American home front went on an unprecedented binge of self-indulgence and the pursuit of pleasure. The Death March and the Japanese POW camps became ancient history, and most Americans didn't want to be reminded of those unpleasant events."[56] By 1994, things had changed so much that the designers of the Smithsonian Air and Space Museum exhibit portrayed the Japanese as the main sufferers during the Pacific War.[57] Opposition to these original plans for the museum exhibit was furious, but the plans showed that the Japanese-as-victims thinking had penetrated to high places.

Fundamental to the power of this myth to override and displace such graphic stories as the accounts of suffering in Japanese prisons is the phenomenon of the unforgettable spectacle. Hiroshima was the paradigm. Ronald Spector states the situation well:

> The sudden, awful end of the war in the radioactive ruins of Hiroshima and Nagasaki has obscured the less spectacular horrors which both sides had inflicted on each other by 1945. The conduct of the Japanese military forces in Southeast Asia and China and their treatment of prisoners of war is well known. Less obvious are the thousands of other deaths from famine and disease caused by the crushing demands of the locust-like Japanese war machine upon the fragile agricultural economies of the countries it occupied.[58]

There were sensitive people who were not going to allow the spectacles to be forgotten, especially pacifists. Lawrence Wittner gives a graphic account of how, few as they were, they were jarred into feverish activity by Hiroshima and Nagasaki.[59] Their activity was aided by watershed events already mentioned as influential in Japan: the Bikini fiasco, the USSBS early surrender doctrine and its use by P.M.S. Blackett, and the Vietnam quagmire were all significant. But the long-term effects of the Cold War, the mid-century eruption of a witch hunt, and the accompanying rampage of the atomic-military-industrial complex played major roles. Five decades after Hiroshima the atomic diplomacy belief is respectable and probably dominant among American intellectuals.

The first organization formed to influence nuclear development and prevent an arms race was begun by Manhattan Project veterans. The Federation of Atomic Scientists leaped into the political arena to caution the world that the bomb had changed things.[60]

Few of the scientists acknowledged a guilty conscience over Truman's use of their product, but Reinhold Niebuhr was not so sure. He thought their activism suspicious and misplaced.[61] The scientists did manage to convince Congress to place nuclear matters under a civilian agency, the AEC, rather than under the Pentagon.

The scientists' other objective was to secure firm international control over nuclear weapons. In this, they were unsuccessful. The nations of the world were not about to be scared into giving up any amount of sovereignty, even if Armageddon threatened. Paul Boyer believes that

> the scientists' manipulation of fear, rather than the particular causes they espoused, seems their principal legacy. Indeed, they may have

served as unwitting advance agents of the very anticommunist hysteria most of them deplored. The emotions they worked so mightily in 1945-1947 to keep alive and intensify created fertile psychological soil for the ideology of American nuclear superiority and an all-out crusade against communism.[62]

The scientists' rhetoric produced another outcome. Spencer Weart believes that the fearful hostilities generated by nuclear weapons and the alarms of the scientists were displaced not only onto those who might use the bombs in future, but onto those "who had already used them."[63] Truman. The scientists who objected to Hiroshima gave a powerful stimulus to the growth of the cult.

While the scientists' movement ran its course by 1950, it left one enduring legacy: *The Bulletin of the Atomic Scientists*, still appearing as a prestigious source of information. As a counterweight to the overpowering printed output of the atomic-military-industrial complex, it may seem feeble; but without the *Bulletin*, our knowledge of the nuclear behemoth would be impoverished.

The Hiroshima story underwrote a more provincial concern: the possible dangers of nuclear power plants. Long before the Three Mile Island event of 1979, the safety of nuclear power was called into question. In 1963, applications to build nuclear reactors at Bodega Head, near a California fault zone, and at Ravenswood in New York City, were violently opposed and ultimately withdrawn by the applying utilities.[64] *Nucleonics Week*, an industry trade journal, charged that nuclear critics used misleading comparisons of nuclear plants with bombs.[65]

In 1969, Sheldon Novick's book, *The Careless Atom*, though not alarmist or exaggerated, was advertised by the publisher with the line "The Hiroshima bomb is alive and ticking—in Indian Point."[66] Another controversy over licensing a nuclear plant in Minnesota saw opponents comparing the plant with Hiroshima.[67]

In 1975, when the Union of Concerned Scientists issued a "Scientists' Declaration on Nuclear Power," signed by 2,000 members, it noted that it was "presented to Congress and the President of the United States on the 30th anniversary of the atomic bombing of Hiroshima."[68] The declaration urged a drastic reduction in nuclear power plant starts; the risks were too great. James Bryant Conant signed the declaration, as did George Kistiakowsky, Harold Urey, and Victor Weisskopf, all prominent scientists on the Manhattan Project. The bomb lingered in their minds.

As it did everywhere. When American Catholic bishops issued a pastoral letter on nuclear weapons in 1983, they called for the country to "express profound sorrow over the atomic bombing in 1945. Without that sorrow, there is no possibility of finding a way to repudiate future use of nuclear weapons."[69]

The fall 1994 issue of *Peace Action* (formerly SANE/FREEZE *News*) described plans for the Peace Action Education Fund to join the Japan Congress Against A- and H-Bombs for the fiftieth anniversary of the bombings in 1995. There was a new and surprising element in this story. Burt Glass, program director of Peace Action, writing about workshops held with the Japanese, said "During these presentations, Japanese activists were especially careful to note Japan's role as an aggressor nation in World War II and its treatment of other Asian countries. It became clear to me that the activists I met opposed more than just the first two atomic bombings. They opposed militarism itself."[70] This is a welcome note in the Hiroshima story. Perhaps it will lead to Japanese satisfaction of the claims of the comfort women, and of the survivors of the seventeen million who perished at the hands of the Greater East Asia Co-Prosperity Sphere.

•   •   •

The Manhattan Project was an uneasy amalgam of military rigidity and freewheeling genius, held together by a fervent desire to beat the Germans to atomic weapons. Stewart Udall belittles this motive, trying to make a case for the view that Gen. Leslie Groves could have found out, had he wanted to, that there was no German atomic bomb project.[71] Since Manhattan was a prestigious and affluent operation, and its director a powerful executive, Groves protected his domain from any skepticism about its justification.

Udall makes the case that Groves would do anything to avoid a challenge to Manhattan's mission; but he can make no case against the sincere and urgent devotion of the Manhattan scientists to assuring Hitler's defeat. Whatever foibles one can attribute to them, the Manhattan elite were not power-driven zealots (except for Edward Teller, whose later fanaticism put him in a different class). Following is Udall's condemnation of the whole Manhattan Project, of the expenditure of so much money uselessly, of using a new weapon when it was unnecessary to secure Japan's surrender:

The atomic age would have had a more modest and balanced beginning if Japan had surrendered before the bombs were ready, or if an objective assessment of Germany's plans had influenced our leaders to slow the pace of the Manhattan Project and convert it into a clandestine, postwar-oriented program of research and development. The surprise announcement of the success of this venture in 1946 or 1947 would have added to America's military and moral strength and encouraged a thoughtful global dialogue about the role of the atom in the modern world.[72]

Here, too, is a speculation of zero credibility. Slowing the pace of Manhattan would have brought certain electoral reprisal against the administration that had pulled its punches in the desperate denouement of the Pacific War. And who can believe the operation could have been kept secret for even a month with the war over? Announcing the success of such a venture in 1946 or 1947? Surely any student of the end of World War II realizes that the frantic rush to get back to normalcy would have cut off any decent appropriations for such a visionary and uncompleted project; there might have been nothing to announce in 1947. In the Soviet Union, however, the *Russians* would have produced their bomb in about the same time regardless. And what kind of arms race would we have had then? Imagine the congress of Joe McCarthy, William Jenner, Pat McCarran, Karl Mundt, Bourke Hickenlooper, John Rankin, Parnell Thomas, and Harold Velde when they discovered that Truman had dragged his feet on a weapon that might have saved the lives of 50,000 or more GIs.

"The atomic age would have had a more modest and balanced beginning" if we had slowed down Manhattan and not bombed Hiroshima? Not likely. In addition to the liabilities just mentioned, Harry Truman would have been impelled to *use* the bomb during the dark days in Korea, instead of just thinking about it.[73] Would that have furthered any cause Udall believes in?

Udall's late conversion to the "Japanese-as-victims" belief is perhaps the paradigmatic instance of projecting the sins of Groves' successors back onto an earlier and entirely different era.

Groves's successors were an arrogant and mendacious lot.[74] It is easy to understand the scientists' movement against nuclear excesses, even to understand how the atomic-military-industrial complex turned so many level-headed citizens to antinuclear activism. Even had the peacetime management of the AEC (and its successors, the Nuclear Regulatory Commission, Energy Research and Development Administration, Department of Energy) been modest and self-effacing (only David Lilienthal fits this description), the power and prominence of nuclear bosses would have brought trouble.

Ironically, Bertrand Russell, one of the gurus of the British antinuclear movement, specifically excludes scientists from the ranks of the truly powerful in his 1938 book *Power: A New Social Analysis*:

> We have already noted the curious fact that, although knowledge plays a larger part in civilization now than at any former time, there has not been any corresponding growth of power among those who possess the new knowledge. Although the electrician and the telephone man do strange things that minister to our comfort (or discomfort), we do not regard them as medicine-men, or imagine that they can cause thunderstorms if we annoy them. The reason for this is that scientific knowledge, though difficult, is not mysterious, but open to all who care to take the necessary trouble.[75]

The atomic age changed that. The physicist-managers who controlled the magical atom accumulated power almost beyond imagining. H. Peter Metzger, who by reason of his expertise in biochemistry lectured for the AEC, and thus was almost one of the priesthood, notes that: "As it was the glamour agency of the day, the chairman of the AEC at that time [late 1950s] was as high as number four on the State Department's protocol list. . . . This entitled him to appear at state functions just after the Vice-President, the Secretary of State, and the Speaker of the House."[76]

Lord Acton may not have said it first, but he is credited with saying it best: "Power tends to corrupt and absolute power corrupts absolutely."[77] What Robert Michels said about the leaders of the early trade unions also speaks to the pathologies of the AEC scientists-managers: "he who has once attained to power will not readily be induced to return to the comparatively obscure position which he formerly occupied."[78] Udall, immersed in the prevarications of the AEC, and kinder to his opponents than many, notes that the normal power syndrome was exacerbated by a sacred mission: maintaining the national security. Thus, "The functionaries who executed this policy were not evil men, but rather loyal men who wore blinders and fulfilled their missions with such dedication and zeal that these virtues, in excess, resulted in dishonorable deeds, not unlike the 'good Germans' who valiantly and without moral reflection, followed the orders of their Fuhrer."[79]

No doubt many of the true believers among the atomic establishment were merely excessively concerned about "The Threat." The behavior of some, however, violates any code of integrity imaginable.

AEC activity at the Nevada Test Site was under the direction of Norris Bradbury, and by 1962, more than a decade of bomb tests had been conducted with many claimed instances of fallout damage. The official position of Bradbury's operation was, "There is no danger." Bradbury knew this was not true. Consider Udall's narrative of events before a major test:

> In 1962, members of Norris Bradbury's family were 'living under' fallout in a dangerous corridor of the downwind zone at Zion National Park, due east of St. George. His son, a park ranger, his pregnant daughter-in-law, and his first grandson, age two, resided in a canyon near the park.
>
> Bradbury surely knew that small children—and especially embryonic children in utero—were exceptionally vulnerable to the impacts of low-level radiation. As a result, he made a special trip to Zion and took action to protect his grandchildren. He showered the parents with safety tips ("Keep them indoors on windy days . . . don't let them eat snow," etc.) and provided airline tickets to his daughter-in-law so she and her son could visit relatives during the month-long 1962 tests.[80]

There were many other evil men involved in the three-decade-long effort of the AEC to deny compensation to the affected downwinders. Udall lists some of them. They include lawyers, veterinarians, medical doctors, physicists, and no doubt other elites. The judges of the U.S. Court of Appeals for the Tenth Circuit (Denver) in the *Bulloch* decision of 1985 are among them.[81]

The Eisenhower administration made a sincere effort to negotiate a nuclear test ban treaty with the Soviet Union. Harold Stassen, as Ike's chief disarmament negotiator, seemed to be making progress. The AEC, backed by the Lawrence Livermore weaponeers and by Edward Teller, was determined to sabotage the whole effort. Its position was that a ban could not be enforced; the Soviets would test underground, and underground tests could not be detected more than 200 miles away. Hence a test ban would be detrimental to national security.

To prove this, AEC conducted an underground test at the Nevada site in the fall of 1957. I.F. Stone, a heretic on nuclear weapons as on other topics, noticed inconspicuous news stories saying that this first underground test had been detected in Toronto, Rome, and Tokyo. He did not have resources to cable these places for verification, but he did the next best thing: he called the seismologists at the U.S. Coast and Geodetic Survey. These scientists, not beholden to Lewis Strauss or Edward Teller, told Stone their seismographs had picked up the test all over the continent, for instance in Fayetteville, Arkansas, 1,200 miles away, and Fairbanks, Alaska, 2,600 miles away.[82]

The AEC found out Stone had outflanked them, phoned him, and admitted he was right. But they did not correct their lying press release, and every paper in the country except the *St. Louis Post-Dispatch*, where Stone tipped off a friend, carried the false story. Stassen's efforts were sabotaged; testing went on. In 1989, the Department of Energy, successor to AEC, acknowledged 802 tests of nuclear weapons since 1957.[83] How many unacknowledged tests took place we do not yet know.

Secrecy was a major asset of the AEC in its long string of false-hoods. The government often controlled all information about its operations, especially information about the incidence of cancer among workers in nuclear plants. By refusing to give independent scholars access to health and employment records, AEC could pretend that exposure to low-level radiation, even over an extended period, was harmless.

One of the most notorious abuses of the secrecy barrier occurred in the case of Dr. Thomas F. Mancuso, epidemiologist with the Graduate School of Public Health at the University of Pittsburgh.[84] In 1965, Mancuso was given an AEC grant to study the health records of workers in American nuclear weapons plants. By 1975, he had completed a study of workers at the Hanford, Washington plant, with results showing higher than normal levels of cancer. Just to be sure, he brought the most prominent British epidemiologists, Alice Stewart and George W. Kneale, to Pittsburgh to inspect his calculations. They concurred.

The atomic establishment could not tolerate this outcome. It cast doubt on its claim that radiation had to exceed a certain threshold level to damage humans. By then AEC had been replaced by the Energy Research and Development Administration; that organization took Mancuso's grant away, he was denied further access to the

Hanford figures, and he gave up his studies. Alice Stewart, however, regularly visited the United States to lecture and testify before congressional committees; she maintained all along that Mancuso had been right. Finally in 1990, as principal investigator for the Three Mile Island Public Health Fund, she regained access to the Hanford records. Her most recent analysis reaffirms the 1975 conclusions, and is accepted by epidemiologists, even some on government payrolls.[85] The government's long struggle to conceal bad news only reinforced the image of the atomic establishment as a lying bully.

Every controversy that arose left the nuclear people looking bad. Take the matter of weapon overkill. Why were the nuclear operators (working, of course, with and even for the military) so intent on ridiculous numbers of warheads? Any observer of the American (or Soviet) nuclear arsenal knew that the number of warheads was entirely divorced from any need for them. As early as 1954, in an editorial "The Bang Gets Bigger—Why?" the *New Republic* asked;

> What is the purpose of doubling and tripling our thermonuclear weapons? The largest possible enemy target that they are intended to obliterate is Moscow. Five million humans live in Moscow's 235 square miles; the five megaton bomb was powerful enough to devastate this area.
>
> No other potential target approaches Moscow in size. So, forsaking all other considerations, what military justification is there for a 12 megaton bomb?[86]

There was no answer then; there has never been one.[87] As J. Carson Mark, who retired in 1973 as head of the theoretical division of the Los Alamos Scientific Laboratory wrote a decade later, warhead goals were set in accordance with the beliefs of the most rabid nuclear promoters in Congress, Senators Brien McMahon and Henry M. Jackson, both of whom publicly stated that the United States should possess every nuclear weapon that it could possibly manufacture. As Mark observed, these goals "did not reflect any judgment of what might actually be needed in the event of a war."[88]

Accurate charges of overkill in the 1950s and later seemed to legitimate charges of overkill levied at the Hiroshima and Nagasaki bombs.

Survivability: How many converts to the atomic diplomacy thesis were made by reaction to the unbelievable claims of cold warriors such as Edward Teller and Herman Kahn that we could survive a nuclear war?[89]

Preventive war: Air force general Orvil Anderson, by April 1950 commandant of the Air War College and a convert to an unlimited nuclear arsenal, told a reporter in August of that year that the fighting had already begun (in Korea), and that he would have no trouble explaining to Christ why he wanted to "break up Russia's five A-bomb nests in a week."[90] Secretary of the Navy Francis P. Matthews, during a ceremony at Boston Naval Shipyard, declared that we should be willing to institute a war "to compel cooperation for peace."[91] Secretary of Defense Louis Johnson was saying the same thing privately. Anderson and Matthews were fired. Even some of the supporters of a limited nuclear arsenal were appalled. But the idea was out in plain sight.

Fallout from testing has been discussed very briefly here; its repercussions were widespread.[92] Tests at the Pacific site, above-ground tests in Nevada, and underground tests after the Limited Test Ban Treaty all caused damage to people. The AEC did its best to keep the lid on. Stewart Udall describes this contemptible effort in a section of his book titled, "Big Lies, Big Cover-Ups."[93] To this scenario he had been a witness, and his accounts are corroborated by a long string of whistle-blowers and investigative reporters, some still on AEC payrolls when they first exposed the commission's mendacity. Two of the most vocal whistle blowers, John Gofman and Arthur Tamplin, were prestigious enough to rate photographs in J. Samuel Walker's authorized study of the AEC from 1963 to 1971.[94]

Walker devotes twenty-six pages to Gofman and Tamplin as critics of AEC's radiation standards. They are treated gingerly until the final paragraph. There Walker expresses his basic support of the Commission:

> Gofman and Tamplin's contribution to the debate over radiation was more rhetorical than substantive. . . . While Gofman and Tamplin succeeded in helping prompt the AEC to tighten its regulations, they also needlessly alarmed the public with their implausible estimates of cancer potentially caused by nuclear power and their allegations that the AEC was indifferent to the hazards of radioactivity. They did not offer their views as constructive criticism but as immutable and incontestable truth. Gofman and Tamplin had some valid complaints about their treatment by the AEC . . . but this hardly seemed to justify *the self-*

righteous, uncharitable, and often inaccurate allegations they levelled at the AEC and others who questioned their positions. [italics added][95]

Significantly, Walker does not record the outcome of a long study by the National Academy of Sciences, which was reported well within the time frame of his book. *The New York Times* did record this study: Anthony Ripley, in "Political Shifts Threaten Growth of Atomic Power," 26 March 1972, says that the AEC had been forced to change its role from ally of the nuclear industry to arbiter. Partly, this was due to environmentalists' victories in safety litigations. But there was a new factor: "In addition, critics of the nuclear industry who were routinely ridiculed or dismissed as 'kooks' for almost two decades are now finding willing ears on both the Atomic Energy Commission and the Congressional Joint Committee on Atomic Energy." As to the credibility of the two critics whom Walker derogates as "needlessly alarming the public":

> A committee of the National Academy of Sciences and National Research Council reported in a long study that the amount of radiation allowable for the general population should be lowered. This was seen as vindicating the position of two dissident scientists at the Lawrence Livermore Laboratory of the commission, Arthur Tamplin and John Gofman.[96]

Did Gofman and Tamplin needlessly alarm the public? Perhaps. But their excess looks good compared to the "self-righteous, uncharitable" inaccuracies of the AEC.[97] Gofman and Tamplin will enter the Pearly Gates long before Lewis Strauss, Merrill Eisenbud, Edward Teller, Glenn Seaborg and their host of prevaricating underlings transit Purgatory.

There is no question what independent scholars—meaning those not on government or industry payrolls—think about the credibility of nuclear industry advocates in power disputes. J. William Fulbright, observing the equally contentious course of the Vietnam War, endorsed the cynical but warranted opinion that academic expertise was no less marketable than boxes of detergent on the grocery shelf.[98] H. Jack Geiger's "Generations of Poison and Lies" in the 5 August 1990 *New York Times* represents the conclusions of an independent group of physicians who studied fallout from Hanford and other AEC installations. He found that even more contemptible than actual damage to humans was concealing from them the extent to which they had been exposed: "Secrecy is the ultimate crime."[99]

George Wald, Nobelist in Physiology/Medicine, analyzed AEC credibility in 1976. In "The Nuclear Power-Truth Maze," Wald found the whistle-blowers usually accurate, and AEC officials willing to compromise on safety to promote the nuclear industry—even when those officials were hired from the best universities.[100]

Daniel Ford's *The Cult of the Atom*, written in 1982 when large numbers of internal AEC documents were becoming available, shows in chilling detail how the commission stonewalled, suppressed, denied, and ignored the warnings of its own safety experts.[101] To adopt new and more stringent safety standards in the 1980s would be to acknowledge that the whistle blowers were right; AEC had been derelict all along. The incident at Three Mile Island had proven it. Three major design faults that AEC safety people had repeatedly warned against had combined with inept operators to produce "one of the worst industrial accidents in history."[102]

The AEC successors to Manhattan were involved in other absurdities, but since these do not involve damage to people, only to the planet, I mention them but briefly.

The atomic establishment proclaimed time and again that far from being a menace to mankind, atomic power would usher in a shining age of health and affluence. Electricity would be too cheap to meter. The deserts would be made to bloom, mountains would be leveled, a sea-level canal in Panama would be dug with a few H-bombs, medical use of isotopes would all but end disease, airplanes would be built that would cross oceans on a thimbleful of fuel.[103] The bankruptcy of all these fantasies reinforced suspicions of the whole nuclear enterprise, going back to the beginning.

Official histories of the AEC and its successors, enlightening as they may be, are still official histories. They may reveal more than just the tip of the iceberg, but there is a vast arena of hidden activities. Energy Secretary Hazel O'Leary has courageously led the Clinton administration in exposing many secrets from the early years of the atom. The Committee on Human Radiation Experiments, established on her recommendation, has begun to present its findings.[104] They reinforce critics of the atomic establishment, and help explain a resurgence of Truman-bashing. Some of it is justified; Truman was too quick to hit the panic button in 1950, for instance. But the bombs on Hiroshima and Nagasaki were necessary to end a vicious war. What came after was a new dispensation.

•　　　•　　　•

The arrogance and mendacity of the atomic establishment were exacerbated by a number of domestic and international events. By 1949, the Cold War and its domestic analog, the witch hunt, dominated American media and afflicted the conduct of government.[105] These were two sides of the same coin, both fueled by American anticommunism and messianism, by Soviet truculence and early acquisition of nuclear weapons, and by discoveries of Soviet espionage that apparently gave the Russians atomic secrets.

These shocks of mid-century explain much of what followed. Domestic and international events were interwoven, bringing on massive armaments and hysteria about subversion. There is no clear starting point for this process, but the sixteen months from September 1949 to December 1950 were particularly virulent. By the end of 1950, the United States was firmly in the grip of megadeath merchants and loyalty inquisitors.

In September 1949, the Soviet Union exploded an atomic device, announced by Truman on 23 September. This was years earlier than some had predicted. On 1 October, Mao Tse-tung proclaimed the existence of the People's Republic of China, ending hopes of a vast American constituency for the triumph of China's great Christian leader, Chiang Kai-shek.

On 21 January 1950, a federal court convicted former State Department official Alger Hiss of perjury for denying that he had spied for the Soviet Union. Truman announced his decision to build hydrogen bombs, each thousands of times more destructive than the Hiroshima bomb, on 30 January. On 3 February, Klaus Fuchs, a physicist who had worked at Los Alamos, confessed giving atomic information to the Soviets.

Sen. Joseph McCarthy of Wisconsin began his red-baiting career 9 February in a speech at Wheeling, West Virginia. A short time later he fingered Owen Lattimore, a sinologue at Johns Hopkins University, as the "top Soviet spy" in the United States, and the boss of Alger Hiss.

On 25 June, North Korea attacked across the 38th parallel, providing what many thought was proof that the Soviet plan for aggressive world conquest was under way. Truman quickly moved to defend South Korea. On 17 July, Julius and Ethel Rosenberg were arrested for atomic spying. In September 1950, Truman approved NSC-68, a blueprint for massive increases in all defense categories.[106]

Perhaps the most fateful event was in October, when Chinese Communist armies joined the war in Korea, first in a brief skirmish, then on 28 November in a full scale attack, decimating the U.S. Eighth Army and forcing it into inglorious retreat. Less talked about, but on the domestic front more consequential than McCarthy's rantings, on 21 December Patrick Anthony McCarran, senator from Nevada and a fanatical anticommunist, established under his Senate Committee on the Judiciary a Subcommittee on Internal Security, which for a decade paced the inquisition.[107]

These happenings help explain the growth of nuclear overkill and anticommunist hysteria, but they are not justifications.[108]

During this crucial mid-century period, resistance to such chauvinistic excesses was relatively weak. Peace forces, antinuclear activists, and Hiroshima cultists were largely quiescent. The scientists' movement ran its course, lending in the process some strength to the movement for a world federation that would have sovereign powers over weapons.[109] But that too failed to change the rush of the major powers to build nuclear arsenals. The War Resister's League, Fellowship of Reconciliation, Henry Wallace's Progressive Party campaign for the presidency in 1948, and various lesser organizations struggled but failed in the cause of peace and disarmament.

Nineteen fifty-seven was the year of rebirth for the peace and antinuclear forces. There are two major explanations of what happened. Spencer Weart places emphasis on the shock of Sputnik, which promised swift delivery of nuclear warheads to distant targets.[110] Lawrence Wittner believes the fallout damage from nuclear testing was the major factor.[111] In any case, activists such as J.B. Priestly in Britain and Norman Cousins in the United States spearheaded a new antinuclear drive. Britain's Campaign for Nuclear Disarmament and America's National Committee for a SANE Nuclear Policy became broad-based channels for public protest.

Whatever the primary stimulus for the 1957 revival, the underlying foundation was still the spectacle of 1945. Weart notes:

> The movement's message was embodied in a set of familiar images, bundled together and thrust in the public's face. A British pamphlet explained how bombs would kill people everywhere "in a lingering and horribly painful manner . . . just as they are still dying in Hiroshima." This was the movement's most characteristic picture, the world as Hiroshima.[112]

The most explosive popular protest, however, came in the 1960s with the war in Vietnam. Attempting to suppress the forces of Ho Chi Minh, a veteran Communist, by working through a puppet anti-Communist regime in the southern part of Vietnam was arguably the worst blunder in American foreign policy. Citizen outrage at that brutal war not only set college campuses ablaze, it brought out a middle class constituency that believed the government was lying and not to be trusted.[113] Many who became disillusioned with American terror bombing in Vietnam became converts to the Hiroshima guilt trip.

There is a significant generational difference here. Converts to the Hiroshima cult among those who had reached adulthood during World War II are few. Mark Stoler once put the matter to me beautifully, "For the generation that fought World War II, the bomb ended the greatest horror of their lives. For their children, the bomb began the greatest horror of their lives." Any teacher who has plumbed the attitudes of the 1960s generation knows how powerful and widespread the disillusionment of the young became. Government lies, area bombing of Vietnamese peasants, chemical defoliants, massacres such as My Lai, and the killings at Kent State caused millions of young people to distrust their parents and country. This was the climate of revolt from which the Hiroshima Cult obtained its adherents.

Paul Boyer, who in one chapter seems to argue that Vietnam was so all-absorbing that antinuclear sentiment took a backseat during those protests, observes in another that P.M.S. Blackett's anti-Hiroshima book got a serious hearing for the first time in the cultural and political climate of the 1960s.[114] Stewart Udall explicitly identifies his "moral qualms" about Vietnam as the stimulus that led him to think about and question his former heroes, Stimson and Truman, decide that the entire atomic fraternity was corrupt, and finally come to membership in the Japanese-as-victims cult.[115]

Barton Bernstein, in his 1974 review of the bomb controversy, writes that the atomic diplomacy position of William Appleman Williams "met indifference or hostility until the mid-sixties when opposition to the Vietnam War created sympathy for critical analyses of American foreign policy."[116] Gaddis Smith, reviewing Gar Alperovitz's second edition for the *New York Times* in 1985, notes that although the book never mentioned Vietnam, its attack on U.S. foreign policy aroused strong feelings, pro or con, among the disputants on Vietnam.[117] J. Samuel Walker's review of the 1974 to 1989 literature on the bomb controversy also credits Vietnam with part of the attention paid to Alperovitz.[118]

Hostility toward the Hiroshima bombing underlay much of the anti-Vietnam War literature; often it surfaced. *Teach-ins: USA* noted that opponents of the University of Michigan teach-in knew that the best way to get under the skin of the participants was with "Drop the Bomb" signs.[119] William A. Williams used the imagery of "a moral A-bomb" to describe the American course in Vietnam. Arthur Waskow denigrated thermonuclear weapons; Anatol Rapoport talked about nuclear age dehumanization; Eric Bentley deplored Hiroshima as retribution by the United States and wondered if we were also "evening up the score" in Vietnam. On the British side, Bertrand Russell's slim volume *War Crimes in Vietnam* has six references to Hiroshima or nuclear war.[120]

American willingness to terror bomb another Asian nation, which so powerfully influenced Japanese opinion, also impressed some Americans. Many suspected, correctly, that Richard Nixon wanted to use nukes on Vietnam. In April 1972, Vietnam Veterans Against the War heard from a GI in Hawaii that nuclear weapons were targeted on Hanoi. As Tom Wells reports, after this news (rumor?) got out, "Protesters responded with leaflets, rallies, traffic stoppages, building occupations, and student strikes in scores of cities."[121]

How this terrible war worked in the minds of many Americans can best be seen in the anguished account of Stewart Udall. In a chapter titled "Notes on a Journey," he tells how as a Johnson administration cabinet officer he gradually came to question the war; how his congressman-brother Morris came out publicly against it; and then the biggest crisis "in the fall of 1969 when Scott, our second son, deserted the army and sought refuge in Canada."[122] This was the beginning of his long journey to a repudiation not only of the atomic-military establishment of the 1960s, but of the Truman administration that he had once proudly supported.

Without Vietnam, the Japanese-as-victims cult in the United States would still be puny. In Japan, need for a counterweight to its own evil deeds made Hiroshima a strategic and welcome symbol. And the United States played into its hands.

8

What if the Bomb Had Not Been Used?

Overshadowing every other consideration, continuation of the Pacific War, had Truman not used atomic bombs in August, would have produced unmitigated evil. The extent of the evil would have depended on the duration of the war. Hiroshima cultists' fanaticism blinds them to everything except the casualties from the atom. The prospect, however, was for far greater casualties, from (1) continued Japanese mistreatment of prisoners and slave laborers; (2) intensified disruption of food supplies and transportation throughout the empire; (3) continued land and sea battles with losses like that of the *Indianapolis*; and (4) continued conventional bombing by Gen. Curtis LeMay's B-29s. These things together would have produced *monthly death rates* well in excess of the Hiroshima-Nagasaki total.[1]

Assume that the war had gone on just until 1 November, which was X-Day for OLYMPIC, and Paul Nitze's target date for probable Japanese surrender without bombs or Russians. In those two and one-half months, we would have seen the following.

(1) Conditions in the POW and labor camps would have deteriorated faster than before, due to destruction of transport, Japanese rage at continued Allied victories, Terauchi's orders to kill all prisoners when the Allies invaded Singapore, and accelerated effects of nutritional inadequacies. There would have been lowered resistance of prisoners, and greatly increased mortality. The 200,000-400,000 persons in Terauchi's jurisdiction would have been exterminated.[2]

Photographs of prisoners released from Japanese camps in the late summer and fall of 1945 show emaciation comparable to prisoners found in Hitler's concentration camps. All observers of the end of the Pacific War agree: starvation and disease were taking a higher toll every week. The testimony of a prominent British observer is typical:

185

As British troops moved into the occupied territories, the Supreme Commander's wife, Lady Edwina Mountbatten, often went ahead of them on a tour of prison camps in her role as head of St. John's Ambulance. She reported later, "There is no doubt that had the war gone on a few more weeks there would have been no prisoners left alive. They were absolutely at their last gasp in the Dutch East Indies area, and the tragedy is that so many did die in the last weeks before the surrender, and even after it."

Mrs. Vivian Skinner was a Queen Alexandra nursing sister with the Relief Agency for Prisoners-of-War and Internees. . . . She told the author, "There is no doubt many of those who died in the last weeks would have still been alive had the Japanese not hoarded drugs and insulin. There were plenty in their stores."[3]

There is no countervailing testimony. The prisoners were at death's door—despised and neglected by a bushido management that saw surrender as cowardly.

(2) Starvation of indigenous peoples throughout East Asia, South Asia, and the Pacific would have increased markedly. This starvation was not well publicized. In wartime, news is defined as the events and outcomes of military struggles, not as difficulties in the lives of civilians. Hiroshima cultists particularly avoid coming to grips with the havoc wreaked on populations conquered by the Japanese. Their travail does not seem to be worthy of note.

Fortunately, the United Nations Economic and Social Council established a Working Group for Asia and the Far East, which was charged with surveying war damage. This group reported to Lake Success (original location of the United Nations) in 1947. Recall that the British blockade of Germany in World War I only caused mass starvation toward the end. Note that the disruptive effect of Japanese conquest peaked in the closing months of the war, when food-producing areas were being fought over for the second time, and prewar stocks had disappeared. Consider these UN findings, not on the most populous country, China, which was covered by American reporters and hence whose problems were known in the United States, but on countries that figure not at all in the American calculus of war damage. On Indonesia:

All of the male and most of the female European population totalling 130,000 was interned, and from 500,000 to 1,000,000 Indonesians as well as many Chinese were used for forced labour.

About 30,000 Europeans and 300,000 Indonesian internees and forced labourers died during the occupation. The health of the half million labourers on the estates was so seriously affected by their starvation-diet that they were useless as workers after the liberation. The total number who were killed by the Japanese, or who died from hunger, disease, and lack of medical attention is estimated at 3,000,000 for Java alone, and 1,000,000 for the Outer Islands.[4]

On India:

Although the war directly touched Indian soil only in the north-eastern corner and the Andaman and Nicobar Islands, and involved several east coast cities in comparatively minor air raids, India emerged from the war with great damage and loss to her man-power and resources. India's military casualties were about 180,000 killed, wounded, and missing. It is estimated that 130 million Indians suffered from under-nourishment under the best peacetime conditions. The poor harvest coinciding with the elimination of rice exports from Burma and the diversion to military purposes of transit needed to move grain from surplus to deficiency areas had tragic results. These factors were mainly responsible for a famine in Bengal which resulted in a million and a half deaths.[5]

Japan was responsible for these deaths. How many more would have been caused between 15 August and 1 November had the atom bomb not been dropped we can never know.

(3) Fighting continued, in August 1945, even though the last major land battle for Americans (Okinawa) was over. There were still skirmishes in the Philippines, Java, and Southeast Asia. Japanese submarines still roamed the seas, as did those of the Allies. The military killing fields were on the wane, in contrast to slaughters elsewhere; but kamikazes, torpedoes, and naval gunfire still took a toll.

(4) Many thousands of Japanese on the home islands would have been killed by LeMay's bombers. Some Hiroshima cultists deny this, claiming that conventional bombing of cities "had been made a low priority by August 1945 on the basis of Air Force experience in Europe."[6] This is false. Priority for transportation targets, lesser priority for urban bombing, may have been put on paper by the Joint Target Committee after its conferences with Paul Nitze and United States Strategic Bombing Survey (USSBS) members in the summer;

this hardly determined LeMay's actions. Tactical considerations, mostly weather, made precision bombing difficult until October. Thus the Twentieth Air Force programmed "rapid destruction of a large number of Japanese cities" for late August and September. In Michael Sherry's words,

> Summer plans for future bombing campaigns, those not carried out because of the war's sudden end, measured the widening circles of the destructive impulse. When the last cities were finished off, targets would still have to be found, and it was doubtful that transportation alone could absorb all the capacity. Operations analysts proposed moving on to "all urban areas with a population greater than 30,000 peoples," some 180 towns in all. They would be wiped out by November, when it was said, "the back of Japan will have been completely broken," as if it was not already and as if planners had no idea of effecting earlier surrender.[7]

So LeMay's targets were towns containing a minimum of 5,400,000 people, to be leveled by the end of October. How many deaths? Certainly more by far than in Hiroshima and Nagasaki.

Put all these killings, even at such rock-bottom estimates, together, and 300,000 *deaths per month* seems the very least one could expect—with no atom bombs, no set-piece land battles, no kamikaze attacks on a massed invasion fleet.

And if the majority opinion of the Japanese leaders interrogated immediately after the war had turned out to be right—that the war would have lasted into 1946—the carnage doubles, or triples. Marquis Kido claimed to have saved twenty million Japanese lives by engineering an August surrender.[8] Togo Shigenori also places the anticipated slaughter *sans* atom in the millions.[9] If they exaggerate, the extent of their exaggeration measures the power of the atom's Shermanesque appearance. The atom saved many lives in the Pacific War. It also saved many lives in unfought future wars. To understand this, we must go back a century.

Alfred Nobel (1833-1896) was not just an oil magnate and a brilliant inventor, he was fluent not only in his native Swedish, but in Russian, German, French, and English. The poet Shelley influenced Nobel's literary style; his cosmopolitanism and atheism he acquired from Voltaire and Diderot. He was personally averse to quarrels and confrontations; the legal disputes over royalties from some of his inventions he attributed to lawyers in his various companies.

Though he experienced the American Civil War and the Crimean War firsthand, Nobel's biographers attribute his lifelong devotion to peace to his basic nature and extensive reading. Michael Evlanoff and Marjorie Fluor write, "His intense interest in history left him no delusions about the horrors of past wars. In days long gone, a defeated country saw its entire population enslaved, its cities burned, its women raped, its war prisoners brutally put to death. Nobel's mind whirled with these facts during his sleepless nights."[10]

Several of his female friends became active in the peace movements of the day, such as the Gesellschaft der Friedensfreunde and the Fourth World Peace Congress. His own program for peace had two components, one modest and practical, the other utopian. The first, long-term approach was to encourage agreements between governments that would require them to submit all disputes to binding international arbitration. He thus foresaw the basic principles of both the League of Nations and the United Nations. What he failed to foresee was the durability of ethnic pride and national sovereignty. But he made the prize for contributing to world peace the core of his magnificent bequests.

The other path to peace, which few today are aware of, he probably first articulated to Bertha von Suttner in 1876: "I should like to invent a substance or a machine with such terrible power of mass destruction that war would thereby be made impossible forever."[11] It was a thought that he clung to, and expressed frequently, almost to the end of his life. If explosives could only be perfected to a terrifying enough dimension, the mere knowledge of their existence would deter wars. Erik Bergengren cites Nobel as saying, "War would, as it were, choke itself."[12]

Not only did he hope that his factories would put an end to war before Bertha von Suttner's congresses could, in an 1890 statement he allegedly told the German arms magnate E. Schneider:

> A mere intensification of the deadly precision of war weapons will not secure peace for us. The limited effect of explosives is a big obstacle to this. To remedy this defect war must be made as death-dealing to the civil population at home as to the troops at the front. Let the sword of Damocles hang over every head, gentlemen, and you will witness a miracle—all war will stop short instantly, if the weapon is bacteriology.[13]

Here he anticipated Douhetian attack on whole populations, though he did not foresee atomic weapons as the means.

Did Oppenheimer and company, in 1945, finally achieve the apocalyptic fright that Nobel dreamed of more than a half century earlier?

The list of those who believe that the Hiroshima/Nagasaki inoculation discouraged major war and further use of nuclear weapons is long and impressive. Surprisingly, one of the earliest to take this position was Leo Szilard. In January 1944, arguing to Vannevar Bush that to prevent a nuclear arms race there must be international control of uranium deposits, Szilard held that this control "will hardly be possible . . . unless high efficiency atomic bombs have actually been used in this war and the fact of their destructive power had deeply penetrated the mind of the public."[14] Szilard later changed his mind about use of the bomb, but the earlier position is in his notes.

Edward Teller, too, while waffling and ambivalent about use of the bomb, wrote Szilard in July 1945 that the only hope for survival lay in getting the facts about the bomb before the people, and "For this purpose actual combat use might even be the best thing."[15] Vannevar Bush was of like mind. The atom bomb "means the end of world war. Fear will prevent it."[16]

Henry Stimson, maligned by the Hiroshima cultists, nonetheless may have been right when he concluded his 1947 analysis of the reasons behind the bombing by noting that "Hiroshima and Nagasaki . . . made it wholly clear that we must never have another war. This is the lesson men and leaders everywhere must learn, and I believe that when they learn it they will find a way to lasting peace."[17] As far as worldwide conflagrations are concerned, who can now say that he was wrong?

Truman, in November 1949, talking to David Lilienthal about reappointment to the Atomic Energy Commission, said he did not want to appoint a "military-minded civilian . . . we're going to use this [atomic power] for peace and never use it for war—I've always said this, and you'll see. It'll be like poison gas (never used again)."[18]

Asada, one of the best of the Japanese historians, concludes his analysis in "Japanese Perceptions of the A-Bomb Decision" this way:

> The last thirty-five years have been a period of unbroken international tension—full of crises, provocations, and local disputes—which

would have exhausted the patience of great powers in the pre-atomic age. But the fact remains that another world war has not occurred. It may be that the use of the "ultimate weapon" in Japan has given awesome credibility to its destructive power,which alone can function as an essential deterrent to nuclear warfare. Future historians might well postulate that Japan's A-bomb experience was a factor that deterred the use of nuclear bombs by the United States in Korea and Vietnam. Thus viewed, the victims of Hiroshima and Nagasaki were not "meaninglessly massacred," as some Japanese critics have charged. On the contrary, those victims, without knowing it, may be said to have served a "noble cause" to prevent another nuclear holocaust.[19]

The opposite position, that if atomic weapons were used once they would be used again, has prestigious backing. Einstein, Oppenheimer, and Harrison Brown believed this.[20] Events so far have not supported them.

There were occasions on which American presidents, and also Soviet general secretaries, were tempted to use nuclear weapons. The most thorough study of such matters, McGeorge Bundy's *Danger and Survival*, concludes that

> . . . since the first two bombs were dropped in August 1945 no government has used a single warhead against an enemy. In my opinion, no government has ever come close. . . . In the age of Radford and LeMay, the doctrines in which they deeply believed—that nuclear weapons should be used whenever needed, even in small wars—these doctrines were disregarded at every moment of choice. A tradition of nonuse took root and grew strong, proving itself most conspicuously in the Vietnam War, where the use of nuclear weapons was the one solution that had no serious advocate. The best consequence of that war is that it reinforced the tradition of nonuse. . . . There is no evidence that the Soviet government has ever come close to using even one of its warheads, and no evidence that Soviet bomb rattling has had any large effect anywhere.[21]

Perhaps Bundy is too optimistic about the thoughts of some presidents during the Vietnam War; about their actions, he is correct.

But consider what might have happened without the examples of Hiroshima and Nagasaki. In the bitter defeat of the Eighth Army in Korea, Truman would have been sorely tempted to use nuclear weapons. After a confusing statement in a press conference on 30

November 1950 that led reporters to believe the use of nuclear weapons was under active consideration, the outrage of the whole world descended on Washington.[22] The White House quickly issued a statement denying that Truman had authorized such use, but the furor was slow to die down. The incident showed the early strength of the inoculation.

When Eisenhower took office, Korea was still ablaze. Veiled threats were made that if the North Koreans and Chinese did not come to terms, atomic bombs would be used. Bundy believes that Secretary of State John Foster Dulles may have favored their use, and that Eisenhower was considering it; both seem to have thought this threat brought the Communists around. Bundy thinks other factors were responsible for the armistice. Whatever the situation, the tradition held.[23]

The Soviet Union might also have used nuclear weapons had there been no prudential event in 1945. The bitterness of the Sino-Soviet feud, and Soviet fear of the "Yellow Peril," caused Kremlin officials to target the People's Republic of China with nuclear missiles at one time.[24] The Soviet clearly threatened China, causing alarm, as Bundy notes, in the Nixon-Kissinger White House.[25] But both sides backed off.

None of these crises saw nuclear weapons used. John Lewis Gaddis' explanation, the growth of a tradition of self-deterrence, has much to commend it. Truman's appreciation of the horror of the atom set the pattern for the last half century. Truman said several times that the atom might never be used again, that it had to be treated differently "from rifles and cannons and ordinary things like that."[26] The result of Truman's thinking, as Gaddis says, was that "The paradox of utility residing in non-use has become a central feature of the nuclear age."[27]

This could never have happened had Truman, and the whole world, not seen the atom in all its destructive fury. No mere demonstration could have produced this outcome.

•   •   •

Yet a third major benefit is attributable to the early end of the war. The Soviet Union was unable to carry out its plans to invade and occupy at least the northernmost Japanese island, Hokkaido, hence Japan was spared the trauma of division, and the world was spared another volatile confrontation of Soviet and American forces. The Soviet Union had long wanted to avenge the 1919-1921 Japanese occupation of the Soviet Far East during the bitter war for Bolshevik control. Stalin had been promised restoration of Southern Sakhalin and the Kurile Islands at Yalta, but his ambition went beyond that. As David Holloway describes events, on 16 August Stalin wrote Truman asking that Soviet forces be allowed to accept surrender of Japanese forces in the northern half of Hokkaido. Then,

> Truman rejected this request on August 18. Stalin, however, was reluctant to give up the idea of landing Soviet forces on Hokkaido. On August 19 Marshal Vasilevskii ordered the Ist Far Eastern Front, whose forces were just about to take southern Sakhalin, to occupy the northern half of Hokkaido as well as the southern Kuriles. On August 21 Vasilevskii sent the Soviet forces a detailed plan for this operation—indicating that the General Staff had planned for this eventuality. On August 22, however, Vasilevskii rescinded the order to occupy Hokkaido . . . Stalin had evidently concluded that the attempt to land forces on Hokkaido would cause a political row—perhaps even an armed clash with the United States.[28]

Were it not obvious what a benefit exclusively American occupation of Japan was to that ravaged nation, Admiral Okada Keisuke wrote in his postwar memoirs, "And, even though Japan had to experience military defeat, what a blessing it was that at least the country was not split in two and that we were able to share our misfortunes and hardships as members of the same single Japanese nation.!"[29] The Japanese Left may not share this sentiment, but Okada certainly speaks for a majority.

Even Calvocoressi, Wint, and Pritchard, who have little good to say about Hiroshima, recognize that a divided Japan would have benefitted none but bruised Russian egos:

> Probably the existence of the bomb frustrated Russian plans for insisting on a joint occupation of Japan, and the consequences of this were incalculable. It avoided endless intrigue, and conflict of puppet parties; probably it saved Japan from a great deal of hardship and made the return to normal life in Japan much quicker. By taking out Japan as a major question of dispute, it probably made the relations of Russia and the United States that much easier to handle. It may even have kept them from war.[30]

•   •   •

Once atomic weapons were proven possible, every country with sufficient resources rushed to build them. This new nuclear arms race, sparked by Soviet-American competition, led to expenditures and genocidal capacity beyond imagining. "National Security" itself became a religion, armaments absorbed a major portion of government budgets, and large constituencies of antinuclear activists sprang up in the West.

These antinuclear efforts are wholly legitimate. The belief that the world would be better off had mankind not learned to split the atom is tenable. The pressure point for this discussion, however, is: Did the *use* of atomic bombs in Japan initiate, exacerbate, or prolong the arms race and the Cold War that accompanied it?

Hiroshima cultists often fail to distinguish between *developing* nuclear weapons, which some approved for the purpose of eliminating the Nazi threat, and the *detonation* of those weapons to end the Pacific War. In fact, most cultists assume that because nuclear weapons are now perceived as evil, the dropping of those first two rudimentary bombs was also evil.

Like the apparent preference for starving the Japanese instead of shocking them with a bomb, this judgment cannot be assumed; it must be argued. Few cultists even begin to make the argument. One who does is Stewart Udall: "Hiroshima heralded the advent of what would be called the atomic age. It also served as the starter's gun for a weapons race between the United States of America and the Union of Soviet Socialist Republics that would carry the world to the edge of a nuclear abyss."[31]

But was Hiroshima the starter's gun for a weapons race? Successful Soviet penetration of the Manhattan Project *long before Hiroshima* signalled a weapons race already going strong. Can Udall show us a plausible scenario in which Stalin abjures nuclear weapons if the United States does not use the ones it developed in 1945? Of course he cannot.

The Hiroshima and Nagasaki bombings did, however, stimulate the Soviet program. The significant question is whether this stimulus had a long-term effect on the ultimate escalation of nuclear armaments to absurdity. There is no reason to think it did.

Actual use of the bombs is difficult to disentangle from the policy of keeping their development, or trying to keep their development, secret from the Russians and the world. Perhaps had the advice of Niels Bohr, Gen. George Marshall, Henry Stimson, and others to inform Stalin fully of Anglo-American progress been followed, the Russians might not have adopted their own crash program, and the pace of the early nuclear race might have been slowed. But the fundamental ideological and geopolitical causes of Soviet-American conflict would not have been alleviated. The many provocative events on both sides of the globe did not depend on Hiroshima and Nagasaki.

The mid-century shocks to American complacency (Berlin blockade, Communist victory in China, Soviet domination of Eastern Europe, the Hiss, Rosenberg, and Fuchs cases, Korea and the defeat of the U.S. Eighth Army) would in no way have abated in the absence of Hiroshima. For the Soviets, equivalent challenges were abrupt suspension of Lend-Lease aid, amalgamation and rearmament of the Western zones of Germany, withdrawal of support from UNRRA, Secretary James Byrnes' provocative Stuttgart speech of September 1946, Kennan's X article, the Truman Doctrine, the Operation Crossroads atomic tests of July 1946, and so on.[32]

Had there been no use of the bombs, one early stage of the Soviet-American arms race might have been delayed, but the race itself would have gone on, much as if Stalin had given his first order for all-out development not after Hiroshima, but after Byrnes brandished atomic weapons at the September 1945 Council of Foreign Ministers Conference in London. The prime stimuli for the arms race did not occur in August 1945; they came after the United States developed its visceral fear of Soviet aggression, and the Soviet Union reciprocated.

David Holloway, the most authoritative expositor of the Soviet nuclear program, summarizes his chapter on "Hiroshima":

> Stalin had not taken the atomic bomb seriously until Hiroshima had shown in the most dramatic way that it could be built. The Soviet Union now mobilized its resources to catch up. These reasons for building the bomb—to restore the emerging balance of power, and to acquire a new and potent symbol of power—would have existed even if Niels Bohr's advice to inform Stalin had been followed. The bomb would still have affected the balance of power, and would still have been a symbol of the economic and technological might of the state. Stalin would still have wanted a bomb of his own.[33]

If Holloway is right, Martin Sherwin's castigation of Truman miscarries. Sherwin labels the Franck Report as prescient, and says the American "proclaimed desire of having such weapons abolished by international agreement" will not be credible to other nations *because* we used the bomb in secret and without warning. Thus "Hiroshima and Nagasaki, the culmination of the process, became the symbols of a new American barbarism, reinforcing charges, with dramatic circumstantial evidence, that the policies of the United States contributed to the origins of the Cold War."[34]

Of course many American actions contributed to the origins of the Cold War. But the "barbarism" of terror bombing was established at Guernica, Warsaw, Hamburg, Dresden, and Tokyo. American "barbarism" at least had a therapeutic outcome. Einstein is right, "The Allies responded in kind . . . with greater effectiveness—and they were morally justified in doing so."[35]

There is another counterfactual hypothesis to consider here. Suppose, instead of using the new weapon on Japan in 1945, Truman had first used atomic bombs against Soviet allies (North Korea, China) who were chewing up MacArthur's troops in the Battle of the Chongchon River, Korea, November 1950.[36] What pace would the arms race have attained then?

Possession of nuclear weapons did reinforce American messianism and truculence. Gar Alperovitz and Kai Bird may be right in believing that without nuclear weapons, the United States might not have rearmed Germany nor intervened in the Korean War.[37] But this is irrelevant to the Hiroshima question. Truman did not let this genie out of the bottle. The United States would have had nuclear weapons as soon as it did no matter who was president. And in all probability, any president would have made ending the war quickly with minimum loss of life his top priority, would have known from intercepts that the Japanese peace party was impotent and the dominant generals were determined to fight a final battle of the homeland, and would have brought the new weapon into play exactly as Truman did. One would hope, however, that with the war over, a different president might not have succumbed so quickly to the chimera of national security, or have gone off as eagerly in search of places to intervene against Communism.[38]

•   •   •

One argument against use of the bomb against Japan does score. Karel van Wolferen is assuredly right that if the bombs had not been dropped, the Japanese cult of victimhood could not have grown as fast:

> Mushroom clouds, it sometimes seems, have become all but mandatory in the war films made by the established Japanese studios. Here is victimhood in its ultimate guise: the atomic bombing of Hiroshima and Nagasaki. The belief in Japanese uniqueness has received very special support from these events: the Japanese did not just suffer, they suffered uniquely; one might even speak of national martyrdom. It has become common in Japan to consider the dropping of the atomic bomb as the worst act of the war. Some even see it as the crime of the century. . . . And for a week in August the nation indulges in a media-generated display of self-pity. . . . Hiroshima is lifted out of history; it is a shrine to Japanese martyrdom.[39]

Who can gainsay this analysis? Of course, the firebombing of Japanese cities would have led to a victimhood cult of some dimension. No conceivable ending of the war could have given the Japanese a sense of their own responsibility for what befell them. They did not see, and their military did not tell them, how horribly the millions died who were their victims. But Hiroshima and Nagasaki were the perfect focus for martyrdom.

Does this victimization argument, the creation of martyrdom, outweigh the good that was done by ending the war so early? Assuredly not, especially since we cannot know how long it would have gone on, how massive the destruction would have been in Japan, or how many of all races and peoples would have been liquidated in the death throes of the empire. We will have to live with the martyrdom sanctioned by Hiroshima. Many of us would not have lived at all had those first two bombs not been used.

Notes

Chapter 1: Why Did Truman Drop the Bomb?

1. John Ray Skates, *The Invasion of Japan: Alternative to the Bomb* (Columbia: University of South Carolina Press, 1994), 69.
2. Omar Bradley and Clay Blair, *A General's Life* (New York: Simon and Schuster, 1983), 172.
3. Geoffrey Perrett, *Days of Sadness, Years of Triumph* (Baltimore: Penguin, 1974), 410.
4. Douglas MacArthur, *Reports of General MacArthur, The Campaigns of MacArthur in the Pacific*, vol. 1 (Washington, D.C.: Government Printing Office, 1966), 394.
5. Samuel A. Stouffer, et al, *The American Soldier: Combat and Its Aftermath*, vol. 2 (Princeton: Princeton University Press, 1949), 469.
6. Maurice Matloff, *Strategic Planning for Coalition Warfare, 1943-1944* (Washington, D.C.: Government Printing Office, 1959), 5.
7. Glen H. Perry, *"Dear Bart": Washington Views of World War II* (Westport, Conn.: Greenwood, 1982), 249.
8. Ronald H. Spector, *Eagle Against the Sun* (New York: Free Press, 1985), 494-502.
9. Cited in John Toland, *The Rising Sun* (New York: Bantam, 1970), 745. William L. O'Neill, in *A Democracy at War* (New York: Free Press, 1993), 416, takes the same view of "casualty shock" at this time; it induced Marshall to consider use of poison gas. Although most Americans considered it unpatriotic to criticize the war effort, Hearst, Scripps-Howard, McCormick-Patterson, and a few other anti-Roosevelt and generally isolationist newspapers complained that American commanders were too indifferent to the safety of their soldiers. Battles that came in for criticism in the Pacific War were Attu, Peleliu, Tarawa, and Iwo Jima. See Spector, *Eagle*, 181, 259, 266, 420, 494-503.
10. Toland, *Rising*, 746.

199

11. Cited in Charles F. Brower IV, "Sophisticated Strategist: General George A. Lincoln and the Defeat of Japan, 1944-45," *Diplomatic History* 15 (Summer 1991): 326. See also Conrad C. Crane, *Bombs, Cities, and Civilians* (Lawrence: University Press of Kansas, 1993), 136.

12. Brower considers the long dispute over whether siege or invasion was the best way to induce surrender of Japan. The argument went on almost to the end of the war, with Marshall usually winning.

13. Hanson Baldwin, *Battles Lost and Won* (New York: Harper & Row, 1966), 380.

14. Roy E. Appleman, et al, *Okinawa: The Last Battle* (Washington, D.C.: Department of the Army, 1948), 473. Gerhard L. Weinberg notes the absence of any reference to the trauma of Okinawa in several prominent discussions of the decision to drop the bomb; see "Some Thoughts on World War II," *Journal of Military History* 56 (October 1992): 667. The historical context of the Okinawa battle is well presented in Ian Gow, *Okinawa 1945: Gateway to Japan* (Garden City, N.J.: Doubleday, 1985); and in George Feifer, *Tennozan: The Battle of Okinawa and the Atomic Bomb* (New York: Ticknor and Fields, 1992).

15. On the Masada mass suicide, see Yigael Yadin, *Masada* (New York: Random House, 1966).

16. Most accounts of the war state that no organized Japanese unit surrendered. There was one, however; see "Daily Summary of Enemy Intelligence," G-2 Estimate of the Enemy Situation, No. 1196, 13/14 Jul 1945, Quintin S. Lander Papers, Box 12, U.S. Army Military History Institute, Carlisle Barracks, Pa.; also No. 1211. Lt. Col. Takenaga of the Japanese 1st Independent Mixed Battalion surrendered on 3 May with 5 other officers, 4 warrant officers, and 33 enlisted men, in the Wewak area of New Guinea.

17. Spector, 540. The suicide factor is also discussed in John W. Dower, *War Without Mercy* (New York: Pantheon, 1986), chap. 3.

18. Murakami Hyoe, *Japan: The Years of Trial, 1919-52* (Tokyo: Japan Culture Institute, 1982), 135-41, 151.

19. Ruth Benedict, *The Chrysanthemum and the Sword* (Boston: Houghton Mifflin, 1946).

20. Tsurumi Shunsuke, *An Intellectual History of Wartime Japan* (London and New York: KPI, 1986), 81.

21. Charlotte Carr-Gregg, *Japanese Prisoners of War in Revolt* (New York; St. Martin's Press, 1978).

22. Asada Teruhiko, *The Night of a Thousand Suicides* (New York: St. Martin's Press, 1972).

23. C.C.S. 643/3, Estimate of the Enemy Situation, 6 July 1945, C.C.S. 381 (6-4-43), sec. 2, pt. 5, Records of the JCS, RG 218, NA; Gar Alperovitz,

Atomic Diplomacy: Hiroshima and Potsdam (New York: Penguin, 1985), expanded and updated edition, 28.

24. Michael S. Sherry, *The Rise of American Air Power* (New Haven: Yale University Press, 1987), 297, 409.

25. Tien-wei Wu, "An Exhibit of World War II in Asia Without Chinese Holocaust Would be Incomplete," typescript in possession of Professor Wu at Southern Illinois University, Carbondale, 1994, 3.

26. Nakamura Masanori, *The Japanese Monarchy* (Armonk, N.Y.: M.E. Sharpe, 1992), 69.

27. P.J. Philip, "6,300 Canadian Soldiers AWOL of 15,600 Called to Go Overseas," *New York Times*, 21 January 1945.

28. Hanson Baldwin, "The 'Let Down' Problem," *New York Times*, 2 April 1945.

29. Robert F. Futrell, *Ideas, Concepts, Doctrine: Basic Thinking in the United States Air Force, 1907-1960* (Maxwell Air Force Base, Alabama: Air University Press, 1989), 164.

30. Brower, 325.

31. JCS 924/15, Rpt by JSP, sub: Pacific Strategy, 25 April 1945; cited in U.S. Department of Defense, *The Entry of the Soviet Union into the War Against Japan* (Washington, D.C.: Government Printing Office, 1955), 65.

32. Edward J. Drea, *MacArthur's ULTRA: Codebreaking and the War Against Japan* (Lawrence: University Press of Kansas, 1992), 204.

33. Drea, 207, 209.

34. Bruce Rae, "Okinawa is a Lesson for Invasion of Japan," *New York Times*, 27 May 1945.

35. "Army Bars Relaxing Its Discharge Rules In View of Bitter Battles in the Pacific," *New York Times*, 1 June 1945.

36. Robert J.C. Butow, *Japan's Decision to Surrender* (Stanford: Stanford University Press, 1954), 69.

37. U.S. Department of Defense, *Entry of the Soviet Union*, 76.

38. Robert H. Ferrell, ed., *Off The Record: The Private Papers of Harry S. Truman* (New York: Harper & Row, 1980), 47.

39. Drea, 209-10.

40. Ibid., 223.

41. Ibid., 210.

42. Forrest C. Pogue, *George C. Marshall, Statesman* (New York: Viking, 1987), 18.

43. Minutes of Meeting Held at the White House on Monday, 18 June 1945 at 1530, *Foreign Relations of the United States* (Hereafter *FRUS*) *The Conference of Berlin (Potsdam) 1945*, vol. 1 (Washington, D.C.: Government Printing Office, 1960), 905.

44. The most prominent analysis of prospective OLYMPIC casualties is Barton Bernstein, "A postwar myth: 500,000 U.S. lives saved," *Bulletin of the Atomic Scientists* 42 (June/July 1986): 38-40. In 1994, Bernstein reanalyzed the relevant documents and advised the Smithsonian curators that the Truman administration's estimate of casualties was 63,000 rather than the earlier figure Bernstein put at 229,000. See Eugene L. Meyer, "Smithsonian Stands Firm On A-Bomb Exhibit," *Washington Post,* 19 January 1995; and John Kifner, "Hiroshima: A Controversy That Refuses to Die," *New York Times,* 31 January 1995. This new figure was accepted by the Smithsonian, triggering a bitter attack from veteran's groups, which had accepted the earlier figure. This numbers game will go on forever. More important, however, Bernstein accepts Truman's great concern to minimize American casualties; 63,000 was far too many. Truman biographers agree; the president was casualty-shy. See Robert H. Ferrell, *Harry S. Truman: A Life* (Columbia: University of Missouri Press, 1994); 210-17, and David McCullough, *Truman* (New York: Simon and Schuster, 1992), 399-401.

45. *FRUS, Berlin,* 907.

46. Ibid., 909.

47. Drea, 222.

48. Denis Warner, Peggy Warner, and Commander Sadao Seno, *The Sacred Warriors: Japan's Suicide Legions* (New York: Van Nostrand Reinhold, 1982), 298.

49. Gar Alperovitz, "Beyond the Smithsonian Flap: Historians' New Consensus," *Washington Post,* 16 October 1994.

50. "Buck's Last Fight," *Time* (25 June 1945): 30.

51. Spector, 543.

52. *FRUS, Berlin,* 873-83. See also Butow, 25, on the control of Japan's government by the militarists. Loose talk about "Japan was ready to surrender" occurs in all Hiroshima cultists' accounts. This is based on two errors: (1) accepting the U.S. Strategic Bombing Survey conclusions as legitimate, and (2) semantic legerdemain—confusing the elitist but impotent peace party with "Japan." The Japanese state was simply not controlled by the peace party.

53. Butow, 75. This account of Japanese overtures to Moscow depends largely on Butow chap. 6.

54. Ibid., chap. 9.

55. Alperovitz, *Atomic,* 225.

56. Butow, chap. 9.

57. Truman, in Ferrell, 56.

58. Geoffrey Warner, "To End a War: The Decision to Drop the Bomb," in David Carlton and Herbert M. Levine, eds., *The Cold War Debated* (New York: McGraw-Hill, 1988), 38.

59. Truman, in Ferrell, 49. Alperovitz, *Atomic*, 51, truncates and thus misrepresents this passage.
60. Ibid., 53-54.
61. Butow, 142-49. Alperovitz misrepresents Truman here also (233). Truman did not translate *mokusatsu*, the press did.
62. G-2 Estimate of the Enemy Situation, Summary 1202; see note 12.
63. Undated, untitled document beginning "The paramount consideration in strategic air attack . . ." Box 21, folder July 1945, Papers of Carl A. Spaatz, LC. These JTG-USSBS meetings are described from the perspective of Paul Nitze in chapter two.
64. "Report on USSBS and JTG Conferences," undated, Box 21, Spaatz Papers.
65. Undated, untitled document beginning "In examining the similarities and differences . . . ." Box 21, Spaatz Papers.
66. *FRUS, Berlin*, 2: 1291.
67. Butow, 142-43.
68. G-2 General HQ U.S. Army Forces, Pacific (Willoughby) to G-3 (same HQ) 28 July 1945, S.J. Chamberlin Papers, U.S. Army Military History Institute, Carlisle Barracks, Penn.
69. Willoughby in Drea, 216.
70. Drea, 222.
71. Truman to James L. Cate, 12 January 1953, in Wesley F. Craven and James L. Cate, eds., *The Army Air Forces in World War II, Vol. 5, The Pacific: Matterhorn to Nagasaki* (Chicago: University of Chicago Press, 1953), 712-13.
72. Drea, 222.
73. "Medical Service in the Asiatic and Pacific Theaters," unpublished ms., Center of Military History, Washington, D.C., chap. 15, "From Olympic to Blacklist," 18.
74. W.B. Shockley to Edward L. Bowles, 21 July 1945, Proposal for Increasing the Scope of Casualty Studies, Edward L. Bowles Papers, Box 34, LC.
75. Robert L. Messer, "New Evidence on Truman's Decision," *Bulletin of the Atomic Scientists* 41 (August 1985): 55.
76. HQ Sixth Army, *G-2 Estimate of the Enemy Situation, Olympic Operation*, Box 1843, RG 165, NA.
77. Joint Intelligence Committee, *Japanese Reaction to an Assault Against Northern Honshu*, 6 August 1945, JCS/CCS 381, Box 615, RG 218, NA; Joint War Plans Committee 398/1, *Plan for the Invasion of Northern Honshu*, 9 August 1945, Box 615, RG 218, NA.
78. Maj. Gen. Clayton Bissell, Memorandum for the Chief of Staff, "Estimate of Japanese Situation for Next 30 Days," 12 August 1945, File #2, Box 12, OPD Executive Files, RG 165, NA.

79. See Butow, chap. 10.
80. John W. Dower, "Rethinking World War II in Asia," *Reviews in American History* 12 (June 1994): 165. See also Karel van Wolferen, *The Enigma of Japanese Power* (New York: Knopf, 1989), 416: "Theories about Japanese readiness to stop fighting before Hiroshima are not based on convincing evidence and reveal ignorance concerning the Japanese political system of the times. They overlook the fact that in 1945 there was no apparatus in Japan that could have chosen peace and rendered any peace negotiations credible."
81. Gar Alperovitz, "Did We Have to Drop the Bomb?" *New York Times,* 3 August 1989.
82. See note 49. When I explained how ill-informed Col. Ennis was ("What New Consensus?" *Washington Post,* 30 November 1994), Alperovitz then wrote it off ("Enola Gay: A New Consensus," *Washington Post,* 4 February 1995) as trivial: "My article on the modern consensus did not, in fact, rely on the 1946 studies with which Mr. Newman quarrels. I preferred to use most of the available space for more important matters."
83. Edward J. Reese, Military Reference Branch, National Archives, to author, 30 October 1989.
84. R.F. Ennis, Memorandum for Chief, Strategic Policy Section, S&P Group, OPD: Subject: Use of Atomic Bomb on Japan, 30 April 1946, ABC 471.6 Atomic, (17 August 1945) Sec. 7, RG 165, NA.
85. See Butow's account, 118-20
86. Ennis, Memorandum.
87. Skates, *The Invasion of Japan,* 256.
88. Report of Reconnaissance and Survey . . . HQ IX Corps, 209-20, Box 4104, RG 94, Washington National Records Center (Suitland).
89. Weld quoted in Robert R. Palmer, Bell I. Wiley, and William R. Keast, *The Procurement and Training of Ground Combat Troops* (Washington, D.C.: Government Printing Office, 1948), 647.
90. Ibid.
91. Edmund J. Winslett, "Defense of Southern Kyushu," 3 June 1946, Winslett Papers, U.S. Army Military History Institute, Carlisle Barracks, Penn., 7.
92. Ibid., 11.
93. HQ, V Amphibious Corps, *The Japanese Plan for the Defense of Kyushu,* 30 November 1945, Marine Historical Center, Washington, D.C.
94. British Combined Operations Observers (Pacific), *Report on Operation Olympic and Japanese Counter-Measures,* 4 April 1946, CAB 106, #97, Public Records Office, Kew, London.
95. Assistant Chief of Staff, HQ Sixth Army (Col. H.V. White), *The Japanese Plans for the Defense of Kyushu,* 31 December 1945, John J. Tolson Papers, U.S. Army Military History Institute, Carlisle Barracks, Penn.

96. Lt. Comdr. Philip Gustafson, USNR, "What if We Had Invaded Japan?" *Saturday Evening Post* (5 January 1946): 17-18, 93-94.
97. K. Jack Bauer and Alvin D. Coox, "Olympic—Ketsu-Go," *Marine Corps Gazette* 49 (August 1965): 42.
98. Ibid., 44.
99. LTC Matsumoto Keisuke, "Preparations for Decisive Battle in Southern Kyushu in Great East Asia War," briefing to US-Japan Military History Exchange Conference, 25 October 1987, 91. Copy in Center of Military History, Washington, D.C.
100. See Tibbets interview in Robert Del Tredici, *At Work in the Fields of the Bomb* (New York: Harper & Row, 1987), 161.
101. J. Samuel Walker, "The Decision to Use the Bomb: A Historiographical Update," *Diplomatic History* 14 (Winter 1990): 111. Barton Bernstein is the definitive source on this, and his "Roosevelt, Truman, and the Atomic bomb, 1941-1945: A Reinterpretation," *Political Science Quarterly* 90 (Spring 1975): 23-69, has not been bettered.
102. Stanley Goldberg, "Racing to the Finish: The Decision to Bomb Hiroshima and Nagasaki," paper at American Historical Association Convention, Chicago, 6 January 1995, 2.
103. Ibid., 3-4.
104. Ibid., 12.
105. See chapter three.
106. Martin Sherwin, *A World Destroyed* (New York: Vintage, 1977), 221.

Chapter 2: Was Japan Ready to Surrender?

1. David MacIsaac, *Strategic Bombing in World War Two* (New York: Garland, 1976), 22.
2. Ibid., chap. 4.
3. John Kenneth Galbraith, *A Life in Our Times* (Boston: Houghton Mifflin, 1981), chap. 14.
4. Paul H. Nitze, *From Hiroshima to Glasnost: At the Center of Decision* (New York: Grove Weidenfeld, 1989), 35.
5. Ibid., 36-37.
6. James Beveridge, *History of the United States Strategic Bombing Survey (Pacific)* (Washington, D.C.: Government Printing Office, 1946), unpaginated appendix. Part of Historical Manuscript File, U.S. Department of the Army Center of Military History, Washington, D.C.
7. Strobe Talbott, *The Master of the Game: Paul Nitze and the Nuclear Peace* (New York: Knopf, 1988), 37. Gregg Herken in *Counsels of War* (New York: Oxford University, 1987), 46-51, makes the same point.

8. Paul H. Nitze, "Atoms, Strategy and Policy," *Foreign Affairs* 34 (January 1956): 198.

9. USSBS, *Summary Report (Pacific War)* (Washington, D.C.: Government Printing Office, 1946), 26. An identical paragraph appears on page 13 of USSBS, *Japan's Struggle to End the War* (Washington, D.C.: Government Printing Office, 1946).

10. Gar Alperovitz, *Atomic Diplomacy, Hiroshima and Potsdam* (New York: Penguin, 1985), 10-11; Hanson Baldwin, *Great Mistakes of the War* (New York: Harper & Brothers, 1950), 100-1; P.M.S. Blackett, *Fear, War, and the Bomb* (New York: Whittlesey House, 1949), 10, 38; Paul Boyer, *By the Bomb's Early Light* (New York: Pantheon, 1985), 186; Gregg Herken, *Counsels of War* (New York: Oxford University Press, 1987), 25; Paul Keckskemeti, *Strategic Surrender; The Politics of Victory and Defeat* (Stanford: Stanford University Press, 1958), 193; Robert L. Messer, "New Evidence on Truman's Decision," *Bulletin of the Atomic Scientists* 41 (August 1985): 51; Leon V. Sigal, *Fighting to a Finish* (Ithaca: Cornell University Press, 1988), 9; the authors of a planned Smithsonian National Air and Space Museum exhibit on the end of World War II— see Ken Ringle, "Enola Gay, at Ground Zero," *Washington Post*, 26 September 1994.

11. Barton J. Bernstein, ed. *The Atomic Bomb: The Critical Issues* (Boston: Little, Brown, 1976), 52-53; Robert J.C. Butow, *Japan's Decision to Surrender* (Stanford: Stanford University Press, 1954), 33, 46, 66, 124; William L. O'Neill, *A Democracy at War* (New York: Free Press, 1993), 415.

12. Author interview with Nitze, 25 January 1994.

13. On Masada, see chapter one. General Marshall told David Lilienthal that the Japanese "were determined and fanatical, like the Morros, and we would have to exterminate them, almost man by man. So we thought the bomb would be a wonderful weapon as a protection and preparation for landings. But we didn't realize its value to give the Japanese such a shock that they would surrender without complete loss of face." David E. Lilienthal, *The Atomic Energy Years, 1945-1950* (New York: Harper & Row, 1964), 198. Russell Brines, *Until They Eat Stones* (Philadelphia: Lippincott, 1944) is enlightening about the Japanese suicide complex. See also John W. Dower, *War Without Mercy* (New York: Pantheon, 1986), chap. 3.

14. Records of the U.S. Strategic Bombing Survey, Microfilm Group M1654, roll 1, frame 0045-0046, NA. [Hereafter Microfilm Group Number, roll, and frame.]

15. Thomas R. H. Havens, *Valley of Darkness: The Japanese People and World War Two* (New York: Norton, 1978), 130-32.

16. Yoshida Shigeru, *The Yoshida Memoirs* (Boston: Houghton Mifflin, 1962), 280.

17. Herbert Passin, "The Occupation: Some Reflections," in Carol Gluck and Stephen Graubard, eds., *Showa: The Japan of Hirohito* (New York: Norton, 1992), 111. A.C. Bell, in *A History of the Blockade of Germany, 1914-1918* (London: Committee of Imperial Defense, 1937), 672, shows that although the blockade began in 1915, it did not result in significant deaths until 1918.

18. O'Neill, *A Democracy*, 421.

19. Nishi Toshio, *Unconditional Democracy* (Stanford: Stanford University Press, 1982), 69.

20. Spencer Weart, *Nuclear Fear* (Cambridge: Harvard University Press, 1988), 93.

21. "Report on USSBS and JTG Conferences," undated, in Papers of Carl Spaatz, Box 21, Fol. July 1945, LC.

22. USSBS, *Japan's Struggle*, 1.

23. Ibid., Appendix B, lists twenty-four Japanese leaders; the Survey interviewed fourteen of them. Butow lists fifty-eight whose testimony he used, most interviewed by Far East Command, but many by Butow himself. USSBS claims it could not interview Koiso Kuniaki, Shigemitsu Mamoru, Togo Shigenori and three others because they were under indictment by IMTFE, but they did interview other indictees: Takagi Sokichi, Kido Koichi, and Hirota Koki.

24. M1654, roll 1, 0049-0050.

25. M1654, roll 3, 0416-0417.

26. M1654, roll 1, 0001-0011.

27. M1655, roll 1, 0002

28. M1654, roll 6, 0805-0808.

29. M1654, roll 1, 0090-0093.

30. M1655, roll 2, 0456-0458, quote on 0458.

31. Transcriptions of some of the USSBS interrogations were published by the Navy. Nomura's is in USSBS, Naval Analysis Division, *Interrogations of Japanese Officials*, vol. 2 (Washington D.C.: Government Printing Office, 1946), quotations from 392, 393.

32. M1654, roll 5, 0487-0509.

33. M1654, roll 5, 0503; other quotations from 0504, 0506, 0501, 0503.

34. See Hugh Byas, *Government by Assassination* (New York: Knopf, 1942).

35. M1654, roll 5, 0310-0321, quotes from frame 0315.

36. Arnold Brackman, *The Other Nuremberg: The Untold Story of the Tokyo War Crimes Trials* (New York: William Morrow, 1987), 332.

37. R. John Pritchard and Sonia M. Zaide, eds., *The Tokyo War Crimes Trial*, vol. 13 (New York: Garland, 1981), 31, 180.

38. Ibid., 31,205. *Japan's Longest Day*, 22, says that the emperor told both Kido and Togo that the "new type" of weapon that had been used made Japan powerless to continue.

39. *Interrogations of Japanese Officials*, 2: 313-26, quotes from 320, 322.

40. Ibid., 2: 324.
41. USSBS, *Mission Accomplished* (Washington, D.C.: Government Printing Office, 1946), is a 110-page document containing snippets of testimony from the Tokyo interrogations. With no context, it is hard to know what to make of these isolated bits. Many of them are from very minor figures. On page 48, Okada So, an economist of Kanagawa Prefecture, is quoted saying "I imagined then [after the 17 March air raid on Kobe] that without invasion the allied air power alone would be able to bring Japan to defeat anytime between November and December." I hold this not probative. Okada was a minor figure.
42. M1654, roll 1, 0637.
43. M1654, roll 3, 1076-77.
44. M1655, roll 208A, 0212-25, quote from 0222.
45. M1654, roll 1, 1002-24, quote from 1021-22. Alperovitz, in "Enola Gay: A New Consensus," *Washington Post,* 4 February 1995, challenges my citation of Hiranuma's testimony as evidence that the atomic bomb ended the war. He writes, "Indeed, one of those Newman cites—Baron Hiranuma, president of the Privy Council—made it quite clear in a part of the interview Newman does not mention that the only condition he had felt it worth fighting for was a guarantee for the emperor." Of course. All members of the peace party wanted this; the problem was that the military rulers of the country wanted three additional and wholly unacceptable conditions. Hiranuma realized, and stated, that the Potsdam Declaration did maintain the emperor, so he supported surrender before Hiroshima. Hiranuma also said clearly that the bomb ended the war. There is not one shred of support for Hiroshima cultists in Hiranuma's testimony.
46. M1654, roll 1, 0054-59, quote from 0057. Kawabe was not asked what brought about the end of the war in this interrogation. Leon V. Sigal misrepresents Kawabe's later statements to a member of the U.S. Army Far East Command, in Sigal's *Fighting to A Finish* (Ithaca: Cornell University Press, 1988), 226. In that interrogation, Kawabe said both the atom bomb and Soviet entry were "shocks in a quick succession." He could not say which of the two factors was the more decisive. Statement by Kawabe Torashiro, 21 November 1949, Historical Manuscript File, Reel 237, Office of the Chief of Military History, U.S. Department of the Army, Washington, D. C. Sigal cites only Kawabe's statement about the impact of Soviet entry. Sigal's misrepresentation is repeated in Robert A. Pape, "Why Japan Surrendered," *International Security* 18 (1993): 187-88.
47. M1654, roll 1, 0308-17, quote from 0317.
48. "The Decision for Peace," *ONI Review* 1 (June 1946): 15. This text of the Sakomizu interrogation is more legible than the NA microfilm.

49. M1655, roll 208A, 0350-61, quote from 0357-58.

50. M1654, roll 1, 0217.

51. M1654, roll 1, 0050-53, quote from 0053.

52. M1654, roll 3, 0005-12, quotes from 0010, 0011.

53. M1654, roll 8, 0977-82, quote from 0980.

54. Butow, in Freeman Dyson, *From Eros to Gaia* (New York: Pantheon, 1992), 258.

55. USSBS, *Urban Areas Division, The Effects of Air Attacks on Japanese Urban Economy* (Washington, D.C.: Government Printing Office, 1947), 49.

56. Ofstie, in MacIsaac, *Strategic Bombing*, 132. Lt. Comdr. James A. Field, Jr., in Ofstie's office, wrote an early draft on Japan's surrender that was more judicious than the final publications. It acknowledged that the atomic bomb played a role in surrender, credits the B-29 bombings with great effect, but also states that control of the air "does not assure victory; there are still some things no airplane can accomplish." USSBS (Pacific), Naval Analysis Division, "The Air Effort Against Japan," manuscript dated 26 March 1946, 68, in Field's possession. According to Field, the draft was well-received in USSBS offices until General Anderson saw it. Author interview with Field, 23 November 1993.

57. MacIsaac, *Strategic Bombing*, 103.

58. Ibid., 160.

59. Beveridge, *History*, 22.

60. Statement of Inaba Masao, 23 December 1949, Historical Manuscript File, vol. 1, Office of the Chief of Military History, Center of Military History, Washington, D.C. document number 57692, frame 585.

61. Butow, *Japan's Decision*, 183.

62. Inaba statement, 585.

63. A cogent argument on this matter is Lawrence Freedman and Saki Dockrill, "Hiroshima: A Strategy of Shock," in Saki Dockrill, ed., *From Pearl Harbor to Hiroshima* (London: Macmillan, 1994), 191-212.

64. USSBS, *Japan's Struggle*, 13, is one of many accounts of the "third bomb" rumor.

65. Ibid., 3; Butow, 33.

66. Ibid., 5; Butow 46.

67. Ibid., 7, 13; Butow, 124.

68. Ibid., 12-13; Butow, 66.

69. H.H. Arnold, *Global Mission* (New York: Harper & Row, 1949) wonders whether the rigid 70 group objective is right. It might be enough to have 47, or we might need 170: See pp. 614-15.

70. Edward J. Drea, *MacArthur's ULTRA* (Lawrence: University Press of Kansas, 1992), chap. 8.

71. USSBS, *Japan's Struggle*, 3-5.

72. G-2 General HQ U.S. Army Forces, Pacific (Willoughby) to G-3 (same HQ) 28 July 1945, S.J. Chamberlin Papers, U.S. Army Military History Institute, Carlisle Barracks, Penn.

Chapter 3: Was The Policy of Unconditional Surrender Justified?

1. John Charmley, *Churchill: The End of Glory* (London: Hodder & Stoughton, 1993), 526.
2. M.P.A.H. Hankey, *Politics, Trials and Errors* (Chicago: Henry Regnery, 1950), 31.
3. G.E.M. Anscombe, "Mr. Truman's Degree," in *The Collected Philosophical Papers of G.E.M. Anscombe, Vol. III: Ethics, Religion and Politics* (Minneapolis: University of Minnesota Press, 1981), 62.
4. Herbert Butterfield, "The Scientific versus the Moralistic Approach in International Affairs," *International Affairs* 27 (October 1951): 417.
5. Anne Armstrong, *Unconditional Surrender* (New Brunswick: Rutgers University Press, 1961), 255.
6. Hanson Baldwin, *Great Mistakes of the War* (New York: Harper & Brothers, 1950), 14. Michael Walzer, in *Just and Unjust Wars* (New York: Basic Books, 1977) offers an extended attack on unconditional surrender; his knowledge of the Pacific War, however, is so minimal that I disregard it here. Leon V. Sigal, in *Fighting to a Finish* (Ithaca: Cornell University Press, 1988), shows considerable knowledge of the war, but his devotion to bureaucracy as the key to unlock all mysteries vitiates his analysis of unconditional surrender. See Mark Stoler's review of Sigal in *Journal of American History* 76 (June 1989): 309-10. Gar Alperovitz in *Atomic Diplomacy* (New York: Penguin, 1985), misrepresents the situation (27-33) by, among other things, claiming that "the only real sticking point" keeping Japan from surrendering was the role of the emperor after surrender. The sticking point was the ability of the emperor upon announcement of surrender to control the military.
7. Hankey, 7.
8. Raymond G. O'Connor, *Diplomacy for Victory: FDR and Unconditional Surrender* (New York: Norton, 1971), 2.
9. Earl Pomeroy, "Sentiment for a Strong Peace, 1917-1919," *South Atlantic Quarterly* 43 (October 1944): 325-30.
10. John J. Pershing, *My Experiences in the World War* (New York: Frederick A. Stokes, 1931), 368, 369.
11. Laurence Stallings, *The Doughboys* (New York: Harper & Row, 1963), 345.

12. Stallings, 374. See also David Stevenson, "The Failure of Peace by Negotiation in 1917," *The Historical Journal* 38 (1991): 65-86; and Richard Hough, *Mountbatten* (New York: Random House, 1980), 201.

13. Roosevelt's experiences in World War I are discussed in O'Connor, 4-5; and Frank Freidel, *Franklin D. Roosevelt: The Apprenticeship* (Boston: Little, Brown, 1952), 371-72.

14. Pomeroy, 325. The lessons Roosevelt learned in World War I are derogated in Ernest R. May, *"Lessons" of the Past: The Use and Misuse of History in American Foreign Policy* (New York: Oxford University Press, 1973), 6-7. May faults Roosevelt for assuming "that the future would be like the recent past," and assuming that the major task after World War II would be to prevent the revival of German and Japanese power, rather than of getting along with the Soviet Union. Roosevelt was, of course, overoptimistic about Soviet-American relations, but I fail to see how that error disparages a concern with the revival of German and Japanese militarism.

15. Iokibe Makoto, "American Policy towards Japan's 'Unconditional Surrender,'" *Japanese Journal of American Studies* 1 (1981): 29.

16. Iokibe, 29-30; Harley A. Notter, *Postwar Foreign Policy Preparation 1939-1940* (Washington, D.C.: Government Printing Office, 1949) 126-27; and Hugh Borton, *American Presurrender Planning for Postwar Japan* (New York: Columbia University Press, 1967), 9-11.

17. *FRUS*, 1942, 1: 25-26.

18. *FRUS, The Conferences at Washington, 1941-1942, and Casablanca, 1943*, 506.

19. Ibid., 635.

20. Ibid., 834-35.

21. Ibid., 727.

22. William M. Franklin, "Unconditional Surrender," in Alexander DeConde, ed., *Encyclopedia of American Foreign Policy* (New York: Charles Scribner's Sons, 1978), 991.

23. Churchill, in Robert E. Sherwood, *Roosevelt and Hopkins: An Intimate History* (New York: Harper & Brothers, 1948), 696.

24. Roosevelt, in Ibid.

25. Ibid., 697. Some students of international relations reject entirely the belief that any war could "stay won," although as Hankey notes, the Carthaginian War stayed "won." Sir Michael Howard, in his early writings, was skeptical of the unconditional surrender doctrine, and of the stability of a postwar settlement: *Grand Strategy, Vol. IV* (London: HMSO, 1972), 285. By 1985, however, he wrote "most of us would now agree that 1945 meant not only the end of the war which had begun in 1939, but of that German attempt to expand and establish herself as a hegemonical power. . . . It was the end of half a century of German

wars, and of the Germany which had provoked them." *Lessons of History* (New Haven: Yale University Press 1991), 128.

26. *FRUS, Casablanca*, 506.

27. U.S. Department of State, *The Axis in Defeat* (Washington, D.C.: Government Printing Office, 1945), 4.

28. Roosevelt in John L. Chase, "Unconditional Surrender Reconsidered," *Political Science Quarterly* 70 (June 1955): 264.

29. Churchill, in Ibid., 265. Warren F. Kimball, in *The Juggler: Franklin Roosevelt as Wartime Statesman* (Princeton: Princeton University Press, 1991), 76, says unconditional surrender can be understood on three levels: an agreement to utterly defeat Germany and Japan, a promise to the Soviets that there would be no separate peace with Germany, and a belief that at the end of the war the Allies would be unencumbered by wartime promises.

30. Michael Howard, *War and the Liberal Conscience* (New Brunswick: Rutgers University Press, 1977), 109.

31. Barton Bernstein, "The Perils and Politics of Surrender: Ending the War with Japan and Avoiding the Third Atomic Bomb," *Pacific Historical Review* 46 (November 1977): 5.

32. A good study of the liberal reformers who dominated the first two years of the occupation is Howard Schonberger, *Aftermath of War* (Kent, Ohio: Kent State University Press, 1989). See also John G. Roberts, "The 'Japan Crowd' and The Zaibatsu Restoration," *Japan Interpreter* 12 (Summer 1979): 383-414; and Theodore Cohen, *Remaking Japan* (New York: Free Press, 1987).

33. On Dean Acheson, see *Present At The Creation* (New York: Signet, 1970), 178 and elsewhere. On Lattimore, see Robert P. Newman, *Owen Lattimore and the 'Loss' of China* (Berkeley: University of California Press, 1992), 35.

34. Louis F. Budenz, "Anti-Soviet Gang Here Maneuver For Peace-Now with Japanese," *Daily Worker*, 25 May 1945.

35. See Paul Kecskemeti, *Strategic Surrender* (Stanford: Stanford University Press: 1958), 163-65; and John W. Dower, *War Without Mercy* (New York: Pantheon, 1986), 181, 188-89.

36. On the American Council on Japan, see Howard Schonberger, "The Japan Lobby in American Diplomacy," *Pacific Historical Review* 46 (August 1977): 327-29.

37. Ibid.; Newman, *Owen Lattimore*, 129, 180; John K. Emmerson, *The Japanese Thread* (New York: Holt Rinehart Winston, 1978), chap. 12; Gary May, *China Scapegoat* (Washington, D.C.: New Republic Books, 1979), passim; and John K. Fairbank, *Chinabound: A Fifty-Year Memoir* (New York: Harper & Row, 1982), chap. 25.

38. Brian L. Villa, "The U.S. Army, Unconditional Surrender, and the Potsdam Proclamation," *Journal of American History* 63 (June 1976): 75-76.

39. *FRUS, The Conferences at Malta and Yalta, 1945*, 825-26.

40. Villa, 78. Villa also believes that the Allies used the unconditional surrender doctrine illegitimately in their treatment of Germany after it surrendered. On this controversy, see "The Diplomatic and Political Context of the POW Camps Tragedy," in Gunter Bischof and Stephen E. Ambrose, eds., *Eisenhower and the German POWs* (Baton Rouge: Louisiana State University Press, 1992), 58.

41. Villa, *U.S. Army*, 81. The intelligence people were groping in the dark. Revealing discussions, particularly of the fear that the Japanese army in Manchuria might reject a surrender order from Tokyo and go its own way as it did in the 1930s, are in JIC minutes for 20 and 25 April 1945. See M1642, Roll 2, frames 0068-74, and 0109-12, NA.

42. Harry S. Truman, *Memoirs, Vol. One, Year of Decisions* (Garden City: Doubleday, 1955), 42.

43. Ibid., 207.

44. *FRUS 1945*, 4: 547.

45. *Public Papers of the Presidents of the United States: Harry S. Truman, 1945* (Washington D.C.: Government Printing Office, 1961), 98. Marc Gallicchio gives the best explanation of Truman's unwillingness to overtly modify unconditional surrender in *The Cold War Begins in Asia* (New York: Columbia University Press, 1988), 16, and chap. 3.

46. Minutes of Meeting of the Committee of Three, 12 June 1945, ASW(McCloy), 334.8, Box 19, RG 107, NA.

47. Minutes of Meeting Held at the White House on Monday, 18 June 1945 at 1530, *FRUS Berlin*, 1: 905.

48. Len Giovannitti and Fred Freed, *The Decision to Drop The Bomb* (New York: Coward McCann, 1965), 136.

49. Minutes of Meeting of the Committee of Three, 19 June 1945, ASW(McCloy), 334.8, Box 19, RG 107, NA.

50. Gallicchio, *Cold War Begins in Asia*, 16-17.

51. Draft Memorandum for Mr. McCloy, Lt. Col. Fahey, 28 June 1945, ASW(McCloy), 385-87, Box 38, RG 107, NA

52. Appendix "C", Mark Howe's Draft, attached to document cited in note 51.

53. Memorandum for Colonel Stimson, 29 June 1945, ASW(McCloy), 385-87, RG 107, NA.

54. *FRUS, Berlin*, 1: 895.

55. Cordell Hull, *Memoirs, II* (New York: Macmillan, 1948), 1594.

56. James F. Byrnes, *Speaking Frankly* (New York: Harper, 1947), 206.

57. *FRUS, Berlin*, 2: 1474.
58. Memorandum, Rights and Powers over Japan, 4 September 1945, ASW(McCloy), 387, Box 38, RG 107, NA.
59. Martin J. Sherwin, *A World Destroyed* (New York: Vintage, 1977), 235. Sherwin tries, in "Hiroshima and Modern Memory," *The Nation*, 10 October 1981, 352, to show that unconditional surrender was a mere "political shibboleth" but that it "bound together a fracturing war party in Japan." He fails on both counts.
60. Sigal, 144-45.
61. Togo Shigenori, *The Cause of Japan* (New York: Simon and Schuster, 1956), 311.
62. USSBS papers, M1654, Roll 1, frame 1021, NA.
63. Kase Toshikazu, *Journey to the Missouri* (New Haven: Yale University Press, 1950), 209-10.
64. Kato Masuo, *The Lost War* (New York: Knopf, 1946), 233.
65. Shigemitsu, in Samuel Eliot Morison, *Victory in the Pacific* (Boston: Little, Brown, 1960), 343.
66. Akira Iriye, *Power and Culture* (Cambridge: Harvard University Press, 1981), 263.
67. Memorandum for the President, 2 August 1945, OSS Reports to the White House, Box 1260, April-September 1945, William J. Donovan Papers, U.S. Army Military History Institute, Carlisle, Penn.
68. Shiroyama Saburo, *War Criminal: The Life and Death of Hirota Koki* (Tokyo: Kodansha International, 1978), 245.
69. Northern Territories Issue Association, *Japan's Northern Territories* (Tokyo: The Association: 1974), 33. For a comprehensive account of this issue, see John J. Stephan, *The Kuril Islands* (Oxford: Clarendon Press, 1974), chap. 7.
70. Iokibe Makoto, "Japan Meets the United States for the Second Time," in Carol Gluck and Stephen Graubard, eds., *Showa: The Japan of Hirohito* (New York: Norton, 1992), 96.
71. A useful analysis of the peace forces is in John W. Dower, *Empire and Aftermath* (Cambridge: Harvard University Press, 1979), chap. 7.
72. The best account of the long struggle within the Japanese government over surrender is still Robert J.C. Butow, *Japan's Decision to Surrender* (Stanford: Stanford University Press, 1954). See especially chaps. 7-9. John Ray Skates, in *The Invasion of Japan* (Columbia: University of South Carolina Press, 1994) concludes that unconditional surrender delayed the end of the war significantly. This conclusion assumes that Anami and the militarists could have been suppressed before the August shocks. I see no evidence for this. Sherwin, in *The Nation* article (note 59), makes the same invalid assumption.
73. Butow, 244.

74. Barton J. Bernstein; see note 31.
75. Cited in Lisle A. Rose, *Dubious Victory* (Kent, Ohio: Kent State University Press, 1973), 319. See also Butow, 189-90.
76. A.E. Campbell, "Franklin Roosevelt and Unconditional Surrender," in Richard Langhorne, ed., *Diplomacy and Intelligence During the Second World War* (Cambridge: Cambridge University Press, 1985), 221.
77. Ibid., 220.
78. The phrase "slight reassurance" is Butow's; 191.
79. Richard W. Johnston, "Survey Shows Japs Unaware of Their Defeat." *Washington Post*, 4 September 1945.
80. Congressional Record-Senate (18 September 1945), 8672.
81. Memorandum for the Chief of Staff, 5 September 1945, ASW(McCloy) 387, Box 38, RG 107, NA.
82. See Ienaga Saburo, *The Pacific War* (New York: Pantheon, 1978), 246-57; David E. Sanger, "A Stickler for History, Even if It's Not Very Pretty," *New York Times*, 27 May 1993; Gerhard L. Weinberg, "Some Thoughts on World War II," *Journal of Military History* 56 (October 1992): 662; and Ronald H. Spector, "The Scholarship on World War II," *Journal of Military History* 55 (July 1991): 371.
83. Schonberger, "Japan Lobby"; John W. Dower, "Occupied Japan and the Cold War in Asia," in Michael J. Lacey, ed., *The Truman Presidency* (Cambridge: Cambridge University Press, 1989), 366-409; Michael Schaller, *The American Occupation of Japan* (New York: Oxford University Press, 1985).
84. For an excellent discussion of the German-Japanese contrast, see Ian Buruma, *The Wages of Guilt: Memories of War in Germany and Japan* (New York: Farar Straus Giroux, 1994).
85. Villa, 92.
86. Chase, 78-79. Vojtech Mastny, in "Stalin and the Prospects of a Separate Peace in World War II" *American Historical Review* 77 (December 1972): 1365-88, is less sure than Chase that unconditional surrender influenced Stalin.
87. Truman, *Memoirs, Vol. I*, 209.

Chapter 4: Why No Warning or Demonstration?

1. Richard G. Hewlett and Oscar Anderson, Jr., *The New World*, vol. 1, (Berkeley: University of California Press, 1990), 253.
2. Ibid., 327.
3. Ibid., 328.
4. Ibid., 329.

5. Alexander Sachs to Secretary of War Patterson, 28 June 1946, Sachs Papers, Franklin D. Roosevelt Library. This part of Sachs' advice along with the background of his advice to Roosevelt is in Nat S. Finney, "How F.D.R. Planned to Use the A-Bomb," *Look* 14 (14 March 1950): 23-27.
6. Hewlett and Anderson, 353.
7. Ibid., 355. The Brewster letter is described also in Peter Wyden, *Day One* (New York: Simon and Schuster, 1984), 154; and Dan Kurzman, *Day of the Bomb* (New York: McGraw-Hill, 1986), 309-10.
8. Wyden, 154.
9. Leo Szilard, in Spencer R. Weart and Gertrud Weiss Szilard, *Leo Szilard: His Version of the Facts* (Cambridge: MIT Press, 1978), 197.
10. Ibid., 181.
11. Ibid., 13.
12. Of course some scientists were present-minded and some politicians were future-minded. Wyden also makes this point, 167.
13. Alice Kimball Smith, *A Peril and a Hope* (Chicago: University of Chicago Press, 1965), 51.
14. Szilard, in Weart and Szilard, 207.
15. Ibid., 206.
16. James F. Byrnes, *All In One Lifetime* (New York: Harper, 1958), 284.
17. Szilard, in Weart and Szilard, 184-85.
18. Memorandum of Conversation with General Marshall, 29 May 1945 - 11:45 A.M., Marshall Papers, George C. Marshall Research Library.
19. Minutes of this meeting are in Martin J. Sherwin, *A World Destroyed* (New York: Vintage, 1977), 295-304. This meeting is also discussed at length in Hewlett and Anderson, 356-59; and in Arthur H. Compton, *Atomic Quest* (New York: Oxford University Press, 1956), 236-40.
20. The demonstration high in the air was Edward Teller's pet idea, which he stuck with at least as late as 1960, when he claimed that documents captured from the Japanese proved that such a demonstration would have brought surrender. As far as I know, no researcher has ever seen such documents. Edward Teller, "Bombing of Hiroshima Was a Mistake," *U.S. News & World Report* 49 (15 August 1960): 75.
21. The "uninhabited area" demonstration was the brainchild of Lewis L. Strauss, then assistant to the secretary of the navy, later chairman of the Atomic Energy Commission. He believed that if a lot of trees were knocked down, the Japanese would be scared enough to surrender. Lewis L. Strauss, "I Proposed Bombing an Uninhabited Area," *U.S. News & World Report* 49 (15 August 1960): 72.
22. The fullest discussion of the crusade of the Chicago scientists is in Smith, *A Peril*, Part I and Appendix B.
23. Ibid., 561.

24. Ibid., 562.
25. Ibid., 564.
26. Ibid., 565.
27. Ibid., 565-66.
28. Ibid., 566.
29. Ibid.
30. Ibid.
31. Ibid.
32. Ibid., 567.
33. Ibid.
34. Ibid.
35. Ibid., 567-68.
36. Ibid., 568.
37. Ibid., 44.
38. Ibid., 45.
39. Ibid., 47.
40. Ibid., 46.
41. Wyden, 167.
42. Urey as quoted in "The Talk of the Town," *The New Yorker* 21 (15 December 1945): 24. For a comprehensive analysis of the Franck Report, see Brian L. Villa, "A Confusion of Signals," *Bulletin of the Atomic Scientists* 31 (December 1975): 36-43.
43. Blackett commanded worldwide respect as a scientist. The Japanese were particularly impressed with his stature as a Nobelist.
44. P.M.S. Blackett, *Fear, War, and the Bomb* (New York: Whittlesey House, 1949), 139.
45. Lord Cherwell, "Atomic Bombing The Decisive Weapon," (London) *Daily Telegraph*, 9 December 1948.
46. Compton, 239-40
47. Wyden, 170-71.
48. Sherwin, 304-5
49. U.S. Atomic Energy Commission, *In the Matter of J. Robert Oppenheimer* (Cambridge: MIT Press, 1971), 34.
50. Ibid. Gray was chairman of the AEC Personnel Security Board.
51. McCloy's statement is not in the official minutes. For an account of this incident see Wyden, 172-73.
52. Hewlett and Anderson, 369.
53. Ibid., 370.
54. Szilard, *His Version*, 209-15.
55. Leo Szilard, "President Truman Did Not Understand," *U.S. News and World Report* 49 (15 August 1960): 70.
56. Szilard, *His Version*, 186
57. Wyden, 151.

58. Mitchell Wilson, *Passion to Know* (New York: Doubleday, 1972), 282.

59. Ibid., 284.

60. Mitchell Wilson, "The Myth of Hiroshima," *New York Times,* 27 April 1972.

61. William E. Juhnke, "Teaching the Atomic Bomb: The Greatest Thing in History," in Louise Hawkley and James C. Juhnke, eds., *Nonviolent America* (North Newton, Kans.: Bethel College Press, 1993), 111-12.

62. William L. Laurence, interviewing McCloy, in *Hiroshima Plus 20* (New York: Delacorte Press, 1965), 124-25.

63. Christopher Thorne, *Allies of a Kind* (New York: Oxford University Press, 1978), 533-34.

64. Lawrence Freedman, "The Strategy of Hiroshima," *Journal of Strategic Studies* 1 (May 1978): 77.

65. Ibid., 82. The full Groves statement is in Leslie R. Groves, *Now It Can Be Told* (New York: Harper & Brothers, 1962), 267.

66. On the military importance of Hiroshima, see Pacific War Research Society, *The Day Man Lost* (Tokyo: Kodansha International, 1972), 78-9, 113, 135.

67. Hewlett and Anderson, 365, 390, 393.

68. Sherwin, 302.

69. Freedman, 87. Michael S. Sherry, in *The Rise of American Air Power* (New Haven: Yale University Press, 1987), ridicules the shock thesis. One chapter is titled "The Persistence of Apocalyptic Fantasy." If Sherry had bothered to explore the Japanese literature he might not have been so sure.

70. Freedman cites Basil Liddell Hart on the strategy of shock: "In discussing the value of air power Liddell Hart noted that 'so long as the process is gradual' human beings can accommodate to degradation of their standard of life. 'Decisive results come sooner from sudden shocks than long-drawn out pressure. Shocks throw the opponent off balance. Pressure allows him time to adjust to it.'" Freedman, 87.

71. William Manchester, *The Glory and the Dream* (New York: Bantam, 1974), 383-84.

72. A comprehensive explanation of why Soviet intervention was not as significant in surrender as the bomb is in Lawrence Freedman and Saki Dockrill, "Hiroshima: A Strategy of Shock," in Saki Dockrill, ed., *From Pearl Harbor to Hiroshima* (London: Macmillan, 1994), 205-7. Confirmation of Japanese expectations of Soviet attack is in Amano Masakasu, Chief of Operations, Imperial General Headquarters, Historical Manuscript File, Office of the Chief of Military History, Reel 237, interview of 29 December 1949, 35; Hayashi Saburo, Secretary to War Minister Anami, ibid., interview of 23 December 1949, 396; Kawabe Torashiro, Vice Chief, Imperial General Staff, ibid., interview

of 21 November 1949, 97; Japanese Monograph No. 85, "Preparations for Operations in Defense of the Homeland," AMHI Library (microfilm), 5; and *Japan's Longest Day*, 19.

Others also sometimes claim Soviet entry to be determinative. Robert A. Pape, military historian, makes this claim and supports it by selectively quoting Toyoda Soemu and Kawabe. Both are inconsistent on the relative influence of atoms and Russians. Robert A. Pape, "Why Japan Surrendered," *International Security* 18 (Fall 1993): 187. Gregg Herken, in *The Winning Weapon* (New York: Knopf, 1980), 21, says "Japanese records suggested" that Soviet invasion was the key—but he does not tell us what records.

73. Edward J. Drea, "Missing Intentions: Japanese Intelligence and the Soviet Invasion of Manchuria, 1945" *Military Affairs* 48 (April 1984): 67.

74. Ibid., 69.

75. Ibid., 66.

76. Ibid.

77. Oleg A. Rzheshevsky, "The Soviet Union: The Direct Strategy," in David Reynolds, Warren F. Kimball, and A.O. Chubarian, eds., *Allies At War* (New York: St. Martin's Press, 1994), 50.

78. For instance, Gar Alperovitz, *Atomic Diplomacy*, rev. ed. (New York: Penguin, 1985), 28.

79. CCS 643/3, Estimate of the Enemy Situation as of 6 July 1945, 381 (6-4-43): Sec. 2, Pt. 5, RG 218, NA, 10.

80. Barton Bernstein makes this point in "The Author Replies" (to an Alperovitz/Messer article in the same issue) *International Security* 16 (Winter 1991/92): 216: "But that statement [in CCS 643/3] apparently did not include any judgment on when Japan would surrender. The gap between a government's recognition of 'the inevitability of complete defeat' and the time that it actually surrendered could be weeks or months—and many lives."

81. Hayashi, 404.

82. M1654, roll 1, 0217.

83. Buried somewhere in the 514 rolls of USSBS documents, or in the Historical Documents File there may be additional testimony that has escaped me; I do not think this likely.

84. Testimony of Funada, Konoye, and Toyoda Soemu is in USSBS files, described in chapter two; Ikeda and Kawabe are in Historical Documents file, Reel 237; Abe and Arisue are in Len Giovannitti and Fred Freed, *The Decision to Drop the Bomb* (New York: Coward, McCann, 1965), 333.

85. Testimony of Hata, Hiranuma, Nagano, Sakomizu, and Suzuki in USSBS, cited in chapter two. Inaba and Kido are in Historical Manuscript File, reel 237; Higashikuni is in Giovannitti and Freed, 334.

86. Most Hiroshima cultists ignore the Japanese testimony entirely. Alperovitz lists 547 items in his bibliography; 12 of them are of Japanese writers, but he cites none of them on the cause of Japan's surrender.

87. Togo Shigenori, *The Cause of Japan* (New York: Simon and Schuster, 1956), 315.

88. Pacific War Research Society, *Japan's Longest Day* (Tokyo and Palo Alto: Kodansha International, 1968), 21-22.

89. Kase Toshikazu, *Eclipse of the Rising Sun* (London: Jonathan Cape, 1951), 215, 217.

90. Ienaga Saburo, *The Pacific War* (New York: Pantheon, 1978), 231.

91. Toyoda Toshiyuki, "Japan's Policies Since 1945," in Len Ackland and Steven McGuire, eds., *Assessing the Nuclear Age* (Chicago: Education Foundation for Nuclear Science, 1986), 55.

92. Takemi Taro, "Remembrances of the War and the Bomb," *Journal of the American Medical Society* 250 (5 August 1983): 618.

93. Murakami Hyoe, *Japan: The Years of Trial, 1919-52* (Tokyo: Japan Culture Institute, 1982), 180; Kato Masuo, *The Lost War* (New York: Knopf, 1946), 247; Nakayama Takashi, "Strategic Concept at the End of the War and Defense of the Home Islands," manuscript of lecture 25 October 1987, U.S.-Japan Military History Exchange Conference, Washington, D.C., 31; Nakamura Masanori, *The Japanese Monarchy* (Armonk, N.Y.: M.E. Sharpe, 1992), 83.

94. Robert J.C. Butow, *Japan's Decision to Surrender* (Stanford: Stanford University Press, 1954), 180.

95. See note 62.

96. Freedman, 94.

Chapter 5: Was a Second Bomb Necessary to End the War?

1. Lawrence Freedman, "The Strategy of Hiroshima," *Journal of Strategic Studies* 1 (May 1978): 76-97. Brig. Gen. G.A. Lincoln, chief, Plans & Policy Group, U.S. Army, in a retrospective comment on an early draft by army historians, says of the timetable of events in August 1945: "Psychologically it was most important that the Japanese be given no opportunity to play for time. . . . The accumulated impact of all factors created a sense of urgency which called for, and resulted in, the maximum acceleration in applying all possible means and resources against a rapidly weakening enemy." Memorandum for Director, Historical Division, WDSS; 11 October 1946. Papers of George A. Lincoln, USMA Library, West Point, N.Y.

2. For a good exposition of War Minister Anami's attempt to downplay the importance of the "new weapon," see Edwin P. Hoyt, *Closing the Circle* (New York: Van Nostrand Reinhold, 1982), chap. 14.

3. For Truman's cancellation of the third bomb, see Barton Bernstein, "The Perils and Politics of Surrender: Ending the War with Japan and Avoiding the Third Atomic Bomb," *Pacific Historical Review* 46 (November 1977): 9.

4. The best statement of the case for giving the Japanese more time before using a second bomb is Robert C. Batchelder, *The Irreversible Decision, 1939-1950* (New York: Macmillan, 1961), 150-54. Summaries of many opinions opposed to Nagasaki are in Michael J. Yavenditti, "American Reactions to the Use of Atomic Bombs on Japan, 1945-1947" (Ph.D. diss., University of California, Berkeley, 1970), 228-31. Condemnations of the Nagasaki bombing in more recent literature are John K. Emmerson, *The Japanese Thread* (New York: Holt Reinhart Winston, 1978), 240; Edwin O. Reischauer, *Japan: The Story of a Nation*, 4th ed. (New York: McGraw-Hill, 1990), 179; Stewart L. Udall, *The Myths of August* (New York: Pantheon, 1994), 112-13.

5. Truman as quoted in *Off The Record: The Private Papers of Harry S. Truman*, ed. Robert H. Ferrell (New York: Harper & Row, 1980), 54.

6. Barton J. Bernstein, "Roosevelt, Truman , and the Atomic Bomb, 1941-1945; A Reinterpretation," *Political Science Quarterly* 90 (Spring 1975): 52.

7. Peter Wyden, *Day One* (New York: Simon & Schuster, 1984), 15, 17.

8. Leslie R. Groves, *Now It Can Be Told* (New York: Harper & Brothers, 1962), 342.

9. Maj. Gen. Clayton Bissell to Chief of Staff (Marshall), "Estimate of Japanese Situation for Next 30 Days," War Dept. General & Special Staffs, OPD, File #2, Box 12, RG 165, NA.

10. Richard Rhodes, *The Making of the Atomic Bomb* (New York: Simon & Schuster, 1986), 738.

11. Hoyt, *Closing*, 157.

12. Butow, *Japan's Decision*, 152.

13. Barton J. Bernstein, "The Atomic Bombings Reconsidered," *Foreign Affairs* 77 (January-February 1995): 150.

14. Pacific War Research Society, *Japan's Longest Day* (Tokyo and Palo Alto: Kodansha International, 1968), 19.

15. Ibid., 23-35.

16. H.G. Nicholas, ed., *Washington Dispatches, 1941-1945* (Chicago: University of Chicago Press, 1981), 602.

17. Pacific War Research Society, *Japan's Longest Day*, 27.

18. Ibid., esp. 45-6, 51, 54-75, 87-8, 90-3, 100-10, 113-17, 120-328.

19. Ibid., 42.

20. Samuel E. Morison, *Victory in the Pacific: Vol. XIV of History of United States Naval Operations in World War II* (Boston: Little, Brown, 1960), 353.
21. Gordon W. Prange, *God's Samurai* (Washington, D.C.: Brassey's, 1991), 153.
22. Fuchida, in Ibid., 150.
23. Fuchida, in Ibid., 153.
24. Affidavit of Marquis Kido Koichi, *The Tokyo War Crimes Trial*, vol. 13, edited by R. John Pritchard and Sonia M. Zaide (New York: Garland, 1981), 31, 180-82.
25. Hayashi Saburo, *Kogun: The Japanese Army in the Pacific War* (Quantico, Va.: Marine Corps Association, 1959), 163.
26. Martin J. Sherwin, *A World Destroyed* (New York: Vintage, 1977), 233.
27. Ibid.
28. Robert J.C. Butow, *Japan's Decision to Surrender* (Stanford: Stanford University Press, 1954), 159.
29. Ibid., 163.
30. Sherwin, 234-35
31. This analysis differs from Butow's, 168.
32. Joseph L. Marx, *Nagasaki: The Necessary Bomb?* (New York: Macmillan, 1971), 223.
33. Sherwin, 235.
34. Muste cited in Michael J. Yavenditti, "American Reactions to the Use of Atomic Bombs on Japan, 1945-1947" (Ph.D. diss. University of California, Berkeley, 1970), 228.
35. "Atrocities and War," *Christian Century* 62 (26 September 1945): 62.
36. Yavenditti, 240-41.

Chapter 6: Was Dropping these Bombs Morally Justified?

1. Michael Howard, *Studies in War and Peace* (New York: Viking, 1971), 16-17.
2. John Haynes Holmes, "Editorial Comment," *Unity* (27 September 1945): 99-100.
3. Lewis Mumford, *Values for Survival* (New York: Harcourt, Brace, 1946), 93.
4. Federal Council of Churches of Christ in America, *Atomic Warfare and the Christian Faith* (New York: The Council, 1946), 11.
5. Dwight MacDonald, "The 'Decline to Barbarism,'" *Politics* 2 (August-September 1945): 225.

6. Edgar R. Smothers, S.J., "An Opinion on Hiroshima," *America* 77 (5 July 1947): 379.

7. "America's Atomic Atrocity," *Christian Century* 62 (29 August 1945), page is 974 but incorrectly numbered in the original.

8. Thomas Nagel, "War and Massacre," *Philosophy and Public Affairs* 1 (Winter 1972): 141.

9. Robert Jay Lifton and Richard Falk, *Indefensible Weapons* (New York: Basic Books, 1982), 5, 39.

10. Norman Cousins, "The Literacy of Survival," *The Saturday Review* 29 (14 September 1946): 14.

11. MacDonald, 225.

12. Hanson W. Baldwin, *Great Mistakes of the War* (New York: Harper & Row, 1950), 102.

13. Ralph McGill, "War Is A Hog-Killing Business," *Atlanta Constitution*, 12 August 1945, 10-C.

14. Nagel, 141

15. Barton J. Bernstein, "Eclipsed by Hiroshima and Nagasaki," *International Security* 15 (Spring 1991): 161; Marc Gallicchio, "After Nagasaki: General Marshall's Plan for Tactical Nuclear Weapons in Japan," *Prologue* 23 (Winter 1991): 396-404.

16. Bernstein, 168.

17. Jack Schubert and Ralph E. Lapp, *Radiation: What It Is and How It Affects You* (New York: Viking, 1957), 219-20. See also one of the pathbreaking studies of fallout, David Bradley, *No Place to Hide* (Boston: Little, Brown, 1948).

18. Howard, *Studies*, 243.

19. Robert L. Holmes, *On War and Morality* (Princeton: Princeton University Press, 1989), 117.

20. Richard A. Wasserstrom, ed., *War and Morality* (Belmont, Calif.: Wadsworth, 1970), 98.

21. Ronald Schaffer, *Wings of Judgment* (New York: Oxford University Press, 1985), 20-21.

22. A good explanation without legalistic jargon is Sheldon Cohen, *Arms and Judgment: Law, Morality and the Conduct of War in the Twentieth Century* (Boulder, Colo.: Westview, 1988), chaps. 1 and 2.

23. Cohen, 92.

24. Herbert R. Southworth, *Guernica! Guernica!* (Berkeley: University of California Press, 1977), book 3, chap. 3.

25. John C. Ford, S.J., "The Morality of Obliteration Bombing," in Wasserstrom (note 20), 18, 23.

26. Norman Cousins, "The Non-Obliterators," *The Saturday Review* 27 (8 April 1944): 14.

27. John Hersey, *Hiroshima* (New York: Penguin, 1946).
28. Ford, 20.
29. G.E.M. Anscombe, *Collected Philosophical Papers, Vol. III: Ethics, Religion and Politics* (Minneapolis: University of Minnesota Press, 1981), chap. 7.
30. Ibid., 65.
31. "Congregation," *Oxford Magazine* 76 (3 May 1956): 382. This account was confirmed accurate in a letter from Lord Bullock to the author, 12 May 1994.
32. Anscombe, 62.
33. See chapter 2, and the account in Robert Butow, *Japan's Decision to Surrender* (Stanford: Stanford University Press, 1954), chaps. 6 and 7.
34. Butow, 169 and elsewhere.
35. Butow, 73, 77, 95, 98, 117, 141.
36. P.M.S. Blackett, *Fear, War, and the Bomb* (title of American publication) (New York: Whittlesey House, 1949); in Britain, *Military and Political Consequences of Atomic Energy* (London, 1948) was the first comprehensive statement of the "atomic diplomacy" thesis. Unfortunately, Blackett accepts the flawed USSBS counterfactual proposition that Japan would have surrendered probably by 1 November with no atom bomb, no Soviet intervention, and no invasion.
37. Butow, chaps. 6-8.
38. Anscombe, 62.
39. Ibid., 64.
40. Ibid., 65.
41. Ibid., 68.
42. R.M. Hare, *Applications of Moral Philosophy* (Berkeley: University of California Press, 1972), 15; George I. Mavrodes, "Conventions and the Morality of War," *Philosophy & Public Affairs* 4 (Winter 1972): 129.
43. Anscombe, 58.
44. Cohen to author, 21 April 1994.
45. Anscombe, 71.
46. Michael Walzer, *Just and Unjust Wars* (New York: Basic Books, 1992).
47. Ibid., 258.
48. Ibid.
49. Ibid.
50. Ibid.
51. Ibid.
52. Cohen to author, 21 April 1994.
53. Cited by Walzer, 266-67. One of the many books by servicemen facing the Japanese military in World War II who believe that only the atomic bomb saved their lives is Stephen Harper, *Miracle of Deliverance: The Case for the Bombing of Hiroshima* (New York, Stein and Day, 1985).

Harper argues that the British troops slated to retake Singapore would have been slaughtered had surrender not intervened.

54. Bamba Nobuya, in Bamba and John F. Howes, eds., *Pacifism in Japan* (Vancouver: University of British Columbia Press, 1978), 263.

55. The best source on Japanese biological experimentation and warfare is Sheldon H. Harris, *Factories of Death* (New York: Routledge, 1994).

56. There are few references in the moral literature about the bomb to this hypocrisy. There is a clear statement of it in Lawrence Freedman and Saki Dockrill, "Hiroshima: A Strategy of Shock," in Saki Dockrill, ed., *From Pearl Harbor to Hiroshima* (London: Macmillan, 1994), 209.

57. John W. Dower, *Japan in War and Peace* (New York: New Press, 1993), chap. 3.

58. See Dower, 88-90.

59. Pacific War Research Society, *The Day Man Lost* (Tokyo and Palo Alto: Kodansha International, 1972), 19. Approximately 45 pages of this volume are devoted to discussing the Japanese atomic bomb project.

60. Ibid., 19.

61. Ibid., 26-30.

62. Ibid., 31.

63. Ibid., 36.

64. Ibid., 38.

65. Ibid., 126.

66. Ibid., 183.

67. Ibid.

68. These are my opinions, not necessarily Dower's. Murakami's statement on how Japanese POWs were treated is typical of Japanese opinion: "The prisoners of war taken by the American forces, together with the former Japanese troops disarmed by them at the end of the war, were returned to Japan promptly and smoothly, transport ships being provided generously for the purpose. Treatment of prisoners during the war was, in a word, good; here, it was, rather, a spiritual problem that troubled them. They feared that if they returned to Japan they would be subject to strict punishment and ostracization by the inhabitants of their home districts." Murakami Hyoe, *Japan: The Years of Trial* (Tokyo: Japan Culture Institute, 1982), 226.

69. Asada Teruhiko, *The Night of a Thousand Suicides* (New York: St. Martin's Press, 1972), 51.

70. Tsurumi Shunsuke, *An Intellectual History of Wartime Japan* (London: KPI, 1986), 98, cites Guillain.

71. Barton J. Bernstein, "Shatterer of Worlds: Hiroshima and Nagasaki," *Bulletin of the Atomic Scientists* 31 (December 1975): 18.

72. Alistair Horne, *Monty* (New York: Harper Collins, 1994), xxi-xxii.

73. Norman Cousins, "The Non-Obliterators," *The Saturday Review* 27 (8 April 1944): 14.

74. A.L. Goodhart, *What Acts of War Are Justifiable?* (Oxford: Clarendon Press, 1940), 25.

75. Franklin D. Roosevelt, *The War Messages of Franklin D. Roosevelt* (Washington, D.C.: Government Printing Office, 1943), 32.

76. Cohen to author, 21 April 1994.

77. Hayashi, in Haruko and Theodore Cook, *Japan at War* (New York: Free Press, 1992), 40-43.

78. My count of Japanese prisoner of war camps comes from the map in Peter Calvocoressi, Guy Wint, and John Pritchard, *Total War*, vol. 2, rev. 2d. ed. (New York: Pantheon, 1989), 1202-3.

79. Dower, 295-97; United Nations, Economic and Social Council, *Report of the Working Group for Asia and the Far East*, Supplement 10 (New York: United Nations, 1948): 6-18.

80. Allied War Graves Registration figures in Olive Checkland, *Humanitarianism and the Emperor's Japan, 1877-1977* (New York: St. Martin's Press, 1994), 111.

81. Gavan Daws, *Prisoners of the Japanese* (New York: Morrow, 1994), 363.

82. Laurens van der Post, *The Prisoner and the Bomb* (New York: Morrow, 1971), 22.

83. Haruko and Theodore Cook, 41, 42.

84. Daws, 18.

85. Dower, 300.

86. Daws, 361.

87. The Chinese Alliance for Memorial and Justice, "A Country That Does Not Recognize Its Wrongs Cannot Do Right," *New York Times*, 17 June 1994, A19. The figures in this Chinese-Korean ad are generally supported by historians. See Sheldon H. Harris, *Factories of Death* (New York: Routledge, 1994), on Unit 731 and germ warfare.

88. Quirino, in William Branigin, "50 Years Later, Survivors of Battle of Manila Speak Out," *Washington Post*, 27 October 1994.

89. Reports of General MacArthur, *Campaigns of General MacArthur in the Pacific*, vol. 1 (Washington, D.C.: Government Printing Office, 1966), 459.

90. See Awaya Kentaro, "In the Shadows of the Tokyo Tribunal," in C. Hosoya et al, eds., *The Tokyo War Crimes Trial* (Tokyo: Kodansha International, 1986), 85.

91. Sheldon Harris, *Factories of Death* (London and New York: Routledge, 1994), 22.

92. Calvocoressi, 1201, 1205.

93. Harris, 222.

94. Ibid.

95. Ibid., 159.

96. Ibid., 4.

97. Ibid., 130.

98. Chinese Alliance; see note 87.

99. Calvocoressi, 1201.

100. Ken Ringle, "Enola Gay, at Ground Zero," *Washington Post*, 26 September 1994.

101. Hilary Conroy, "Japan's War in China: Historical Parallel to Vietnam?" *Pacific Affairs* 43 (Spring 1970): 61.

102. Ibid., 71-72.

103. Butow as summarized in Conroy, 63.

104. Maruyama Masao, *Thought and Behaviour in Modern Japanese Politics* (London: Oxford University Press, 1963), 88.

105. Ienaga Saburo, *The Pacific War* (New York: Pantheon, 1978), 181.

106. John J. Stephan, *Hawaii under the Rising Sun: Japan's Plans for Conquest after Pearl Harbor* (Honolulu: University of Hawaii Press, 1984), 1.

107. Joseph C. Grew, *Turbulent Era*, vol. 2 (Boston: Houghton Mifflin, 1952), 1392, 1393-94.

108. Akira Iriye, *Power and Culture* (Cambridge: Harvard University Press, 1981) has a quite different view of Japanese ideology and motivations.

109. Kinoshita Junji, "What the Tokyo Trial Made Me Think About," in Hosoya, 149.

110. B.V.A. Röling, "Question and Answer Period," in Hosoya, 152-53.

111. Richard Hough, *Mountbatten* (New York: Random House, 1980), 209.

112. William Lanouette, *Genius in the Shadows* (New York: Charles Scribner's Sons, 1992), 275.

113. Van der Post, 122.

114. Ibid.

115. Ibid., 131.

116. Andre Ryerson, "The Cult of Hiroshima," *Commentary* 80 (October 1985): 36-40.

117. Van der Post, 135.

118. Albert Einstein as told to Raymond Swing, "Atomic War or Peace," *Atlantic Monthly* 180 (November 1947): 30.

Chapter 7: Why Has the "Japan-as-Victim" Myth Been So Attractive?

1. John W. Dower, *War Without Mercy* (New York: Pantheon, 1986).

2. William Chapman, *Inventing Japan* (New York: Prentice Hall, 1991), 236.

3. Asada Sadao, "Japanese Perceptions of the A-Bomb Decision," in Joe C. Dixon, ed., *The American Military and the Far East* (Colorado Springs: U.S. Air Force Academy, 1980), 202. See also Murakami Hyoe, *Japan: The Years of Trial, 1919-52* (Tokyo: Japan Culture Institute, 1982), 198.

4. Asada, 202.

5. Nakamura Masanori, *The Japanese Monarchy* (Armonk, N.Y.: M.E. Sharpe, 1992), 140.

6. Imi Ryukiochi, "Japan and the Nuclear Age," in Richard S. Lewis and Jane Wilson, eds., *Alamogordo Plus Twenty-Five Years* (New York: Viking, 1971), 79.

7. Michael J. Yavenditti, "The American People and the Use of Atomic Bombs on Japan: The 1940s," *The Historian* 36 (February 1974): 226-30.

8. Ian Buruma, *The Wages of Guilt* (New York: Farar Straus Giroux, 1994).

9. Murakami, 198.

10. Ienaga Saburo, *The Pacific War* (New York: Pantheon, 1978), 255.

11. Buruma, 101.

12. Shiroyama Saburo, *War Criminal: The Life and Death of Hirota Koki* (Tokyo: Kodansha International, 1978).

13. Ienaga, 250.

14. Murakami, 199.

15. Lawrence S. Wittner, *One World or None, Vol. One of The Struggle Against the Bomb* (Stanford: Stanford University Press, 1993), 47.

16. Ibid., 48.

17. Buruma, 45.

18. Asada, 203.

19. Ibid., 208.

20. Ibid., 203.

21. The best commentary on the IMTFE is in two articles by B.V.A. Röling, Dutch jurist who was a member of the Court; "Introduction," and "The Tokyo Trial and the Quest for Peace," in C. Hosoya, N. Ando, Y. Onuma, and R. Minear, eds., *The Tokyo War Crimes Trial* (Tokyo: Kodansha, 1986), 15-28, and 125-33. Other articles in this volume are also perceptive, especially those of Tsurumi Shunsuke, John Pritchard, Awaya Kentaro, and Kinoshita Junji. More readily available are Arnold C. Brackman, *The Other Nuremberg* (New York: William Morrow, 1987); and Lawrence Taylor, *A Trial of Generals* (South Bend, Ind.: Icarus Press, 1981.)

22. For this account of the *Lucky Dragon* incident, I depend on Ralph E. Lapp, *The Voyage of the Lucky Dragon* (New York: Harper and Brothers, 1958); and Roger Dingman, "Alliance in Crisis: The Lucky Dragon Incident and Japanese-American Relations," in Warren I. Cohen and Akira Iriye, eds., *The Great Powers in East Asia, 1953-1960* (New York: Columbia University Press, 1990), 187-214.

23. Robert A. Divine, *Blowing on the Wind* (New York: Oxford University Press, 1978), 11.

24. Ibid.

25. A.M. Halpern, *Changing Japanese Attitudes Toward Atomic Weapons*, Rand Corporation Report, RM-1331 (Santa Monica: Rand Corporation, 1954), 21.

26. Lapp, 119.

27. Halpern, 26. See also Tsurumi Shunsuke, *An Intellectual History of Wartime Japan* (London: KPI, 1986), 115-19.

28. Lapp, 119.

29. On Strauss, see Richard Pfau, *No Sacrifice Too Great* (Charlottesville: University Press of Virginia, 1984).

30. Lapp, 119.

31. Asada, 203.

32. Tanaka Yasumasa, "Japanese Attitudes Toward Nuclear Arms," *Public Opinion Quarterly* 34 (Spring 1970): 29.

33. Dingman, 206. In 1994, Rep. George Miller (D-Calif.) called hearings of the House Natural Resources Committee to probe newly-released materials concerning the extent of fallout from BRAVO; it was far greater than the AEC claimed in 1954. See Gary Lee, "Postwar Pacific Fallout Wider Than Thought," *Washington Post*, 24 February 1994.

34. Thomas A. Bailey, *A Diplomatic History of the American People*, 9th ed. (Englewood Cliffs: Prentice-Hall, 1970), 817.

35. Nishi Toshio, *Unconditional Democracy: Education and Politics in Occupied Japan 1945-1952* (Stanford: Stanford University Press, 1982), xxxi.

36. Ibid., xxxiii. See also Tsurumi, 111.

37. Thomas R.H. Havens, *Fire Across the Sea: The Vietnam War and Japan, 1965-1975* (Princeton: Princeton University Press, 1987), 3-4.

38. Carl Oglesby, "Teaching-In in Tokyo," in Louis Menashe and Ronald Radosh, eds. *Teach-In: U.S.A.* (New York: Praeger, 1967), 322-24.

39. Havens, Passim.

40. Ibid., 133.

41. Ibid., 146-48.

42. Ibid., 160.

43. Ibid., 196.

44. Ienaga, 252.

45. Hattori, in Ibid., 252.

46. Ibid., 256.

47. David E. Sanger, "A Stickler for History, Even if It's Not Very Pretty," *New York Times*, 27 May 1993, A4.

48. "Scholar Wins Ruling on Nanjing Atrocity," *New York Times*, 13 May 1994, A3.

49. Allen S. Whiting, *China Eyes Japan* (Berkeley: University of California Press, 1989), chap. 3.

50. Ibid., 52.

51. F. Sionil Jose, "After Hiroshima, The Second Coming," *New York Times*, 6 August 1988, 25.

52. Asada, 211. See also Karel van Wolferen, *The Enigma of Japanese Power* (New York: Knopf, 1989), 426-28, for his statement on "victimhood in its ultimate guise: the atomic bombing of Hiroshima and Nagasaki."

53. Asada, 205.

54. Henry A. Wallace, Diary, 10 August 1945, Wallace Papers, University of Iowa, Iowa City. Truman told Wallace "the thought of wiping out another 100,000 people was too horrible."

55. Hatana Sumio, "The Pacific War," in Sadao Asada, ed., *Japan and the World, 1853-1952* (New York: Columbia University Press, 1989), 373.

56. William B. Breuer, *The Great Raid on Cabanatuan* (New York: Wiley, 1994), 228.

57. Ken Ringle, "Enola Gay, at Ground Zero," *Washington Post*, 26 September 1994, A10.

58. Ronald H. Spector, *Eagle Against the Sun* (New York: Free Press, 1985), xv-xvi.

59. Lawrence S. Wittner, *Rebels Against War* (New York: Columbia University Press, 1969), 127.

60. For the scientists' movement, see Alice K. Smith, *A Peril and a Hope* (Chicago: University of Chicago Press, 1965).

61. Niebuhr as cited in Paul Boyer, *By the Bomb's Early Light* (New York: Pantheon, 1985), 383.

62. Boyer, 106.

63. Spencer R. Weart, *Nuclear Fear* (Cambridge: MIT Press, 1988), 126.

64. J. Samuel Walker, *Containing the Atom* (Berkeley: University of California Press, 1992), 389.

65. Ibid.

66. Ibid., 395.

67. Ibid., 315-16.

68. Union of Concerned Scientists, *Scientists' Declaration on Nuclear Power*, issued at Cambridge, Mass., 1975.

69. Boyer, 182.

70. "PAEF Builds Ties in Hiroshima, Nagasaki," *Peace Action* 33 (Fall 1994): 2.

71. Stewart Udall, *The Myths of August* (New York: Pantheon, 1994), 36-39.

72. Ibid., 43.

73. A good discussion of deliberations over use of nuclear weapons in Korea is in Wittner, *One World or None*, 260-62.

74. See the account in Barton Bernstein, "Nuclear Deception: The U.S. Record," *Bulletin of the Atomic Scientists* 42 (August/September 1986): 40-43.

75. Bertrand Russell, *Power: A New Social Analysis* (London: Allen and Unwin, 1938), 45.

76. H. Peter Metzger, *The Atomic Establishment* (New York: Simon and Schuster, 1972), 81.

77. John E.E. Dalberg-Acton, First Baron Acton, *Essays on Freedom and Power* (Boston: Beacon, 1948), 364.

78. Robert Michels, *Political Parties* (New York: Dover, 1915), 206.

79. Udall, 179.

80. Ibid., 248-49

81. Ibid., 216; see also Howard Ball, *Justice Downwind* (New York: Oxford University Press, 1986), 204-10; and Philip L. Fradkin, *Fallout* (Tucson: University of Arizona Press, 1989), chap. 9.

82. "Izzy vs. a Mendacious Agency," *Washington Journalism Review* 10 (May 1988): 50.

83. "Known Nuclear Tests Worldwide, 1945 to December 31, 1989," *Bulletin of the Atomic Scientists* 46 (April 1990): 57.

84. This account of the Mancuso affair is taken from the author's conversation with Mancuso 1 November 1994, and from Robert Del Tredici, *At Work in the Fields of the Bomb* (New York: Harper & Row, 1987), 138-41.

85. Matthew L. Wald, "Pioneer in Radiation Sees Risk Even in Small Doses," *New York Times*, 8 December 1992, A1.

86. "The Bang Gets Bigger—Why?" *New Republic* 130 (5 April 1954): 7.

87. Herbert York, in an interview with Robert Scheer, put overkill pungently: "What the plan calls for is, not to exaggerate—the strip mining of the Soviet Union." Robert Scheer, *With Enough Shovels* (New York: Random House, 1982), 269. Even Admiral Hyman Rickover, after a career developing nuclear submarines, reflected that he had gone too far: "For example, take the number of nuclear submarines. . . . At a certain point you get where it's sufficient. What's the difference whether we have 100 nuclear submarines or 200? . . . . You can sink everything on the oceans several times over with the number we have and so can they." Del Tredici, 165.

88. J. Carson Mark, "Research, Development and Production," *Bulletin of the Atomic Scientists* 39 (March 1983): 50.

89. Scheer, *With Enough Shovels*, is good on this as are Robert J. Lifton and Richard Falk, *Indefensible Weapons* (New York: Random House, 1982).

90. Ronald Schaffer, *Wings of Judgment* (New York: Oxford University Press, 1985), 202.

91. Ibid., 249.

92. In addition to the work already mentioned on Bulloch, see Carole Gallagher, *American Ground Zero* (Cambridge: MIT Press, 1993); John G. Fuller, *The Day We Bombed Utah* (New York: New American Library, 1984), and R. J. List, et al., "Meteorological Evaluation of the Sources of Iodine-131 in Pasteurized Milk," *Science* 146 (2 October 1964): 59-64.

93. Udall, 229-38.

94. Walker, 343, 344.

95. Ibid., 361-62.

96. Anthony Ripley, "Political Shifts Threaten Growth of Atomic Power," *New York Times* 26 November 1972, 82.

97. Walker, 362.

98. J. William Fulbright, "The War and Its Effects—III," *Congressional Record*, 90th Cong., 1st Sess., (13 December 1967), S18485.

99. H. Jack Geiger, "Generations of Poison and Lies," *New York Times*, 5 August 1990, sec. 4, 19.

100. George Wald, "The Nuclear-Power-Truth Maze," *New York Times*, 29 February 1976, sec. 4, 15.

101. Daniel Ford, *The Cult of the Atom* (New York: Simon and Schuster, 1982), parts 1 and 2.

102. Ibid., 231.

103. Metzger, chap. 6.

104. Gary Lee, "New Reasons Revealed for Radiation Test Secrecy," *Washington Post*, 15 December 1994.

105. For an attempt to integrate 1945-1955 domestic and foreign events as they played themselves out in the life of a prominent sinologue, see Robert P. Newman, *Owen Lattimore and the 'Loss' of China* (Berkeley: University of California Press, 1992), chaps. 9-27. Other excellent sources on the witch hunt are the books by Adams, Caute, Fried, Griffith, Kutler, Oshinsky, and Reeves, listed in the bibliography.

106. On NSC 68, see Ernest R. May, ed., *American Cold War Strategy: Interpreting NSC 68* (Boston: Bedford/St. Martin's Press, 1993). Of books about the Cold War and its beginnings there is no end. In this area, with the opening of Soviet archives, the best is yet to come.

107. Joe McCarthy made such an unending noise that he is given more credit for the vileness of the witch hunt than he deserves. HUAC was also a major player and receives considerable attention, but the most powerful of the inquisitors, Pat McCarran, is largely overlooked. See Stanley I. Kutler, *The American Inquisition* (New York: Hill & Wang, 1982); and Newman, *Lattimore*, esp. chaps. 21 and 22.

108. Two worthwhile considerations of overkill are David Alan Rosenberg, "American Atomic Strategy and the Hydrogen Bomb Decision," *Journal of American History* 66 (June 1979): 62-87; and Rosenberg, "The Origins of Overkill," *International Security* 7 (Spring 1983): 3-27. See also

Nagai Yonusuke, "The Roots of Cold War Doctrine," in *Origins of the Cold War in Asia,* ed. Nagai and Akira Iriye, 15-42, for a useful perspective on American "crisis theology" and obsessive anticommunism.

109. Smith, part 4.
110. Weart, 241.
111. Wittner, 240.
112. Weart, 242.
113. This author was part of that middle class, and a minor participant in the antiwar movement. See Newman, "The Spectacular Irrelevance of Mr. Bundy," *Today's Speech* 13 (September 1965), for a bitter attack on the credibility of McGeorge Bundy and the Johnson administration he served.
114. Boyer, 192, 358.
115. Udall, 15, 17.
116. Barton J. Bernstein, "The Atomic Bomb and American Foreign Policy, 1941-1945: An Historiographical Controversy," *Peace and Change* 2 (Spring 1974): 6.
117. Gaddis Smith, "Was Moscow Our Real Target?" *New York Times Book Review,* 18 August 1985, 16.
118. J. Samuel Walker, "The Decision to Use the Bomb: A Historiographical Update," *Diplomatic History* 14 (Winter 1990): 99.
119. Menashe and Radosh, 7; the Williams' statement is p. 46; Waskow, 62; Rapoport, 180; Bentley, 260.
120. Bertrand Russell, *War Crimes in Vietnam* (New York: Monthly Review Press, 1967), 44, 70, 79, 83, 92, 100.
121. Tom Wells, *The War Within* (Berkeley: University of California Press, 1994), 537.
122. Udall, 15-17.

Chapter 8: What if the Bomb Had Not Been Used?

1. I assume death rates calculated from Dower and United Nations figures. See chap. 6.
2. Laurens van der Post, *The Prisoner and the Bomb* (New York: Morrow, 1971), 122.
3. Stephen Harper, *Miracle of Deliverance* (New York: Stein and Day, 1986), 183.
4. United Nations, Economic and Social Council, *Report of the Working Group for Asia and the Far East,* Supplement 10 (New York: United Nations, 1948), 14.
5. Ibid., 14-15.

6. Gar Alperovitz, "Beyond the Smithsonian Flap: Historians' New Consensus," *Washington Post,* 16 October 1994.

7. Michael S. Sherry, *The Rise of American Air Power* (New Haven: Yale University Press, 1987), 311-12.

8. Kido in R. John Pritchard and Sonia M. Zaide, eds., *The Tokyo War Crimes Trial,* vol. 13 (New York: Garland, 1981), 31,205.

9. Togo Shigenori, *The Cause of Japan* (New York: Simon and Schuster, 1956), 339.

10. Michael Evlanoff and Marjorie Fluor, *Alfred Nobel* (Los Angeles: Ward Ritchie Press, 1969), 190.

11. Nobel in Erik Bergengren, *Alfred Nobel* (London: Thomas Nelson and Sons, 1962), 189.

12. Ibid., 194.

13. Ibid.

14. Szilard, in William Lanouette with Bela Silard, *Genius in the Shadows* (New York: Charles Scribner's Sons, 1992), 256.

15. Teller in Martin J. Sherwin, *A World Destroyed* (New York: Vintage, 1977), 218.

16. Bush in Lawrence S. Wittner, *Rebels Against War* (New York: Columbia University Press, 1969), 131.

17. Henry L. Stimson, "The Decision to Use the Atomic Bomb," *Harper's Magazine* 194 (February 1947): 107.

18. Truman in David E. Lilienthal, *The Atomic Energy Years, 1945-1950* (New York: Harper & Row, 1964), 594.

19. Asado Sadao, "Japanese Perceptions of the A-Bomb Decision," in Joe C. Dixon, ed., *The American Military and the Far East* (Colorado Springs: U.S. Air Force Academy, 1980), 217. Others who subscribe to the inoculation hypothesis are Lester Bernstein, "Truman and the Bomb," *New York Times,* 13 May 1984; Admiral Robert L. Dennison, Oral History, Harry S. Truman Library, 1971; Dan Kurzman, *Day of the Bomb* (New York: McGraw-Hill, 1986), 310; Louis W. Alvarez, in Jonathan Harris, ed., *Hiroshima: A Study in Science, Politics, and the Ethics of War* (Menlo Park, Calif.: Addison-Wesley, 1970), 73.

20. Albert Einstein, "The Real Problem is in the Hearts of Men," in M. David Hoffman, *Readings for The Atomic Age* (New York: Globe, 1950), 358; J. Robert Oppenheimer, "The New Weapon: The Turn of the Screw," in Dexter Masters and Katharine Way, eds., *One World or None* (New York: Whittlesey House/McGraw-Hill, 1946), 25; Harrison Brown, "Must Destruction Be Our Destiny?" in Hoffman, *Readings,* 300.

21. McGeorge Bundy, *Danger and Survival* (New York: Vintage, 1990), 586-87.

22. Robert J. Donovan, *Tumultuous Years* (New York: Norton, 1982), 307-10.

23. Bundy, 238-45.

24. Raymond L. Garthoff, *Deterrence and the Revolution in Soviet Military Doctrine* (Washington, D.C.: The Brookings Institute, 1990), 85n. 93.

25. Bundy, 533.

26. John Lewis Gaddis, *The Long Peace* (New York: Oxford University Press, 1987), 106.

27. Ibid., 105.

28. David Holloway, *Stalin and the Bomb* (New Haven: Yale University Press, 1994), 13; Stanley Weintraub, "The Three-Week War," *MHQ: The Quarterly Journal of Military History* 7 (Spring 1995): 86-95; and David M. Glantz, "The Soviet Invasion of Japan," *MHQ* 7 (Spring 1995): 96-97.

29. Okada in Maruyama Masao, *Thought and Behavior in Modern Japanese Politics* (London: Oxford University Press, 1963), 124.

30. Peter Calvocoressi, Guy Wint, and John Pritchard, *Total War: The Great East Asia and Pacific Conflict* (New York: Pantheon, 1989), 1207.

31. Stewart L. Udall, *The Myths of August* (New York: Pantheon, 1994), 22.

32. See Michael MccGwire, "National Security and Soviet Foreign Policy," in Melvyn P. Leffler and David S. Painter, eds., *Origins of the Cold War* (London and New York, 1994), 72-75; Lloyd J. Graybar, "The 1946 Atomic Bomb Tests: Atomic Diplomacy or Bureaucratic Infighting?" *Journal of American History* 72 (March 1986), 888-907; William Burr, "Soviet Cold War Military Strategy: Using Declassified History," *Cold War International History Project Bulletin* 4 (Fall 1994): 1, 9-13; Ronald G. Suny, "Second-guessing Stalin," *Radical History Review* 37 (1987): 101-15.

33. Holloway, *Stalin*, 133.

34. Martin J. Sherwin, "The Atomic Bomb and the Origins of the Cold War," in Leffler and Painter, 91.

35. Einstein, in Raymond Swing, "Atomic War or Peace," *Atlantic Monthly* 180 (November 1947): 30.

36. S.L.A. Marshall, *The River and the Gauntlet* (New York: William Morrow, 1953).

37. See Gar Alperovitz and Kai Bird, "The Centrality of the Bomb," *Foreign Policy* (Spring 1994): 3.

38. Herbert S. Dinerstein, *Intervention Against Communism* (Baltimore: Johns Hopkins University Press, 1967).

39. Karel van Wolferen, *The Enigma of Japanese Power* (New York: Knopf, 1989), 427-28.

Chronology through 1946

1875		Japan established control of Okinawa, displacing China
1894-95		Sino-Japanese War: Japan takes control of Korea and Formosa
1904-1905		Russo-Japanese War: Japan takes southern Sakhalin
1931	18 September	Japan invades Manchuria, establishes "independent" Manchukuo
1932		Ishii Shiro establishes first biological warfare lab in Manchukuo
1937	7 July	Japanese attack Chinese troops at Marco Polo Bridge, then invade China
1937	December	Rape of Nanking; 200,000 Chinese massacred
1939	1 September	Germans invade Poland: WW II begins
1940	22 September	Japanese occupy northern Indochina
1941	13 April	Soviet-Japanese Neutrality Pact
	26 July	U.S. freezes all Japanese assets
	14 August	Roosevelt-Churchill Conference: Atlantic Charter
	17 October	Tojo succeeds Konoye as Premier

	7 December	Japanese attack Pearl Harbor, The Philippines, Hong Kong, Malaya
	8 December	U.S., Britain declare war on Japan
	9 December	Yamamoto orders staff to prepare plans for invasion of Hawaii
	11 December	Japan attacks Wake Island, U.S. surrenders 23rd
	25 December	British surrender Hong Kong
1942	2 January	Japanese take Manila
	17 January	Siege of Bataan begins
	15 February	Singapore surrenders to Japanese
	9 April	Japanese take Bataan, Death March begins
	7 May	U.S. surrenders Corregidor
	4-6 June	Battle of Midway
	7 June	Japanese invade Attu, Kiska
	7 August	U.S. troops land on Guadalcanal
	27 August	Japanese troops land on Guadalcanal
1943	14-24 Jan	Casablanca Conference: Churchill and FDR
	24 Janurary	FDR press conference at Casablanca: announces unconditional surrender policy
	9 February	U.S. pacifies Guadalcanal
	5 May	Nishina's atomic laboratory in Tokyo reports that a bomb is feasible
	11-30 May	Battle for Attu: no Japanese survivors
	20-23 November	Battle of Tarawa: heavy casualties
	22-26 November	First Cairo Conference: Churchill, FDR, Chiang Kai-shek
	1 December	FDR clarifies "unconditional surrender" for Japan

1944	28 January	U.S. releases accounts of Bataan Death March. Reports of Japanese atrocities begin to escalate
	1-4 February	U.S. occupies Kwajalein
	17-21 February	U.S. occupies Eniwetok
	6 June	D-Day, Normandy
	17 June-9 July	U.S. victory in Saipan
	19 June	U.S. victory in Battle of the Philippine Sea
	18 July	Koiso replaces Tojo as Japanese Premier
	21 July-10 August	U.S. Marines capture Guam
	24 July-1 August	U.S. Marines capture Tinian
	19 October	MacArthur's troops begin recapture of Philippines; Japanese carry out scorched earth policy
1945	4-11 February	Yalta Conference
	19 February-26	March U.S. captures Iwo Jima
	25 February	First fire-bombing of Tokyo
	3 March	Japanese resistance ends in Manila
	9-10 March	LeMay's great fire raid on Tokyo
	1 April-22 June	Battle for Okinawa
	5 April	Suzuki replaces Koiso as Japanese Premier
	6 April	Japanese begin heavy kamikaze attacks in Okinawa area
	12 April	Roosevelt dies; Truman sworn in
	13 April	B-29 raid destroys Nishina's atomic laboratory
	16 April	Truman affirms unconditional surrender policy

25 April	ULTRA gives MacArthur's HQ first estimate of Japanese strength on Kyushu at time of projected OLYMPIC invasion
1 May	Stimson appoints Interim Committee to advise on atomic matters
8 May	Germany surrenders unconditionally: V-E Day
9 May	Suzuki acknowledges German defeat, says Japan will fight on
11-14 May	Supreme War Council in Tokyo decides to improve relations with Russia; discussion but no decision on ending war by negotiation
25 May	U.S. Joint Chiefs approve OLYMPIC for 1 November
31 May	Interim Committee and scientific advisors reject warning to Japan about atomic bomb
8 June	Emperor endorses cabinet decision to fight to the end
9 June	Suzuki hard line speech to Diet: no surrender
14 June	Truman requests casualty estimates for OLYMPIC
18 June	Crucial meeting of Truman with Joint Chiefs: main topic casualties
22 June	Emperor tells Supreme Council to reconsider fight-to-end decision; agrees to seek negotiated armistice through Soviets
3 July	James F. Byrnes becomes secretary of state
7 July	Emperor orders special envoy to Moscow to get Soviet mediation
8 July	Togo persuades Konoye to make mission to Moscow; get peace without unconditional surrender

16 July   Atomic device tested at Alamogordo:
              Truman learns of success at Potsdam

17 July   Potsdam Conference begins

21 July   Shockley casualty projection reported to
              Stimson

25 July   Truman approves order to drop atomic
              bombs as ready

26 July   Potsdam Declaration to Japan: surrender on
              these terms or face destruction

29 July   ULTRA decrypts: U.S. bombing not
              preventing reinforcement of Kyushu

30 July   Suzuki appears to reject Potsdam terms

6 August   Hiroshima

7 August   Gen. Kawabe in Tokyo: report says
              Hiroshima destroyed by one bomb

8 August   Togo tells emperor Japan must accept
              Potsdam terms

9 August   Soviet troops enter Manchuria, Nagasaki
              bombed, emperor tells Kido Japan must
              surrender now

10 August   Japan accepts Potsdam terms if emperor can
              remain head of government

11 August   U.S. accepts continuing emperor under
              MacArthur's jurisdiction

11 August   Hatanaka leads planning for military coup
              in Tokyo

12 August   Japanese Army and Navy chiefs tell
              emperor must reject American offer and
              fight on; Kido recommends acceptance

13 August   Supreme Council meets all day, deadlocked;
              cabinet also deadlocked

14 August   Emperor summons cabinet, says accept
              American offer; cabinet bows

	14 August	Military dissidents take over palace, kill Gen. Mori, attempt to assassinate Kido
	15 August	Revolt suppressed, emperor broadcast at noon. Suicides begin, among them Minister of War Anami
	15 August	Truman directs USSBS to study bombing in Japan. Murders of POWs in Japanese control continue despite emperor's speech
	2 September	MacArthur accepts formal surrender on USS *Missouri*
	October-November	USSBS interrogates Japanese elites
1946	3 May	IMTFE opens war crimes proceedings in Tokyo; Ishii and other biological warfare operatives protected from prosecution
	1 July	USSBS publishes *Japan's Struggle to End the War*
	August	John Hersey's *Hiroshima* published

Bibliography

Abbrevations:

BAS - Bulletin of the Atomic Scientists
NYT - New York Times
WP - Washington Post

Acheson, Dean. *Present At The Creation*. New York: Signet, 1970.
Acton, Lord. *Essays on Freedom and Power*. Boston: Beacon, 1948.
Adams, John G. *Without Precedent: The Story of the Death of McCarthyism*. New York: Norton, 1983.
Alperovitz, Gar. *Atomic Diplomacy: Hiroshima and Potsdam*. 2d ed. New York: Penguin, 1985.
————. "Beyond the Smithsonian Flap: Historian's New Consensus." *WP*, 16 October 1994.
————. "Did We Have to Drop the Bomb?" *NYT*, 3 August 1989.
————. "Enola Gay: A New Consensus." *WP*, 4 February 1995.
Alperovitz, Gar, and Kai Bird. "The Centrality of the Bomb." *Foreign Policy*, no. 94 (Spring 1994): 3-20.
"America's Atomic Atrocity." *Christian Century* 62 (29 August 1945): 974-96.
Anscombe, G. E. M. *Collected Philosophical Papers Vol III: Ethics, Religion and Politics*. Minneapolis: University of Minnesota Press, 1981.
Appleman, Roy E., et al. *Okinawa: The Last Battle*. Washington, D.C.: U.S. Department of the Army, 1948.
Armstrong, Anne. *Unconditional Surrender*. New Brunswick: Rutgers University Press, 1961.
"Army Bars Relaxing Its Discharge Rules in View of Bitter Battles in the Pacific." *NYT*, 1 June 1945.

243

Arnold, H. H. *Global Mission*. New York: Harper & Row, 1949.

Asada Sadao. "Japanese Perceptions of the A-Bomb Decision." In *The American Military and the Far East,* edited by Joe C. Dixon, 199-217. Colorado Springs: U.S. Air Force Academy, 1980.

Asada Teruhiko. *The Night of a Thousand Suicides*. New York: St. Martin's Press, 1972.

"Atrocities and War." *Christian Century* 62 (26 September 1945): 62.

Awaya Kentaro. "In the Shadows of the Tokyo Tribunal." In *The Tokyo War Crimes Trial,* edited by C. Hosoya, et al., 79-88. Tokyo: Kodansha, 1986.

Bailey, Thomas A. *A Diplomatic History of the American People*. 9th ed. Englewood Cliffs: Prentice-Hall, 1970.

Baldwin, Hanson. *Battles Lost and Won*. New York: Harper & Row, 1966.

———. *Great Mistakes of the War*. New York: Harper & Brothers, 1950.

———. "The 'Let-Down' Problem." *NYT*, 2 April 1945.

Ball, Howard. *Justice Downwind*. New York: Oxford University Press, 1986.

Bamba Nobuya. "Conclusion: Japanese Society and the Pacifist." In *Pacifism in Japan* Bamba Nobuya and John F. Howes, 251-72. Vancouver: University of British Columbia Press, 1978.

"The Bang Gets Bigger—Why?" *New Republic* 130 (5 April 1954): 7.

Batchelder, Robert C. *The Irreversible Decision, 1939-1950*. New York: Macmillan, 1961.

Bauer, K. Jack, and Alvin D. Coox. "Olympic-Ketsu-Go." *Marine Corps Gazette* 49 (August 1965): 32-44.

Bell, A. C. *A History of the Blockade of Germany, 1914-1918*. London: Committee of Imperial Defense, 1937.

Benedict, Ruth. *The Chrysanthemum and the Sword*. Boston: Houghton Mifflin, 1946.

Bergengren, Erik. *Alfred Nobel*. London: Thomas Nelson and Sons, 1962.

Bernstein, Barton, ed. *The Atomic Bomb: The Critical Issues*. Boston: Little, Brown, 1976.

———. "The Atomic Bomb and American Foreign Policy, 1941-1945: An Historiographical Controversy." *Peace and Change* 2 (Spring 1974): 1-16.

———. "The Atomic Bombings Reconsidered." *Foreign Affairs* 77 (January-February, 1995): 135-52.

———. "The Author Replies." *International Security* 16 (Winter 1991/92): 214-21.

———. "Eclipsed by Hiroshima and Nagasaki." *International Security* 15 (Spring 1991): 149-73.

———. "Nuclear Deception: The U.S. Record." *BAS* 42 (August/September 1986): 40-43.

———. "The Perils and Politics of Surrender." *Pacific Historical Review* 46 (November 1977): 1-27.

———. "A Postwar Myth: 500,000 U.S. Lives Saved." *BAS* 42 (June/July 1986): 38-40.

———. "Roosevelt, Truman, and the Atomic Bomb, 1941-1945: A Reinterpretation." *Political Science Quarterly* 90 (Spring 1975): 23-69.

———. "Shatterer of Worlds: Hiroshima and Nagasaki." *BAS* 31 (December 1975): 12-22.

Bernstein, Lester. "Truman and the Bomb." *NYT*, 13 May 1984.

Blackett, P. M. S. *Fear, War, and the Bomb.* New York: Whittlesey House, 1949.

Borton, Hugh. *American Presurrender Planning for Postwar Japan.* New York: Columbia University Press, 1967.

Boyer, Paul. *By the Bomb's Early Light.* New York: Pantheon, 1985.

Brackman, Arnold. *The Other Nuremberg: The Untold Story of the Tokyo War Crimes Trials.* New York: William Morrow, 1987.

Bradley, David. *No Place to Hide.* Boston: Little, Brown, 1948.

Bradley, Omar, and Clay Blair. *A General's Life.* New York: Simon and Schuster, 1983).

Branigin, William. "50 Years Later, Survivors of Battle of Manila Speak Out." *WP*, 27 October 1994.

Breuer, William B. *The Great Raid on Cabanatuan.* New York: Wiley, 1994.

Brines, Russell. *Until They Eat Stones.* Philadelphia: Lippincott, 1944.

Brower, Charles F., IV. "Sophisticated Strategist: General George A. Lincoln and the Defeat of Japan, 1944-45." *Diplomatic History* 15 (Summer 1991): 317-37.

Brown, Harrison. "Must Destruction Be Our Destiny?" In *Readings for the Atomic Age,* edited by M. David Hoffman, 294-303. New York: Globe, 1950.

Budenz, Louis F. "Anti-Soviet Gang Here Maneuver for Peace-Now with Japanese" *Daily Worker,* 25 May 1945.

Bundy, McGeorge. *Danger and Survival.* New York: Vintage, 1990.

Burr, William. "Soviet Cold War Military Strategy: Using Declassified History." *Cold War International History Project Bulletin* 4 (Fall 1994): 1, 9-13.

Buruma, Ian. *The Wages of Guilt: Memories of War in Germany and Japan.* New York: Farar Straus Giroux, 1994.

Butow, Robert J. C. *Japan's Decision to Surrender.* Stanford: Stanford University Press, 1954.

Butterfield, Herbert. "The Scientific versus the Moralistic Approach in International Affairs." *International Affairs* 27 (October 1951): 411-22.

Byas, Hugh. *Government by Assassination.* New York: Knopf, 1942.

Byrnes, James F. *All in One Lifetime.* New York: Harper, 1958.

———. *Speaking Frankly.* New York: Harper, 1947.

Calvocoressi, Peter, Guy Wint, and John Pritchard. *Total War.* vol. 2. rev. 2d ed. New York: Pantheon, 1989.

Campbell, A. E. "Franklin Roosevelt and Unconditional Surrender." In *Diplomacy and Intelligence during the Second World War,* edited by Richard Langhorne, 219-41. Cambridge: Cambridge University Press, 1985.

Carr-Gregg, Charlotte. *Japanese Prisoners of War in Revolt.* New York: St. Martin's Press, 1978.

Caute, David. *The Great Fear.* New York: Simon and Schuster, 1978.

Chapman, William. *Inventing Japan.* New York: Prentice Hall, 1991.

Charmley, John. *Churchill: The End of Glory.* London: Hodder & Stoughton, 1993.

Chase, John L. "Unconditional Surrender Reconsidered." *Political Science Quarterly* 70 (June 1955): 258-79.

Checkland, Olive. *Humanitarianism and the Emperor's Japan, 1877-1977.* New York: St. Martin's Press, 1994.

Cherwell, Lord. "Atomic Bombing The Decisive Weapon." (London) *Daily Telegraph,* 9 December 1948.

Chinese Alliance for Memorial and Justice. "A Country That Does Not Recognize Its Wrongs Cannot Do Right." *NYT,* 17 June 1994.

Cohen, Sheldon M. *Arms and Judgment.* Boulder, Colo.: Westview, 1988.

Cohen, Theodore. *Remaking Japan.* New York: Free Press, 1987.

Compton, Arthur H. *Atomic Quest.* New York: Oxford University Press, 1956.

"Congregation." *Oxford Magazine* 74 (3 May 1956): 382.

Conroy, Hilary. "Japan's War in China: Historical Parallel to Vietnam?" *Pacific Affairs* 43 (Spring 1970): 61-72.

Cook, Haruko Taya, and Theodore Cook. *Japan at War.* New York: Free Press, 1992.

Coox, Alvin D., with Hayashi Saburo. *Kogun: The Japanese Army in the Pacific War.* Quantico, Va.: Marine Corps Assoc., 1959.

Cousins, Norman. "The Literacy of Survival." *The Saturday Review* 29 (14 September 1946): 14.

———. "The Non-Obliterators." *The Saturday Review* 27 (8 April 1944): 14.

Crane, Conrad. *Bombs, Cities, and Civilians.* Lawrence: University Press of Kansas, 1993.

Craven, Wesley F., and James L. Cate. *The Army Air Forces in World War II.* vol. 5. Chicago: University of Chicago Press, 1953.

Daws, Gavan. *Prisoners of the Japanese.* New York: Morrow, 1994.

Del Tredici, Robert. *At Work in the Fields of the Bomb.* New York: Harper & Row, 1987.

Dinerstein, Herbert S. *Intervention Against Communism.* Baltimore: Johns Hopkins University Press, 1967.

Dingman, Roger. "Alliance in Crisis: The Lucky Dragon Incident and Japanese-American Relations." In *The Great Powers in East Asia, 1953-1960,* edited by Warren I. Cohen and Akira Iriye, 187-214. New York: Columbia University Press, 1990.

Divine, Robert A. *Blowing on the Wind.* New York: Oxford University Press, 1978.

Dockrill, Saki, and Lawrence Freedman. "Hiroshima: A Strategy of Shock." In *From Pearl Harbor to Hiroshima,* edited by Saki Dockrill, 191-212. London: Macmillan, 1994.

Donovan, Robert J. *Tumultuous Years.* New York: Norton, 1982.

Dower, John W. *Empire and Aftermath.* Cambridge: Harvard University Press, 1979.

———. *Japan in War and Peace.* New York: New Press, 1993.

———. "Occupied Japan and the Cold War in Asia." In *The Truman Presidency,* edited by Michael J. Lacey, 367-409. Cambridge: Cambridge University Press, 1989.

———. "Rethinking World War II in Asia." *Reviews in American History* 12 (June 1944): 155-69.

———. *War Without Mercy.* New York: Pantheon, 1986.

Drea, Edward J. *MacArthur's ULTRA: Codebreaking and the War against Japan.* Lawrence: University Press of Kansas, 1992.

———. "Missing Intentions: Japanese Intelligence and the Soviet Invasion of Manchuria, 1945." *Military Affairs* 48 (April 1984): 66-73.

Dyson, Freeman. *From Eros to Gaia.* New York: Pantheon, 1992.

Einstein, Albert, as told to Raymond Swing. "Atomic War or Peace." *Atlantic Monthly* 180 (November 1947): 29-32.

Emmerson, John K. *The Japanese Thread.* New York: Holt Rinehart Winston, 1978.

Evlanoff, Michael, and Marjorie Fluor. *Alfred Nobel.* Los Angeles: Ward Ritchie Press, 1969.

Fairbank, John K. *Chinabound: A Fifty-Year Memoir.* New York: Harper and Row, 1982.

Federal Council of Churches of Christ in America. *Atomic Warfare and the Christian Faith.* New York: The Council, 1946.

Feifer, George. *Tennozan: The Battle of Okinawa and the Atomic Bomb.* New York: Ticknor and Fields, 1992.

Ferrell, Robert H., ed. *Off the Record: The Private Papers of Harry S. Truman.* New York: Harper & Row, 1980.

———. *Harry S. Truman: A Life.* Columbia: University of Missouri Press, 1994.

Finney, Nat S. "How F. D. R. Planned to Use the A-Bomb." *Look* 14 (14 March 1950): 23-27.

Ford, Daniel. *The Cult of the Atom.* New York: Simon and Schuster, 1982.

Ford, John C., S.J. "The Morality of Obliteration Bombing." In *War and Morality*, edited by Richard A. Wasserstrom, 15-41. Belmont, Calif.: Wadsworth, 1970.

Foreign Relations of the United States: The Conference of Berlin (Potsdam). Washington, D.C.: Government Printing Office, 1960.

———. *The Conferences at Washington, 1941-1942, and Casablanca, 1943.* Washington, D.C.: Government Printing Office, 1968.

Fradkin, Philip L. *Fallout.* Tucson: University of Arizona Press, 1989.

Franklin, William M. "Unconditional Surrender." In *Encyclopedia of American Foreign Policy*, edited by Alexander DeConde, 986-93. New York: Charles Scribner's Sons, 1978.

Freedman, Lawrence, and Saki Dockrill. "Hiroshima: A Strategy of Shock." In *From Pearl Harbor to Hiroshima*, edited by Saki Dockrill, 191-212. London: Macmillan, 1994.

———. "The Strategy of Hiroshima." *Journal of Strategic Studies* 1 (May 1978): 76-97.

Freidel, Frank. *Franklin D. Roosevelt: The Apprenticeship.* Boston: Little, Brown, 1952.

Fried, Richard M. *Nightmare in Red.* New York: Oxford University Press, 1990.

Fulbright, J. William. "The War and Its Effects: III." *Congressional Record* 90th Cong., 1st sess., 13 December 1967, S18485.

Fuller, John G. *The Day We Bombed Utah.* New York: New American Library, 1984.

Futrell, Robert F. *Ideas, Concepts, Doctrine: Basic Thinking in the United States Air Force, 1907-1960.* Maxwell Air Force Base, Ala.: Air University Press, 1989.

Gaddis, John Lewis. *The Long Peace.* New York, Oxford University Press, 1987.

Galbraith, John Kenneth. *A Life in Our Times.* Boston: Houghton Mifflin, 1981.

Gallagher, Carole. *American Ground Zero.* Cambridge: MIT Press, 1993.

Gallicchio, Marc S. "After Nagasaki: General Marshall's Plan for Tactical Nuclear Weapons in Japan." *Prologue* 23 (Winter 1991): 396-404.

———. *The Cold War Begins in Asia.* New York: Columbia University Press, 1988.

Garthoff, Raymond L. *Deterrence and the Revolution in Soviet Military Doctrine.* Washington, D.C.: The Brookings Institute, 1990.

Geiger, H. Jack. "Generations of Poison and Lies." *NYT,* 5 August 1990.

Giovannitti, Len, and Fred Freed. *The Decision to Drop the Bomb.* New York: Coward McCann, 1965.

Glantz, David M. "The Soviet Invasion of Japan." *MHQ: The Quarterly Journal of Military History* 7 (Spring 1995): 96-97.

Goldberg, Stanley. "Racing to the Finish: The Decision to Bomb Hiroshima and Nagasaki." Paper presented at the American Historical Association Convention, Chicago, Ill., 6 January 1995.

Goodhart, A. L. *What Acts of War Are Justifiable?* Oxford: Clarendon Press, 1940.

Gow, Ian. *Okinawa 1945: Gateway to Japan.* Garden City, N.J.: Doubleday, 1985.

Graybar, Lloyd J. "The 1946 Atomic Bomb Tests: Atomic Diplomacy or Bureaucratic Infighting?" *Journal of American History* 72 (March 1986): 888-907.

Grew, Joseph C. *Turbulent Era.* 2 vols. Boston: Houghton Mifflin, 1952.

Griffith, Robert. *The Politics of Fear.* 2d. ed. Amherst: University of Massachusetts Press, 1987.

Groves, Leslie. *Now It Can Be Told.* New York: Harper & Brothers, 1962.

Gustafson, Philip. "What If We Had Invaded Japan?" *Saturday Evening Post* 218 (5 January 1946): 17-18, 93-94.

Halpern, A. M. *Changing Japanese Attitudes Toward Atomic Weapons.* Santa Monica: Rand Corporation, 1954.

Hankey, Lord M. P. A. H. *Politics, Trials and Errors.* Chicago: Henry Regnery, 1950.

Hare, R. M. *Applications of Moral Philosophy.* Berkeley: University of California Press, 1972.

Harper, Stephen. *Miracle of Deliverance: The Case for the Bombing of Hiroshima.* New York: Stein and Day, 1986.

Harris, Jonathan, ed. *Hiroshima: A Study in Science, Politics, and the Ethics of War.* Menlo Park, Calif.: Addison-Wesley, 1970.

Harris, Sheldon H. *Factories of Death.* New York: Routledge, 1994.

Hatana Sumio. "The Pacific War." In *Japan and the World, 1853-1952,* edited by Sadao Asada, 355-86. New York: Columbia University Press, 1989.

Havens, Thomas R. H. *Fire Across the Sea: The Vietnam War and Japan. 1965-1975.* Princeton: Princeton University Press, 1987.

———. *Valley of Darkness: The Japanese People and World War Two.* New York: Norton, 1978.

Hayashi Saburo with Alvin D. Coox. *Kogun: The Japanese Army in the Pacific War.* Quantico, Va.: Marine Corps Assoc., 1959.

Herken, Gregg. *Counsels of War.* New York: Oxford University Press, 1987.

———. *The Winning Weapon.* New York: Knopf, 1980.

Hersey, John. *Hiroshima.* New York: Penguin, 1946.

Hewlett, Richard G., and Oscar Anderson, Jr. *The New World.* vol. 1. Berkeley: University of California Press, 1990.

Hoffman, M. David, ed. *Readings for the Atomic Age.* New York: Globe, 1950.

Holloway, David. *Stalin and the Bomb.* New Haven: Yale University Press, 1994.

Holmes, John Haynes. "Editorial Comment." *Unity* (27 September 1945): 99-100.

Holmes, Robert L. *On War and Morality.* Princeton: Princeton University Press, 1989.

Horne, Alistair. *Monty.* New York: Harper Collins, 1994.

Hough, Richard. *Mountbatten.* New York: Random House, 1980.

Howard, Sir Michael. *Grand Strategy, vol. IV.* London: HMSO, 1972.

————. *Lessons of History.* New Haven: Yale University Press, 1991.

————. *Studies in War and Peace.* New York: Viking, 1971.

————. *War and the Liberal Conscience.* New Brunswick: Rutgers University Press, 1977.

Hoyt, Edwin P. *Closing the Circle.* New York: Van Nostrand Reinhold, 1982.

————. *Japan's War.* New York: McGraw-Hill, 1986.

Hull, Cordell. *Memoirs, vol. II.* New York: Macmillan, 1948.

Ienaga Saburo. *The Pacific War.* New York: Pantheon, 1978.

Imai Ryukichi. "Japan and the Nuclear Age." In *Alamogordo Plus Twenty-Five Years,* edited by Richard S. Lewis and Jane Wilson, 79-90. New York: Viking, 1971.

Iokibe Makoto. "American Policy towards Japan's 'Unconditional Surrender.'" *Japanese Journal of American Studies* 1 (1981): 19-53.

————. "Japan Meets the United States for the Second Time." In *Showa: The Japan of Hirohito,* edited by Carol Gluck and Stephen Graubard, 91-106. New York: Norton, 1992.

Iriye, Akira. *Power and Culture.* Cambridge: Harvard University Press, 1981.

"Izzy vs. a Mendacious Agency." *Washington Journalism Review* 10 (May 1988): 50.

Johnston, Richard W. "Survey Shows Japs Unaware of Their Defeat." *WP,* 4 September 1945.

Jose, F. Sionil. "After Hiroshima, The Second Coming." *NYT,* 6 August 1988.

Juhnke, William E., "Teaching the Atomic Bomb: The Greatest Thing in History." In *Nonviolent America,* edited by Louise Hawkley and James C. Juhnke, 104-23. North Newton, Kans.: Bethel College, 1993.

Kase Toshikazu. *Eclipse of the Rising Sun.* London: Jonathan Cape, 1951.

————. *Journey to the Missouri.* New Haven: Yale University Press, 1950.

Kato Masuo. *The Lost War.* New York: Knopf, 1946.

Keckskemeti, Paul. *Strategic Surrender: The Politics of Victory and Defeat.* Stanford: Stanford University Press, 1958.

Kifner, John. "Hiroshima: A Controversy That Refuses to Die." *NYT,* 31 January 1995.

Kimball, Warren F. *The Juggler: Franklin Roosevelt as Wartime Statesman.* Princeton: Princeton University Press, 1991.

Kinoshita Junji. "What the Tokyo Trial Made Me Think About." In *The Tokyo War Crimes Trial*, edited by C. Hosoya, et al, 146-51. Tokyo: Kodansha, 1986.

"Known Nuclear Tests Worldwide, 1945 to Dec. 31, 1989." *BAS* 46 (April 1990).

Kurzman, Dan. *Day of the Bomb*. New York: McGraw-Hill, 1986.

Kutler, Stanley I. *The American Inquisition*. New York: Hill & Wang, 1982.

Lanouette, William, with Bela Silard. *Genius in the Shadows*. New York: Charles Scribner's Sons, 1992.

Lapp, Ralph E. *The Voyage of the Lucky Dragon*. New York: Harper and Brothers, 1958.

Laurence, William L. "The Scientists: Their Views Twenty Years Later." In *Hiroshima Plus 20*, edited by the *New York Times*, 114-25. New York: Delacorte Press, 1965.

Lee, Gary. "New Reasons Revealed for Radiation Test Secrecy." *WP*, 15 December 1994.

———. "Postwar Pacific Fallout Wider Than Thought." *WP*, 24 February 1994.

Lifton, Robert J., and Richard Falk. *Indefensible Weapons*. New York: Basic Books, 1982.

Lilienthal, David E. *The Atomic Energy Years, 1945-1950*. New York: Harper & Row, 1964.

List, R. J., et al. "Meteorological Evaluation of the Sources of Iodine-131 in Pasteurized Milk." *Science* 146 (2 October 1964): 59-64.

MacArthur, Douglas. *Reports of General MacArthur: The Campaigns of MacArthur in the Pacific*. 2 vols. Washington, D.C.: Government Printing Office, 1966.

MacDonald, Dwight. "The Decline to Barbarism." *Politics* 2 (August/September 1945): 225, 257-60.

MacIsaac, David. *Strategic Bombing in World War Two*. New York: Garland, 1976.

MccGwire, Michael. "National Security and Soviet Foreign Policy." In *Origins of the Cold War*, edited by Melvyn P. Leffler and David S. Painter, 53-74. London and New York: Routledge, 1994.

McCullough, David. *Truman*. New York: Simon and Schuster, 1992.

McGill, Ralph. "War is a Hog-Killing Business." *Atlanta Constitution*, 12 August 1945.

Manchester, William. *The Glory and the Dream*. New York: Bantam, 1975.

———. *Goodbye, Darkness.* Boston: Little, Brown, 1980.

Mark, J. Carson. "Research, Development and Production." *BAS* 39 (March 1983): 45-51.

Marshall, S. L. A. *The River and the Gauntlet.* New York: William Morrow, 1953.

Maruyama Masao. *Thought and Behaviour in Modern Japanese Politics.* London: Oxford University Press, 1963.

Marx, Joseph L. *Nagasaki: The Necessary Bomb?* New York: Macmillan, 1971.

Mastny, Vojtech. "Stalin and the Prospects of a Separate Peace in World War II." *American Historical Review* 77 (December 1972): 1365-88.

Matloff, Maurice. *Strategic Planning for Coalition Warfare, 1943-44.* Washington D.C.: Government Printing Office, 1959.

Mavrodes, George, I. "Conventions and the Morality of War." *Philosophy & Public Affairs* 4 (Winter 1972): 117-31.

May, Ernest R., ed. *American Cold War Strategy: Interpreting NSC 68.* Boston: Bedford/St. Martin's Press, 1993.

———. *"Lessons" of the Past: The Misuse of History in American Foreign Policy.* New York: Oxford University Press, 1973.

May, Gary. *China Scapegoat.* Washington, D.C.: New Republic Books, 1979.

Menashe, Louis, and Ronald Radosh, eds. *Teach-Ins: U.S.A.* New York: Praeger, 1967.

Messer, Robert L. "New Evidence on Truman's Decision." *BAS* 41 (August 1985): 50-56.

Metzger, H. Peter. *The Atomic Establishment.* New York: Simon and Schuster, 1972.

Meyer, Eugene L. "Smithsonian Stands Firm on A-Bomb Exhibit." *WP*, 19 January 1995.

Michels, Robert. *Political Parties.* New York: Dover, 1959.

Morison, Samuel Eliot. *Victory in the Pacific.* Boston: Little, Brown, 1960.

Mumford, Lewis. *Values for Survival.* New York: Harcourt, Brace, 1946.

Murakami Hyoe. *Japan: The Years of Trial, 1919-52.* Tokyo: Japan Culture Institute, 1982.

Nagai Yonosuke. "The Roots of Cold War Doctrine." In *Origins of the Cold War in Asia*, edited by Nagai Yonosuke and Akira Iriye, 15-42. New York: Columbia University Press, 1977.

Nagel, Thomas. "War and Massacre." *Philosophy and Public Affairs* 1 (Winter 1972): 123-44.

Nakamura Masanori. *The Japanese Monarchy.* Armonk, N.Y.: M. E. Sharpe, 1992.

Nakayama Takashi. "Strategic Concept at the End of the War and Defense of the Home Islands." *JGSDF Staff College,* 25 October 1987. U.S. Army Center of Military History, Washington, D.C.

Newman, Robert P. *Owen Lattimore and the 'Loss' of China.* Berkeley: University of California Press, 1992.

———. "The Spectacular Irrelevance of Mr. Bundy." *Today's Speech* 13 (September 1965): 30-34.

———. "What New Consensus?" *WP,* 30 November 1994.

Nicholas, H. G., ed. *Washington Dispatches, 1941-1945.* Chicago: University of Chicago Press, 1981.

Nishi Toshio. *Unconditional Democracy.* Stanford: Stanford University Press, 1982.

Nitze, Paul H. "Atoms, Strategy and Policy." *Foreign Affairs* 34 (January 1956): 187-98.

———. *From Hiroshima to Glasnost: At The Center of Decision.* New York: Grove Weidenfeld, 1989.

Northern Territories Issue Association. *Japan's Northern Territories.* Tokyo: The Association, 1974.

Notter, Harley A. *Postwar Foreign Policy Preparation 1939-40.* Washington, D.C.: Government Printing Office, 1949.

O'Connor, Raymond G. *Diplomacy for Victory: FDR and Unconditional Surrender.* New York: Norton, 1971.

Oglesby, Carl. "Teaching-In in Tokyo." In *Teach-Ins: U.S.A.,* edited by Louis Menashe and Ronald Radosh, 322-24. New York: Praeger, 1967).

O'Neill, William L. *A Democracy at War.* New York: Free Press, 1993.

Oppenheimer, J. Robert. "The New Weapon: The Turn of the Screw." In *One World or None,* edited by Dexter Masters and Katharine Way, 22-25. New York: Whittlesey House/McGraw-Hill, 1946.

Oshinsky, David. *A Conspiracy So Immense: The World of Joe McCarthy.* New York: Macmillan/Free Press, 1983.

Pacific War Research Society. *The Day Man Lost.* Tokyo and Palo Alto: Kodansha International, 1972.

———. *Japan's Longest Day.* Tokyo and Palo Alto: Kodansha International, 1968.

"PAEF Builds Ties in Hiroshima, Nagasaki." *Peace Action* 33 (Fall 1944): 2.

Palmer, Robert R., et al, *The Procurement and Training of Ground Combat Troops* Washington, D.C.: Government Printing Office, 1948.

Pape, Robert A. "Why Japan Surrendered." *International Security* 18 (Fall 1993): 154-201.

Passin, Herbert. "The Occupation: Some Reflections." In *Showa: The Japan of Hirohito*, edited by Carol Gluck and Stephen Graubard, 107-30. New York: Norton, 1992.

Perrett, Geoffrey. *Days of Sadness, Years of Triumph.* Baltimore: Penguin, 1974.

Perry, Glen H. *"Dear Bart": Washington Views of World War II.* Westport: Greenwood, 1982.

Pershing, John J. *My Experiences in The World War.* New York: Frederick A. Stokes, 1931.

Pfau, Richard. *No Sacrifice Too Great.* Charlottesville: University Press of Virginia, 1984.

Philip, P.J. "6,300 Canadian Soldiers AWOL . . . ." *NYT,* 21 January 1945.

Pogue, Forrest C. *George C. Marshall, Statesman.* New York: Viking, 1987.

Pomeroy, Earl. "Sentiment for a Strong Peace, 1917-1919." *South Atlantic Quarterly* 43 (October 1944): 325-30.

Prange, Gordon, with Donald M. Goldstein and Katherine V. Dillon. *God's Samurai.* Washington, D.C.: Brassey's, 1991.

Pritchard, R. John, and Sonia M. Zaide, eds. *The Tokyo War Crimes Trial.* 27 vols. New York: Garland, 1981.

Rae, Bruce. "Okinawa is a Lesson for Invasion of Japan." *NYT,* 27 May 1945.

Reeves, Thomas C. *The Life and Times of Joe McCarthy.* New York: Stein and Day, 1982.

Reischauer, Edwin O. *Japan: The Story of a Nation.* 4th. ed. New York: McGraw-Hill, 1990.

Rhodes, Richard. *The Making of the Atomic Bomb.* New York: Simon & Schuster, 1986.

Ringle, Ken. "Enola Gay, at Ground Zero." *WP,* 26 September 1994.

Ripley, Anthony. "Political Shifts Threaten Growth of Atomic Power." *NYT,* 26 November, 1972.

Roberts, John G. "The 'Japan Crowd' and the Zaibatsu Restoration," *Japan Interpreter* 12 (Summer 1979): 383-414.

Röling, B.V.A. "Introduction." In *The Tokyo War Crimes Trial*, edited by C. Hosoya et al, 15-28. Tokyo: Kodansha, 1986.

————. "The Tokyo Trial and the Quest for Peace," In *The Tokyo War Crimes Trial*, edited by C. Hosoya et al, 125-33. Tokyo: Kodansha, 1986.

————. "Question and Answer Period," In *The Tokyo War Crimes Trial*, edited by C. Hosoya et al, 152-58. Tokyo: Kodansha, 1986..

Roosevelt, Franklin D. *The War Messages of Franklin D. Roosevelt.* Washington, D.C.: Government Printing Office, 1943.

Rose, Lisle A. *Dubious Victory.* Kent, Ohio: Kent State University Press, 1973.

Rosenberg, David Alan. "American Atomic Strategy and the Hydrogen Bomb Decision." *Journal of American History* 66 (June 1979): 62-87.

————. "The Origins of Overkill." *International Security* 7 (Spring 1983): 3-27.

Russell, Bertrand. *Power: A New Social Analysis.* London: Allen and Unwin, 1938.

————. *War Crimes in Vietnam.* New York: Monthly Review Press, 1967.

Russell, Richard. *Congressional Record—Senate.* 18 September 1945, 8672.

Ryerson, Andre. "The Cult of Hiroshima." *Commentary* 80 (October 1985): 36-40.

Rzheshevsky, Oleg A. "The Soviet Union: The Direct Strategy." In *Allies at War*, edited by David Reynolds, Warren Kimball, and A. O. Chubarian, 27-54. New York: St. Martin's Press, 1994.

Sanger, David E. "A Stickler for History, Even if It's Not Very Pretty." *NYT*, 27 May 1993.

Schaffer, Ronald. *Wings of Judgment.* New York: Oxford University Press, 1985.

Schaller, Michael. *The American Occupation of Japan.* New York: Oxford University Press, 1985.

Scheer, Robert. *With Enough Shovels.* New York: Random House, 1982.

"Scholar Wins Ruling on Nanjing Atrocity." *NYT*, 13 May 1994.

Schonberger, Howard. *Aftermath of War.* Kent, Ohio: Kent State University Press, 1989.

————. "The Japan Lobby in American Diplomacy." *Pacific Historical Review* 46 (August 1977): 327-59.

Schubert, Jack, and Ralph E. Lapp. *Radiation: What It Is and How It Affects You.* New York: Viking, 1957.

Sherry, Michael. *The Rise of American Air Power*. New Haven: Yale University Press, 1987.

Sherwin, Martin, "The Atomic Bomb and the Origins of the Cold War." In *Origins of the Cold War*, edited by Melvyn P. Leffler and David S. Painter, 77-94. London and New York: Routledge, 1994.

———. "Hiroshima and Modern Memory," *The Nation* 233 (10 October 1981): 399-53.

———. *A World Destroyed*. New York: Vintage, 1977.

Sherwood, Robert E. *Roosevelt and Hopkins: An Intimate History*. New York: Harper and Brothers, 1948.

Shirayama Saburo. *War Criminal: The Life and Death of Hirota Koki*. Tokyo: Kodansha International, 1978.

Sigal, Leon V. *Fighting to a Finish*. Ithaca: Cornell University Press, 1988.

Skates, John Ray. *The Invasion of Japan*. Columbia: University of South Carolina Press, 1994.

Smith, Alice Kimball. *A Peril and a Hope*. Chicago: University of Chicago Press, 1965.

Smith, Gaddis. "Was Moscow Our Real Target?" *NYT Book Review*, 18 August 1985, 16.

Smothers, Edgar R., S.J. "An Opinion on Hiroshima." *America* 77 (5 July 1947): 379-80.

Southworth, Herbert R. *Guernica! Guernica!* Berkeley: University of California Press, 1977.

Spector, Ronald H. *Eagle Against the Sun*. New York: Free Press, 1985.

———. "The Scholarship on World War II." *Journal of Military History* 55 (July 1991): 369-72.

Stallings, Laurence. *The Doughboys*. New York: Harper & Row, 1963.

Stephan, John J. *Hawaii under the Rising Sun: Japan's Plans for Conquest after Pearl Harbor*. Honolulu: University of Hawaii Press, 1984.

———. *The Kuril Islands*. Oxford: Clarendon Press, 1974.

Stevenson, David. "The Failure of Peace by Negotiation in 1917." *The Historical Journal* 34 (1991): 65-68.

Stimson, Henry L. "The Decision to Use the Atomic Bomb." *Harper's Magazine* 194 (February 1947): 97-107.

Stoler, Mark, Review of Leon V. Sigal. "Fighting to a Finish." *Journal of American History* 76 (June 1989): 309-10.

Stouffer, Samuel, et al. *The American Soldier: Combat and Its Aftermath*. vol. 2. Princeton: Princeton University Press, 1949.

Strauss, Lewis L. "I Proposed Bombing an Uninhabited Area." *U.S. News and World Report* 49 (15 August 1960): 71-73.

Suny, Ronald G. "Second-Guessing Stalin." *Radical History Review* 37 (1987): 101-15.

Szilard, Leo. "President Truman Did Not Understand." *U.S. News & World Report*
49 (15 August 1960): 68-71.

Takemi Taro. "Remembrances of the War and the Bomb." *Journal of the American Medical Association* 250 (5 August 1983): 618-19.

Talbott, Strobe. *The Master of the Game: Paul Nitze and the Nuclear Peace.* New York: Knopf, 1988.

"The Talk of the Town," (interview with Harold Urey). *The New Yorker* 21 (15 December 1945): 23-24 .

Tanaka Yasumasu. "Japanese Attitudes Toward Nuclear Arms." *Public Opinion Quarterly* 34 (Spring 1970): 26-42.

Taylor, Lawrence. *A Trial of Generals.* South Bend, Ind.: Icarus Press, 1981.

Teller, Edward. "Bombing of Hiroshima Was a Mistake." *U.S. News & World Report* 49 (15 August 1960): 75-76.

Thorne, Christopher. *Allies of a Kind.* New York: Oxford University Press, 1978.

Togo Shigenori. *The Cause of Japan.* New York: Simon and Schuster, 1956.

Toland, John. *The Rising Sun.* New York: Bantam, 1970.

Toyoda Toshiyuki. "Japan's Policies Since 1945." In *Assessing the Nuclear Age,* edited by Len Ackland and Steven McGuire, 55-64. Chicago: Educational Foundation for Nuclear Science, 1986.

Truman, Harry S., *Memoirs, Vol. One, Year of Decisions.* Garden City, N.J.: Doubleday, 1955.

Tsurumi Shunsuke. *An Intellectual History of Wartime Japan.* London and New York: KPI, 1986.

Udall, Stewart. *The Myths of August.* New York: Pantheon, 1994.

United Nations, Economic and Social Council. *Report of the Working Group for Asia and the Far East.* New York: United Nations, 1948.

U.S. Atomic Energy Commission. *In the Matter of J. Robert Oppenheimer* Cambridge: MIT Press, 1971.

U.S. Department of Defense. *The Entry of the Soviet Union into the War against Japan.* Washington, D.C.: Government Printing Office, 1955.

U.S. Department of State. *The Axis in Defeat.* Washington, D.C.: Government Printing Office, 1945.

U.S. Strategic Bombing Survey, Urban Areas Division. *The Effects of Air Attacks on Japanese Urban Economy.* Washington, D.C.: Government Printing Office, 1947.

———. Naval Analysis Division. *Interrogation of Japanese Officials.* 2 vols. Washington, D.C.: Government Printing Office, 1946.

———. *Japan's Struggle to End the War.* Washington, D.C.: Government Printing Office, 1946.

———. *Summary Report (Pacific War).* Washington, D.C.: Government Printing Office, 1946.

Van der Post, Laurens. *The Prisoner and the Bomb.* New York: Morrow, 1971.

Van Wolferen, Karel. *The Enigma of Japanese Power.* New York: Knopf, 1989.

Villa, Brian L. "A Confusion of Signals." *BAS* 31 (December 1975): 36-43.

———. "The U.S. Army, Unconditional Surrender, and the Potsdam Proclamation." *Journal of American History* 63 (June 1976): 66-92.

Wald, George. "The Nuclear-Power-Truth Maze," *NYT,* 29 February 1976.

Wald, Matthew L. "Pioneer in Radiation Sees Risk Even in Small Doses." *NYT,* 8 December 1992.

Walker, J. Samuel. *Containing the Atom.* Berkeley: University of California Press, 1992.

———. "The Decision to Use the Bomb: A Historiographical Update." *Diplomatic History* 14 (Winter 1990): 97-114.

Walzer, Michael. *Just and Unjust Wars.* 2d ed. New York: Basic Books, 1992.

Warner, Denis, Peggy Warner, and Commander Sadao Seno. *The Sacred Warriors: Japan's Suicide Legions.* New York: Van Nostrand Reinhold, 1982.

Warner, Geoffrey. "To End a War: The Decision to Drop the Bomb." In *The Cold War Debated,* edited by David Carlton and Herbert M. Levine, 34-40. New York: McGraw-Hill, 1988.

Wasserstrom, Richard A., ed., *War and Morality* (Belmont, Calif.: Wadsworth, 1970).

Weart, Spencer R., and Gertrud Weiss Szilard. *Leo Szilard: His Version of the Facts.* Cambridge: MIT Press, 1978.

———. *Nuclear Fear.* Cambridge: Harvard University Press, 1988.

Weigley, Russell. *The American Way of War.* Bloomington: Indiana University Press, 1977.

Weinberg, Gerhard, L. "Some Thoughts on World War II." *Journal of Military History* 56 (October 1992): 667.

Weintraub, Stanley. "The Three-Week War." *MHQ: The Quarterly Journal of Military History* 7 (Spring 1995): 86-95.

Wells, Tom. *The War Within.* Berkeley: University of California Press, 1994.

Whiting, Allen S. *China Eyes Japan.* Berkeley: University of California Press, 1989.

Wilson, Mitchell. "The Myth of Hiroshima." *NYT,* 29 April 1972.

———. *Passion to Know.* New York: Doubleday, 1972.

Wittner, Lawrence. *One World or None.* Stanford: Stanford University Press, 1993.

———. *Rebels Against War.* New York: Columbia University Press, 1969.

Wu, Tien-wei. "Expansion of UN Security Council and Problems of Japanese Permanent Membership." *Journal of Studies of Japanese Aggression Against China* (May 1994): 63-69.

Wyden, Peter. *Day One.* New York: Simon and Schuster, 1984.

Yadin, Yigael. *Masada,* New York: Random House, 1966.

Yavenditti, Michael J. "The American People and the Use of Atomic Bombs on Japan: the 1940s." *The Historian* 36 (February 1974): 226-30.

———. "American Reactions to the Use of Atomic Bombs on Japan, 1945-1947." Ph.D. diss., University of California, Berkeley, 1970.

Yoshida Shigeru. *The Yoshida Memoirs.* Boston: Houghton Mifflin, 1962.

Additional Reading on the Asian Holocaust

Allen, Louis. *The End of the War in Asia.* London: Hart-Davis, McGibbon, 1976.

Behr, Edward. *Hirohito: Behind the Myth.* New York: Villard, 1989.

Berry, William. *Prisoner of the Rising Sun.* Norman: University of Oklahoma, 1971.

Braddon, Russell. *The Other Hundred Year's War.* Lincoln: Collins, 1983.

Coleman, John S., Jr. *Bataan and Beyond.* College Station: Texas A&M Press, 1978.

Falk, Stanley. *Bataan*. New York: Norton, 1962.

Fitzpatrick, Bernard. *The Hike Into the Sun*. Jefferson, NC: McFarland, 1993.

Fletcher-Cooke, John. *The Emperor's Guest*. London: Hutchinson, 1971.

Fujita, Frank. *Foo: A Japanese-American Prisoner of the Rising Sun*. Denton: University of North Texas, 1993.

Haney, Robert E. *Caged Dragons: An American POW in WWII Japan*. Ann Arbor: Sable, 1991.

Harries, Meirion, and Susie Harries. *Soldiers of the Sun*. New York: Random, 1991.

Hayes, Thomas. *Bilibid Diary*. Hamden, Conn.: Archon, 1987.

Hubbard, Preston John. *Apocalypse Undone*. Nashville: Vanderbilt University, 1990.

Irwin, Gregory J. W. *Facing Fearful Odds*. Lincoln: University of Nebraska, (forthcoming).

James, D. Clayton, ed. *South to Bataan, North to Mukden*. Athens: University of Georgia, 1971.

Kerr, E. Bartlett. *Surrender and Survival*. New York: Morrow, 1985.

Kinvig, Clifford. *River Kwai Railway*. London, Brassey, 1992.

Knox, Donald. *Death March: The Survivors of Bataan*. New York: Harcourt Brace Jovanovich, 1981.

LaForte, Robert S., and others. *With Only the Will to Live*. Wilmington, Del.: Scholarly Resources, 1994.

Lawton, Manny. *Some Survived*. Chapel Hill: Algonquin Books, 1984.

Marek, Stephen. *Laughter in Hell*. Caldwell, ID: Claxton, 1954.

Onorato, Michael P. *Forgotten Heroes*. Westport and London: Meckler, 1990.

Russell of Liverpool, Lord. *The Knights of Bushido: A Short History of Japanese War Crimes*. London: Cassel, 1958.

Sinclair, Robert. *The Burma-Siam Railway*. London: Imperial War Museum, 1984.

Stewart, Sydney. *Give Us This Day*. New York: Norton, 1956.

Timperly, H. J. *What War Means: The Japanese Terror in China*. London: Gollancz, 1938.

Wainwright, Jonathon M. *General Wainwright's Story*. New York: Doubleday, 1946.

Index